SURVEILLANCE, DATAVEILLANCE AND PERSONAL FREEDOMS:
Use and Abuse of Information Technology

Symposia of the
columbia human rights law review
available in hardbound books

LEGAL RIGHTS OF CHILDREN:
Status, Progress and Proposals

SURVEILLANCE, DATAVEILLANCE AND PERSONAL FREEDOMS:
Use and Abuse of Information Technology

A SYMPOSIUM
Edited by the Staff of

columbia human rights
law review

SURVEILLANCE

DATAVEILLANCE

and

PERSONAL

FREEDOMS

USE AND ABUSE OF INFORMATION TECHNOLOGY

Foreword by NAT HENTOFF

R. E. BURDICK, Inc., Publishers
Fair Lawn, New Jersey 07410

225622

International Standard Book Number: 0-913638-03-X.
Library of Congress Catalogue Card Number: 73-80006

Original text published as pages 1-235 of the
COLUMBIA HUMAN RIGHTS LAW REVIEW, Volume 4, Number 1,
Copyright © 1972 by *Columbia Human Rights Law Review,*
which is published in association with the
Columbia University Institute of Human Rights.

Revised and augmented text of hardbound book edition
Copyright © 1973 by R. E. Burdick, Inc.,
12-01 12th Street, Fair Lawn, New Jersey 07410

Published simultaneously in Canada
by the Book Center, Inc.,
1140 Beaulac Street, St.-Laurent 382, Quebec.

Printed in the United States of America.

CONTENTS

FOREWORD

IN HIS DISSENTING OPINION in *Laird v. Tatum* (1972)—a case involving Army secret surveillance of lawful civilian political activities—Justice William O. Douglas noted:

> The Constitution was designed to keep Government off the backs of the people. The Bill of Rights was added to keep the precincts of belief and expression of the press, of political and social activities free from surveillance. The Bill of Rights was designed to keep agents of Government and official eavesdroppers away from assemblies of people. The aim was to allow men to be free and independent and to assert their rights against Government. There can be no influence more paralyzing of that objective than Army surveillance. When an Intelligence officer looks over every nonconformist's shoulder in the library or walks invisibly by his side in a picket line or infiltrates his club, the America once extolled as the voice of liberty heard around the world is no longer cast in the image which Jefferson and Madison designed, but more in the Russian image.

As Justice Douglas would agree—and has so said in a number of judicial opinions and in other public statements—no less paralyzing than Army surveillance is secret spying on the citizenry by agents of civilian law enforcement agencies. Never before in the history of this country has such secret surveillance—with its concomitant accumulation of computerized dossiers—been so pervasive. All the more dangerous to the personal freedoms of every citizen is that this degree of surveillance has been made much more omnivorous because of the swift advance in the technology of surveillance.

As I write this, for instance, I have just received in the morning mail a report that Texas police are testing a new electronics device that can "see" people through walls and closed doors. The instrument's electromagnetic waves penetrate walls and doors to a distance of some thirty feet and are set in motion by anything over sixteen inches tall. (People attending private meetings in Texas are hereby advised to conduct their discussions while crawling.)

For several years, I have been engaged in research on the serious incursions into our Constitutional rights by the rapidly spreading growth of secret surveillance while also studying the evolution of surveillance technology itself. An invaluable source of information on both counts are the remarkably well researched and carefully analyzed materials in *Surveillance, Dataveillance and Personal Freedoms: Use and Abuse of Information Technology.*

I understate the case, I think, when I say that this is an essential book for any American concerned with protecting his own liberties and the ineluctably intertwining liberties of all other citizens. It is not a "technical" book in the sense that it is difficult to absorb. I am neither a lawyer nor, to say the least, an expert in the terminology of technology; but I found the book thoroughly—and absorbingly—accessible. I should add that experts in Constitutional law and in surveillance technology will also find this volume of unusual value because much of what it contains has not appeared elsewhere.

It is my hope that this book is as widely distributed and as widely read as possible. It certainly should be included in many high school and college courses on that vital interdisciplinary subject of how we can remain free citizens and avoid the coming of what former Congressman Cornelius Gallagher has called "post-Constitutional America."

Unless the citizenry—and their representatives in Congress and in state and local legislative bodies—awake, we are approaching the time when, as former Attorney General Ramsey Clark has warned, "a person can hardly speak his mind to any other person without being afraid that the police or someone else will hear what he thinks. Because of our numbers and the denseness of our urban society, it will be difficult enough in the future for us to secure some little sense of privacy and individual integrity. We can trap ourselves; we can become the victims of our technology and we can change the meaning of man as an individual."

This book shows precisely—and chillingly—how we, without knowing about it, are allowing ourselves to be thus trapped.

It is difficult for me to imagine anyone reading this book who will not thereby become justifiedly alarmed at the real possibility that "the meaning of man as an individual" can and will be changed unless the citizenry reclaim and reaffirm their liberties as proclaimed in the Bill of Rights.

New York, N. Y.   NAT HENTOFF
March 1973

PREFACE

ONLY A FEW MONTHS AGO, the *Columbia Human Rights Law Review* published a symposium on the subject of government surveillance and the right to privacy. The propriety of widespread government surveillance has been a critical issue in American politics. Indeed recent developments including the Watergate bugging affair, the National Academy of Sciences' publication of a landmark empirical evaluation of computers and privacy, and the Supreme Court's abortion decision articulating a 14th Amendment right to privacy, have sparked intensified consideration of the relationship that personal privacy and government regulation ought to have in our democracy.

This *Columbia Human Rights Law Review*'s symposium already has been cited in several court decisions and law review articles, as well as in the popular press including CBS Radio News, *The Village Voice* and *Playboy* magazine. The Board of Editors is particularly gratified that this collection of articles is now being presented in a more durable and widely promoted format.

Arthur R. Miller, a leading critic and scholar in the privacy and liberty debate, and author of *The Assault on Privacy*, introduces our discussion with a broad-gauged outline of the privacy environment. Senator Sam J. Ervin's article presents information from his recently concluded hearings (Hearings on Federal Data Banks, Computers and The Bill of Rights, 92d Cong., 1st Sess. 1971) to highlight one aspect of the privacy threat—surveillance by the military. Nicholas Katzenbach, former Attorney General and now General Counsel and Vice President for the nation's major computer firm, IBM, discusses the use and abuse of computers in criminal justice information systems. "Surveillance: The Social Science Perspective" by ACLU attorney and Rutgers Law Professor Frank Askin is the first systematic attempt to document the "chilling effect" of government surveillance. Michael A. Baker, co-author of the National Academy of Sciences' report, *Databanks in a Free Society*, has written a social science critique of the privacy consciousness of those who manage our records. Mr. Baker's article has been specially expanded and updated for inclusion in this hardcover edition.

The articles written by the staff members of the *Columbia Human Rights Law Review* confront three major threats to personal privacy. A former Editor-in-Chief of the journal, Donald R. Davis, reviews the growth of political surveillance and databanks and evaluates the potential response from various Constitutional remedies. "Police Use of

Remote Camera Systems for Surveillance of Public Streets," an article co-authored by Robert R. Belair and Charles D. Bock, two third-year Columbia University law students and respectively the Editor-in-Chief and the Writing and Revisions Editor of the *Columbia Human Rights Law Review*, presents the first thorough empirical and legal discussion of police remote-controlled television systems and street surveillance. In the last article John P. Flannery, a former Managing Editor of the journal, looks at the burgeoning personal information collection activities of the private sector and outlines its legal consequences.

Three people deserve particular recognition for editing this book. Donald R. Davis, who was the Editor-in-Chief during the year that this material was compiled, is, of course, greatly responsible for the book's development. In addition, William J. Muller and Miriam A. Bender, members of the Editorial Board of the *Columbia Human Rights Law Review* played a vital role in the book's production.

New York City
March 1973

ROBERT R. BELAIR
Editor-in-Chief
Columbia Human Rights Law Review

COMPUTERS, DATA BANKS AND INDIVIDUAL PRIVACY: An Overview

ARTHUR R. MILLER*

Do you think your telephone has been tapped, your mail opened, or your activities and associations monitored? Many Americans have recently had cause to consider such possibilities although our nation is supposedly committed to democratic principles, the freedom of the individual, and citizen privacy. But if you have not fallen victim to this type of paranoia, perhaps you have wondered who can look at your tax returns or who has access to your employer's personnel files, your financial or military records, test scores, or insurance applications?

Concern over privacy is hardly irrational. In our increasingly computerized life, whenever a citizen files a tax return, applies for life insurance or a credit card, seeks government benefits or interviews for a job, a dossier is opened on him and his informational profile is sketched.[1] It now has reached the point at which whenever we fly on a commercial airline, stay at one of the national hotel chains, or rent a car, we are likely to leave distinctive electronic tracks in the memory of a computer that can reveal much about our activities, habits and associations. Few people seem to appreciate the fact that modern technology is capable of monitoring, centralizing and evaluating these electronic entrees no matter how numerous and scattered they may be.

Americans today are scrutinized, measured, watched, and quizzed more than at any time in our history.[2] The increase in both

---

* Visiting Professor of Law, Harvard University School of Law; author, THE ASSAULT ON PRIVACY: COMPUTERS, DATA BANKS, AND DOSSIERS (1971).

1. The kind of information typically required includes name, address, age, sex, health, education, previous training and employment, present occupation, marital status, draft status, and professional and credit references.

2. *See generally* MILLER, THE ASSAULT ON PRIVACY: COMPUTERS, DATA BANKS, AND DOSSIERS (1971) [hereinafter cited as MILLER]; DUGGAN, IRWIN AND MCCARTIN, eds. THE COMPUTER UTILITY, IMPLICATIONS FOR HIGHER EDUCATION

private and governmental data-gathering activities, combined with ever broader applications of modern information technology, have caused anxiety over the inroads being made on our traditional bastions of physical and informational privacy. One major concern is that the computer may become the heart of a surveillance system that will turn society into a transparent world in which our homes, finances and associations are bared to the most casual observer.[3]

A brief recital of some of the blessings and blasphemies of the new technology makes the computer-privacy dilemma abundantly clear. In various medical centers, doctors are using computers to monitor physiological changes in the bodies of heart patients.[4] The quest is to isolate those alterations in body chemistry that precede a heart attack, providing an *early warning system* so that treatment is not delayed until the actual heart attack has rendered the patient moribund for all practical purposes.[5]

Other plans include giving everyone an identification number at birth for tax, banking, education, social security and draft purposes[6] which would be done in conjunction with the computerization of a wide range of records. Thus, in the future, if a person falls ill away from home, a local doctor can use his identification number to retrieve the patient's medical history and drug reactions from a distant central data bank, thereby immensely speeding diagnosis and treatment.

The immediate goal is to eliminate much of the existing multiplicity in record-keeping while at the same time expediting the business of society. Long-range objectives include developing a checkless, cashless economy, improving the information bases available for rational planning, providing better governmental services to people, and promoting the more equitable allocation of human and natural resources.[7]

(1970); WIENER, THE USE OF HUMAN BEINGS (Paper ed., 1970); ROSZAK, THE MAKING OF A COUNTER CULTURE (paper ed., 1969); FERKISS, THE TECHONOLOGICAL MAN (1969); LONG, THE INTRUDERS (1967).

3. *See* MILLER, note 2 *supra* at 38: WESTIN, PRIVACY AND FREEDOM 65 (1967); Countryman, *The Diminishing Right of Privacy: The Personal Dossier and the Computer*, 49 TEX. L. REV. 837 (1971). *See generally Hearings on Federal Data Banks, Computers and the Bill of Rights, Before the Subcomm. on Constitutional Rights of the Senate Comm. on the Judiciary* 92d Cong. 1st Sess. (1971) [hereinafter cited as *Senate Hearings*].

4. *See* Stevens, *Now—The Automated Physical Check-up,* READER'S DIGEST 95 (July, 1944). For related discussions of medical use of the computer, *see How Computers Help MDs Diagnose,* BULLETIN INTERUNIVERSITY COMMUNICATIONS COUNCIL 3-6 (April, 1966). Freed, *Legal Aspects of Computer use in Medicine,* 32 LAW AND CONTEMPORARY PROBLEMS 674 (1967); N.Y. Times 47, col. 6 (June 18, 1968).

5. *See* note 4, *supra* and accompanying text. *See also* MILLER, note 2 *supra* at 4.

6. *See* MILLER, note 2 *supra* at 4, 20-23.

7. *See* O'Brien, *The Bank of Tomorrow Today,* COMPUTERS AND AUTOMATION 26 (May, 1968). *Electronic Money,* FORBES 42 (April 1, 1967); WEISS, THE MARKETING

But the same electronic sensors that can warn us of an impending heart attack might be used to locate us, track our movements, and measure our emotions and thoughts. For example, experiments are underway in the field of telemetry and significant breakthroughs are on the horizon.[8] And some criminologists already have suggested that a prisoner be subjected to sensor implantation as a condition of parole.[9] Law enforcement people then could monitor his activities and perhaps take him into custody should his *aggression level* become *too high.*[10]

Similarly, the identification number given us at birth might come a leash around our necks, subjecting us to constant monitoring and making credible the fear of the fabled womb-to-tomb dossier. In a computerized society those who control the recordation and preservation of personal data will have a degree of power over the individual that is at once unprecedented and subject to abuse.

Close scrutiny and evaluation of the implications of information technology on individual privacy are especially appropriate today because of the rising interest in many quarters for the establishment of governmental and private data centers. The extent to which federal agencies and private companies are using computers and microfilm technology to collect, store, and exchange information about the activities of private citizens is rapidly increasing. During the past year we have read of the Department of Housing and Urban Development's Adverse Information File, the National Science Foundation's data bank on scientists, the Customs Bureau's computerized data bank on *suspects*, the Civil Service Commission's *investigative* and *security* files, and the State Department's Passport Lookout Service.[11] There also have been disturbing revelations about the Justice Department's intelligence bank, the Department of Transportation's National Driver Register of 2.6 million drivers, the Secret Service's

---

IMPLICATIONS OF THE CHECKLESS SOCIETY (1968); Kramer and Livingston, *Cashing in on the Checkless Society,* 45 HARV. BUS. REV. 141 (Sept.-Oct. 1967). *See generally* INFORMATION SUPPORT PROGRAM BUDGETING AND THE CONGRESS (1968); Macy, *Automated Government—How Computers Are Being Used in Washington to Streamline Personnel Administration to the Individual's Benefit,* SATURDAY REV. 25 (July 23, 1966); Note, *Privacy and Efficient Government: Proposals for a National Data Center,* 82 HARV. L. REV. 400 (1968).

8. *See* Schwitzgebel, *Electronic Innovation in the Behavioral Sciences: A Call to Responsibility,* 22 AMERICAN PSYCHOLOGIST 364 (1970); *Berry, Project Brain Control,* reprinted in 111 CONG. REC. 16,181, 16,182 (July 9, 1965); Note, *Anthropotelemetry: Dr. Schwitzgebel's Machine,* 80 HARV. L. REV. 403, 407 (1966). *See also* FERKISS, TECHNOLOGICAL MAN 166-67 (1969).

9. *See* MILLER, note 2, *supra* at 45-46.

10. *Id.* at 46. How one distinguishes between excitement generated by antisocial or aberrational behavior and that caused by watching a football game is extremely difficult to say.

11. MILLER, note 2, *supra* at 5-7.

dossiers on *undesirables*, *activists*, and *malcontents*, and the surveillance activities of the United States Army.[12]

This list merely represents a sampling of the federal government data banks that have been brought to light; even now only the tip of the iceberg may be visible. Still below the surface are the implications of several provisions in President Nixon's welfare reform proposal (the Family Assistance and Manpower Training Acts), which would give the Department of Health, Education and Welfare authority to computerize and exchange individualized data with state welfare agencies and lead to the establishment of a national job applicant data bank.[13]

By and large, most data-gathering activities are well intended efforts to achieve socially desirable objectives. For example, in the law enforcement field one objective of computerized filebuilding is said to be the elimination of organized crime and the preservation of *law and order*. In a similar vein, the FBI and the Army justify their intelligence operations in terms of combating subversion or quelling campus disruptions and riots in our urban centers by knowing whom to watch or seize in times of strife.[14] As to the information activities of credit grantors, private investigators and insurance companies, it simply is good business to know as much as possible about a man before you lend him money, employ him, or insure his life.[15]

But there is a negative side to the problem of mushrooming data banks—particularly those that bear the imprimatur of a governmental organization. Consider the information practices of the United States Army. It was revealed early in 1970 that for some time Army intelligence units had been systematically keeping watch on the *lawful* political activity of a number of groups and preparing *incident* reports and dossiers on individuals engaged in a wide range of *legal* protests. This monitoring not only covered members of radical or militant groups but included such nonviolent organizations as the NAACP, the ACLU, the Southern Christian Leadership Conference, the Women Strike for Peace, and allegedly extended to newsmen,

---

12. *See generally Senate Hearings* note 3, *supra;* MILLER, note 2, *supra* at 40; Ervin, *The Final Answer: The People in Control,* 14 TRIAL MAGAZINE (March/April (1971)).

13. *See* S. 2,986, 91st Cong., 1st Sess. (1969); H. REP. NO. 14,173, 14,174, 14,175, 91st Cong., 1st Sess. (1969); H. REP. NO. 15,440 91st Cong., 2d Sess. (1970) (proposed Family Assistance Act); S. 2,838, 91st Cong., 1st Sess. (1969); H. REP. NO. 13,472, 13,518, 91st Cong., 1st Sess. (1969) (proposed Manpower Training Act). *See also* MILLER, note 2, *supra* at 21-22, 142 for discussion of these bills with respect to the information they will bring into government files.

14. *Senate Hearings,* note 3 *supra* at 1253, 1270, 1261 (Army surveillance directives); *id.* at 1315 (FBI Civil Disturbance System).

15. *See* MILLER, note 2 *supra* at 67-79. *See also* Karst, *The Files: Legal Controls over the Accuracy and Accessibility of Stored Personal Data,* 21 LAW AND CONTEMPORARY PROB. 342 (1966) for the kinds of information gathered and the problems engendered.

congressmen, and a former governor who is now a federal judge. And, as the hearings before Senator Sam Ervin's Subcommittee on Constitutional Rights made clear, the military pursued their surveillance activities with an unrestrained fervor and in a few short years numerous Americans fell under their scrutiny.[16] Although there is some justification for certain types of information collection that are directly relevant to the Army's duties, the development of dossiers on people pursuing lawful social and political, activities bears little relationship to the duties of the military even during periods of social unrest. This overreaching is especially offensive when many of those being scrutinized are extremely unlikely to be involved in illegal civil disorders, and the selection of suspects seems to be governed by a very simplistic *these are the good guys and those are the bad guys* approach. Not only was the Army's filebuilding difficult to justify, but it was undertaken without sufficient appreciation of the fact that the creation and exposure of dossiers on people who are politically active could deter them from exercising their right to assemble, speak freely, or petition the government.[17]

The emergence of a number of information systems in law enforcement magnifies both this threat to personal privacy and the potential *chilling effect* of informational surveillance.[18] The FBI's constantly expanding National Crime Information Center (NCIC) provides state and city police forces with immediate access to computerized files on many people. Although until recently it only contained data on fugitives and stolen property, plans are underway to add arrest records and other types of sensitive information. Moreover, NCIC is the keystone of an emerging information network that will eventually tie together the nation's law enforcement information centers. By the end of 1969, it was exchanging data with state and local police agencies in every state except Alaska.[19] State and local law enforcement surveillance systems also are becoming increasingly sophisticated—several with the aid of funding under the Law Enforcement Assistance Administration program of the Justice Department.

When a citizen knows that his conduct and associations are being put *on file* and that the information might be used to harass or

---

16. *See Senate Hearings,* note 3 *supra* at 1427.

17. *See* Askin, *Police Dossiers and Emerging Principles of First Amendment Adjudication,* 22 STAN. L. REV. 196 (1970); Note, *The Chilling Effect in Constitutional Law,* 69 COLUM. L. REV. 808 (1969).

18. *See* note 17 *supra* and accompanying text; MILLER, note 2, *supra* at 38. *See also* Tatum v. Laird, 444 F.2d 947 (1971), *cert. granted,* No. 71-288 (1971); Anderson v. Sills, 106 N.J. Super. 545, 256 A.2d 298 (Ch. Div. 1969), *rev'd and remanded,* 56 N.J. 210, 265 A.2d 678 (1970); Transcript, *Assault on Privacy,* ABC Television broadcast (Sat., Jan. 8, 1972); Transcript, *Under Surveillance,* CBS Television broadcast (Thurs., Dec. 23, 1971).

19. *See* MILLER, note 2 *supra* at 147.

injure him, he may become more concerned about the possible content of that file and less willing to risk asserting his expressional rights. The effect may be to encourage Americans to keep a politic silence on all occasions. We cannot afford to allow constitutional guarantees to be debilitated by any type of coercion. Claims of governmental efficiency or the war against crime and subversion must not be allowed to justify every demand for gathering personal data.

We can take little comfort from the present Administration's repeated assertions that it has *inherent* power to wiretap and engage in surveillance whenever it decides there is a threat to *internal security*,[20] especially since the Administration has offered no guidelines as to how the government plans to use this power and what safeguards will protect us against misuse of the resulting files. Indeed, the contents of the FBI memoranda stolen from its Media, Pennsylvania, office earlier this year portray a conscious effort to harass and frighten citizens through systematic intelligence activities.

Because this atmosphere is conducive to the development of a *record prison* mentality, it is not surprising that some commentators are suggesting that contemporary government surveillance efforts are an invitation to a police state or a return to McCarthyism.[21] Thus, it is not sufficient that governmental agencies assure us that surveillance and filebuilding are not being engaged in for repressive purposes. For many, the appearance of repression has the impact of reality.

Data-gathering and dossier-building are as prevalent in private industry as in government. Personal information can be used for commercial purposes, such as generating a list of prospective consumers. *Reader's Digest* reportedly has used a computer to produce a mailing list consisting of its subscribers' neighbors,[22] a tactic that proved surprisingly effective. "The approach had a kind of 'all the neighbors are doing it' quality," said one commentator, "but more significantly, the individual was pleased that the *Reader's Digest* knew him and could relate him to others on his block."[23]

The commercial use of cybernetics may go beyond this relatively benign method of soliciting business. The line between using the tech-

---

20. *See* Comment, *Warrantless Electronic Surveillance of Dissident Domestic Organizations under the National Security Exception,* 5 VALP. UNIV. L. REV. 651 (1971); Comment, *Privacy and Political Freedom: Application of the Fourth Amendment to National Security Investigations,* 17 U.C.L.A. L. REV. 1205 (1970). *Cf.* United States v. Sinclair, Criminal No. 44375 (E.D. Mich., Jan. 25, 1971) and United States v. Smith, 312 F. Supp. 425 (C.D. Cal. 1971) in which the Administration's assertions were refuted.

21. *See, e.g.,* Donner, *The Theory and Practice of American Political Intelligence,* NEW YORK REVIEW OF BOOKS 27 (April 22, 1971). *See generally Senate Hearings,* note 3 *supra.*

22. N.Y. Times 41, col. 1 (July 30, 1968). *Cf.* Lamont v. Comm. of Motor Vehicles, 269 F. Supp. 880 (S.D.N.Y. 1967), *affirmed per curiam,* 386 F.2d 449 (2d Cir. 1967).

23. N.Y. Times 41, col. 1 (July 30, 1968).

nology to communicate with a customer and employing it to manipulate his attitudes is nebulous and is likely to be transgressed frequently. For example, one New Jersey firm is developing a comprehensive data bank on doctors so that drug companies can promote their products in a way that will appeal to the habits and personality of individual doctors.[24]   And the nation's credit bureaus have been moving toward computerization since 1965; eventually, a computerized network will provide information instantaneously anywhere in the country.[25] The consumer reporting industry cannot be faulted for embracing the new technology, but too little attention has been given to preserving the privacy of the people on whom dossiers are maintained. All too often this indifference has resulted in misuse of information, gross inaccuracies, shoddy investigative practices that propagate gossip, rumor, and vindictive remarks, and a failure to acknowledge the crippling potential of information—or misinformation.[26]

Few people realize that they sign away a portion of their privacy when they apply for credit. Credit bureau and investigative agency files bulge with information on mortgages, make of car, salary, size of family; the resulting collage of data frequently produce an intimate sketch of the subject's economic life. To augment this profile, many companies regularly comb newspapers, court records and other public files for bits of personal data that are thought to be relevant.[27]

A new federal statute—the *Fair Credit Reporting Act*[28]—is the first step in eliminating a few of the abuses of the unregulated buying and selling of personal information. Generally, it gives individuals some control over the flow of personal information by providing access to their files in consumer reporting agencies and establishing a procedure for correcting errors. But the *Act* is full of loopholes[29] and its success depends on a level of consumer sophistication that

---

24. *See* MILLER, note 2 *supra* at 67-78.

25. *Id.* at 16-20 and notes thereto.

26. *See, e.g.,* Menard v. Mitchell, 430 F.2d 486 (D.C. Cir. 1970), *decision upon remand* 328 F.Supp. 718 (D.D.C. 1971). *Senate Hearings,* note 3 *supra* at 492, 510 (testimony and exhibits presented by San Francisco Mayor Joseph Alioto).

27. *See Hearings on Commercial Credit Bureaus Before a Subcomm. of the House Comm. on Government Operations* 125-26, 90th Cong., 2d Sess. (1968).

28. 15 U.S.C. § 1681 *et seq.* (1970). Similar acts, exhibiting varying degrees of effectiveness, have been passed by the same states. *See, e.g.,* CALIF. CIVIL CODE § § 1750 *et seq.* (1970); MASS. GEN. LAWS, ch. 93, § § 44-47 (1969); N.Y. SESS. LAWS, ch. 300 (1970).

29. The *Act* does not take cognizance of the problems raised by consumer reporting in the computer age; for example, it does not define who can or should have access to a file, prescribe the length of time certain dangerous or embarrassing material may be maintained or determine the scope of proper investigative information gathering.

seems unrealistic. Hopefully, the *Act* represents only the first skirmish in the legislative battle for individual privacy.

Until recently, informational privacy has been relatively easy to protect because: 1) large quantities of information about individuals have not been available; 2) the available information generally has been decentralized; 3) the available information has been relatively superficial; 4) access to information has been difficult to secure; 5) people in a highly mobile society are difficult to keep track of; and 6) most people are unable to interpret and infer revealing information from data.[30] But these protections were part of a by-gone era. New efforts must now be made to give people effective control over the circulation of data relating to them. Testimony before several congressional   committees has revealed the way in which our personal privacy has been intruded upon by scientific means.[31] Revelations concerning the widespread use of spike and parabolic microphones, a variety of gadgets for electronic eavesdropping, and cameras equipped with modern optical devices that enable photographs to be taken at a distance under adverse weather or light conditions, demonstrate that we do not necessarily enjoy physical privacy in our homes, or offices or on the street.[32] And now, ever increasing resort to the computer, laser technology, and microminiaturization techniques has begun to erode our informational privacy.

It should be evident to all that we live in an information based society. As recording processes have become cheaper and more efficient, data collection has intensified and been accompanied by a trend toward centralization. It is a form of Parkinson's Law—as capacity for information handling has increased, there has been a tendency to engage in more extensive manipulation and analysis of recorded data, which, in turn, has motivated the collection of data pertaining to a larger number of variables. The availability of electronic data storage and retrieval has accelerated this pattern, as evidenced by the increased detail of tax forms and the drastic expansion of governmental, industrial, and academic questionnaires.

There are many risks lurking in this spiraling collection of data. As information cumulates, the contents of an individual's computerized dossier appear more and more impressive, and despite the "soft-

---

30. *See* MILLER, note 2 *supra* at 26.

31. *See, e.g., Senate Hearings,* note 3 *supra; Hearings on Computer Privacy Before Subcomm. on Administrative Practice and Procedure of the Senate Comm. on the Judiciary,* 90th Cong., 2d Sess. (1968); *Hearings on Retail Credit Company Before the Subcomm. on Invasion of Privacy of the House Comm. on Government Operations,* 90th Cong., 2d Sess. (1968); *Hearings on the Computer and Invasion of Privacy Before a Subcomm. of the House Comm. on Government Operations,* 89th Cong., 2d Sess. (1966).

32. Note, *Police Use of Remote Camera Systems for the Surveillance of Public Streets,* 4 COLUM. HUMAN RIGHTS L. REV. 143 (1972).

ness" of much of the data, it imparts a heightened sense of reliability to the user which makes it less likely that an independent evaluation will be made or that the data will be verified. Many people have come to feel that their success or failure in life ultimately may turn on what other people put in their file and an unknown programmer's ability—or—inability—to evaluate process and interrelate that information. Technology's threats to privacy are created not only by those who desire to injure others or who can obtain some personal advantage by doing so. Unthinking information managers and users are as capable of injuring people by unintentionally rendering a record inaccurate, losing it or disseminating its contents to unauthorized parties as are those acting out of malice or for personal aggrandizement.[33] The fact is that a computerized file has a certain indelible quality, which means adversities cannot be overcome with time absent an electronic eraser and a compassionate soul willing to use it.

The centralization of information from widely divergent sources also creates serious risks of using data out of context. Information can be entirely accurate and sufficient in one context and wholly incomplete and misleading in another. A *fair* rating, for instance, actually may denote very different levels of performance in two different contexts.

The problem of contextual accuracy is best illustrated by one of the most dangerous types of personal information currently maintained—the unexplained and incomplete arrest record. Consider the potential effect of a computer entry: "arrested, criminal trespass; sentenced, six months." Without more data how will the user know that our computerized man was demonstrating for desegregation in the South in the 1950's or equal employment opportunities in the North in the 1960's and was convicted under a statute that was overturned on appeal as an unconstitutional restraint on free speech?[34]

In an era of great social activism on the part of the young, with counterpoint demands from other groups for *law and order*, arrests are bound to increase. It is now common for hundreds of demonstrators to be arrested in connection with one incident. Using recent experience as a guide, only a small fraction of the group will be prosecuted and an even smaller number convicted. All of them, however, will have arrest

---

33. *See* MILLER, note 2 *supra* at 27-28, 147-48; BOGUSLAW, THE NEW UTOPIANS 97-98 (paper ed., 1965). *Cf.* Clurman and Provorny, *Publicity and Inspection of Federal Tax Returns,* 46 TAXES 144 (1968).

34. *See, e.g.,* Menard v. Mitchell, 430 F.2d 486 (D.C. Cir. 1970), *decision upon remand* 328 F.Supp. 718 (D.D.C. 1971). *Cf.* Thom v. New York Stock Exchange, 306 F.Supp. 1002 (S.D.N.Y. 1969), *aff'd,* 425 F.2d 1074 (2d Cir. 1970), *cert. denied,* 398 U.S. 905 (1970); United States v. Rickenbacker, 309 F.2d 462 (2d Cir. 1962), *cert. denied,* 371 U.S. 962 (1963). *See also* COMPUTERWORLD 12 (Feb. 18, 1970).

records. Unless these records are accurately updated, their circulation may have an improperly prejudicial effect.

And these records *will* circulate. In our information-oriented society, data about people is valuable, especially if it is derogatory. Credit grantors, employers, detective agencies, insurance companies, political operatives, and government investigators will pay for it or, on occasion, steal it. We recently had a warning of this in New York when a number of consumer reporting agencies were prosecuted for bribing New York policemen to reveal the content of fingerprint and arrest records to them.[35]

It also seems evident that the rewards of getting at a data center's enormous store of information may well offset the technical difficulty of gaining access to the computerized files and deciphering them, which occasionally are offered as reasons why machine readable information is inherently more secure than manually stored data. Even if the cost of securing access to computerized information is higher than the cost of dredging out the information in a more traditional form of record, the centralized quality and compactness of a computerized dossier creates an incentive to invade it because the payoff for doing so successfully is much larger.

Perhaps the greatest dangers lie in the *information buddy system* that promotes the dissemination of personal information throughout the government and the private sector. It is a striking fact that many, if not most, bank and corporate security officers, private detectives, and field investigators for consumer reporting companies are former federal or local law enforcement agents.[36] The result is a subterranean information exchange network that functions on a mutual back-scratching basis or can be invoked for a fee. This network's existence means that decisions are being made about us based on reports from unknown sources we can never confront that contain information whose accuracy we can never challenge.

What then is the solution? As an initial matter one would hope that good judgment and self-regulation on the part of the information gathering and using communities would suffice. Those who handle individualized data—whether it be in the context of financial profiles in a credit bureau, student records in a school system, medical files in a hospital, intelligence information in a law enforcement computer, welfare lists in a governmental agency, or personnel data in a large corporation—have an obligation to guard the privacy of the human

---

35. *See* MILLER, note 2 *supra* at 26-38 for this and similar examples of the individual's loss of control over information concerning himself once it reaches the data bank.

36. *Id.* at 67.

beings whose lives are reflected in those dossiers. There are many ways in which this might be achieved, including the use of a wide range of technical, administrative, and procedural protections that might be imposed on all information systems containing personal data.[37] These safeguards are currently available so that the only question is how to promote their utilization.

Ultimately, however, we must look to Congress to achieve the much needed balance between exploitation of the new information technology and preservation of personal privacy. One highly desirable legislative approach would be to prohibit governmental, and perhaps even nongovernmental, organizations from collecting certain types of sensitive data when there is no clear social justification for doing so that outweighs the risks to personal privacy. A somewhat different, and in various ways more drastic, solution involves imposing a statutory duty of care on everyone who handles personal information and enacting comprehensive privacy-oriented regulations for data banks and many information gathering activities. Enforcement of the legislation could be delegated to an information agency that would act like an ombudsman to redress grievances and insure that information handlers adhere to an administratively established code of conduct. At the very least, Congress must act to bring governmental surveillance within carefully defined limits that are consistent with societal self-preservation and individual freedom.

As the 1972 election approaches, the political appeal of being for privacy is becoming apparent. Unfortunately, some of the activity to date is reminiscent of Leacock's Man, who jumped on his horse and rode off in all directions at once. Proposals have been made to regulate credit bureaus, mailing list companies, the census, employee privacy, government questionnaires, polygraphs, and psychological testing; but only the *Fair Credit Reporting Act* has become law.[38] Fortunately, Senator Ervin and Congressmen Gallagher, Koch, and Mikva have sensed the need for a broadly conceived approach to the problem and their efforts deserve our attention and support.[39]

---

37. For discussions of technical safeguards, see generally Kramer and Livingston, *Cashing In on the Checkless Society*, 45 HARV. BUS. REV. 141, 143 (Sept. - Oct., 1967); Petersen and Turn, *System Implications of Information Privacy*, 30 AFIPS CONFERENCE PROCEEDINGS 291, 294-95 (1967); Graham, *Protection in an Information Processing Utility*, 11 COMMUNICATIONS OF THE ACM 365 (1968); Peters, *Security Considerations in a Multi-Programmed Computer System*, 30 AFIPS CONFERENCE PROCEEDINGS 283, 284 (1967). Administrative safeguards are discussed in MILLER, note 2 *supra* at 248-257. Procedural protections are also discussed in MILLER, note 2 *supra* at 245-248. In addition, see Peters, *supra* at 284; Ruggles, *On the Needs and Values of Data Banks, in Symposium—Computers, Data Banks, and Individual Privacy*, 53 MINN. L. REV. 211, 219 (1968).

38. 15 U.S.C. § 1681 *et seq.* (1970).

39. *See, e.g., Senate Hearings*, note 3 *supra* (before Senator Ervin's subcommittee); Ervin, *The First Amendment: A Living Thought in the Computer Age*, 4 COLUM. HUMAN RIGHTS L. REV. 13 (1972); *Hearings on the Computer and Invasion of Privacy Before a Subcomm. of the House Comm. on Government Operations*, 89th Cong., 2d Sess. (1966)

We must overcome our all-too-often complacent attitude toward the management of our affairs by what frequently are astigmatic administrators in both the government and the private sector. The very real benefits conferred by information technology are obscuring the price that may be exacted in terms of personal freedom. The computer is precipitating a realignment in the patterns of power and is becoming an increasingly important decision-making tool in practically all of our significant governmental and nongovernmental institutions. As society becomes more information oriented, the central issue that emerges to challenge us is how to contain the excesses and channel the benefits of this new form of power.

If the concept of personal privacy is fundamental to our tradition of individual autonomy, and if its preservation really is desirable, then the expenditure of considerable effort on its behalf and the development of greater sensitivity to the dangers of information abuse is imperative.[40] Otherwise, some day we might awaken from our apathy to discover that the mantle of policymaking is being worn by specially trained technicians who have found the time to master the machine and are manipulating it for their own purposes.

---

40. One requisite to increased awareness of the potential dangers and benefits of computers and data banks is the continued public examination of the privacy questions involved in hearings such as those conducted by Senator Sam J. Ervin. *See generally Senate Hearings*, note 3 *supra*. Another is the building of legal literature dealing with such problems. *See, e.g., Symposium—Computers, Data Banks, and Individual Privacy*, 53 MINN. L. REV. 211, 219 (1968).

THE FIRST AMENDMENT:
2 | A Living Thought in the Computer Age

SAM J. ERVIN, Jr.*

Sherwood Anderson wrote words about America as true today as they were in the third decade of this century:

> America ain't cemented and plastered yet. They're still building it. . . . All America asks is to look at it and listen to it and understand it if you can. Only the understanding ain't important either; the important thing is to believe in it even if you don't understand it, and then try to tell it, put it down. Because tomorrow America is going to be something different, something more and new to watch and listen to and try to understand; and, even if you can't understand, believe.

Anyone seeking to understand contemporary America must deal with our national experience with computer technology. They must understand that it has become an essential tool in the "cementing and plastering" of our nation. They must understand that it has at once presented our country its greatest hope and its greatest challenge; keeping faith with our historical heritage and commitment to freedom, while enjoying the fruits of a rich industrialized society under a democratic constitution.

Throughout our nation the people involved with computer technology have charge of a great national resource which will affect the course of our economic and social progress. More important, insofar as it affects the exercise of governmental power and the power of large special interest groups, the new technology may help determine the course of freedom and human rights in our land.

---

* U.S. Senator, North Carolina.

1. Based on an address before the Spring Joint Computer Conference of the Federation of Information Processing Societies, Atlantic City, N.J., May 20, 1971.

In the process, I believe Americans could find wisdom in Sherwood Anderson's advice "to believe" in America. I say this because, as we grasp for the new computer technology and seek theories of systems analysis for our social problems, Americans may tend to forget to look to their own history. Some, in their haste to solve today's problems, may fear to translate America's promise of freedom into the program language of the computer age.

Those who are initiated into the technological mysteries of computer hardware and software may take great pride. Through their deeds and genius they have helped people go to the moon, produce music, create art, conduct off-track betting, run railroads and administer welfare systems. They help maintain our national defense and they keep our economy running. They aid in catching criminals and they establish instant credit. They locate marriage-mates for people and they prejudge elections almost before the votes are cast.

A tape storage system has been described which will make it possible to store a dossier on every living person in the United States and to retrieve any one of them in a maximum of 28 seconds. With such feats to their credit, these people know better than anybody that in the application of their knowledge, they play a major role in the economic and social well-being of our society. They are responsible for bringing to our nation all the wondrous blessing of computer technology, especially scientific methods of processing information.

They can bend these machines to their will and make them perform feats undreamed of ten or even five years ago.

They have a special understanding of the new information flow charts for the vast data systems in our government.

They hold the access code to control over the technology as it affects the individual in our society.

They may hold the key to the final achievement of the rule of law which is the promise of our constitution.

With this body of knowledge, therefore, they bear special responsibility for the preservation of liberty in our country. That they have accepted this responsibility is clear from the *Privacy* themes of many recent conferences of computer professionals, equipment manufacturers, and computer users in the governmental and private sectors.

Their power is not limited to their technical expertise, but is augmented by the sheer numbers in the computer-related professions.

Advertisements on TV, radio, in newspapers, and even on buses daily remind the public of the inducements and rewards of a career in computer and data processing fields.

In the Federal Government, their numbers are growing. An inventory of automatic data processing equipment shows that in 1952 there were probably two computers in government. In 1971, there were 5,961.[2]

In 1960, there were 48,700 man-years used in federal automated data processing functions. This includes systems analysis and design, programming, equipment selection and operation, key punching, equipment maintenance and administrative support. In 1970, there were about 136,504 man-years used in direct ADP work.

A recent illuminating report by the National Association for State Information Systems shows that in 35 states in 1971, over twenty-four and a half thousand people were engaged in ADP. Twenty-eight states together spent 181 million dollars of their budgets on such personnel.[3]

To glance through their professional journals, newspapers and bulletins each month is to be constantly amazed at the breadth and reach of the theories and accomplishments.[4] It also deepens a layman's wonder at the complex language which sometimes defies translation into ordinary English.

For all of these reasons, the general public stands in superstitious awe of the skills and knowledge, the machines and instruments, and the products derived and transmitted by them. For the uninitiated, the computer print-out bears a mystique and an aura of scientific rationality which makes it appear infallible. This is true for most lawyers and probably for most people in political life.

There is a theory abroad today in academic circles that America is divided into two worlds. One of them is the world of science and technology,[5] inhabited by people who are part of a technological and electronic revolution. In the other world are said to live all the rest of the people whose ideas and values are based on an earlier age.

In accordance with their theory, some have tried to stamp the scientist with motives and values different from those of other Ameri-

2. INVENTORY OF AUTOMATIC DATA PROCESSING EQUIPMENT IN THE UNITED STATES FISCAL YEAR 1971, GENERAL SERVICES ADMINISTRATION, at 15. A report providing information on the digital electronic computers installed throughout the U.S. Government, which defines "computer" as a configuration of EDPE components which includes one central processing system concept which recognizes the growing importance of configurations with more than one central processing unit. This report responds to requirements of P.L. No. 89-306, Stat. (Oct. 30, 1965) and S. Doc. No. 15 (1965), REPORT TO THE PRESIDENT ON THE MANAGEMENT OF AUTOMATIC DATA PROCESSING IN THE FEDERAL GOVERNMENT.

3. 1970 NASIS REPORT, INFORMATION SYSTEMS TECHONOLOGY IN STATE GOVERNMENT at 18, developed by the State of Illinois and the National Association for State Information Systems, Council of State Governments.

4. See generally COMPUTERWORLD (a weekly periodical servicing the computer community): DATAMATION: DATA MANAGEMENT; and BUSINESS AUTOMATION.

5. See, e.g., Brzezinksi, Between Two Ages, America's Role In The Technotronic Era, although all authors do not engage in such distinctions with the same judgments or purposes.

cans; with goals oriented only toward efficiency or shorn of compassion, or, alternatively, with exclusive ability to determine social priorities. I cannot agree with this analysis, for I believe there is a yearning in every human heart for liberty, and for the freedom to express oneself according to the dictates of conscience. Despite a man's commitment to a chosen profession, he wants the freedom to fulfill himself as an individual and to use his God-given faculties free from the coercion of government.

So I do not believe Americans dwell in two worlds. Regardless of our origins, I believe we share a common heritage and a common destiny in that we are all engaged in searching for freedom. We share, according to the mandates of the Constitution, a common understanding that the best protection for that freedom rests on the limitations on the power of government and on the division of that power.

I cannot agree with such an analysis for another reason. Since the Senate Constitutional Rights Subcommittee began its study of computers, data banks and the Bill of Rights, I have received many letters from computer specialists, systems designers, engineers, programmers, professors and others in the scientific community which prove that despite, and perhaps because of their professions, they share the same concern about invasion of privacy as all other Americans, the same apprehensions about excesses of governmental surveillance and inquiries. Above all, they realize, perhaps better than others, that while the information technology they deal with can extend the intellect of man for the betterment of society, it also extends the power of government a millionfold.[6]

It makes it possible for government to administer more efficiently and to offer vastly better services to the taxpayers.

At the same time, it extends and unifies official power to make inquiries, conduct investigations, and to take note of the thoughts, habits and behavior of individuals. Of course, government has always had such power, but on a much smaller scale than today. Similarly, men possessing the power of government have always had the capacity for bad motives, simple errors or misguided purpose. There have always been problems with errors in the manual files. Now, computers may broadcast the image of these errors throughout a national information system.

---

6. *Hearings on Federal Data Banks, Computers and the Bill of Rights Before the Subcomm. on Constitutional Rights of the Senate Comm. on the Judiciary*, 92d Cong., 1st Sess. [Feb. 23-25 and Mar. 2-4, 9-11, 15 and 17 (1971)] [hereinafter cited as *1971 Hearings*]. Testimony of Robert Bigelow, attorney, describing concern of professional computer organizations and press, *id.* at 680; Bibliography, lists of public discussions on privacy and computers in the United States and abroad, *id.* at 692 *et seq.;* Testimony of Professor Caxton Foster, University of Mass., Department of Computer and Information Sciences, *id.* at 707.

What the electronic revolution has done is to magnify any adverse effects flowing from these influences on the life of the individual and on his proper enjoyment of the rights, benefits and privileges due a free man in a free society.

I reject the notion of division of Americans on the basis of scientific and technological values. If I had the unhappy and well-nigh impossible task of distinguishing two types of Americans, I believe I would distinguish between those who understand the proper limits and uses of governmental power and those who do not.

However much we try to rationalize decisions through the use of machines, there is one factor for which the machine can never allow. That is the insatiable curiosity of government to know everything about those it governs. Nor can it predict the ingenuity applied by government officials to find out what they think they must know to achieve their ends.

It is this curiosity, combined with the technological and electronic means of satisfying it, which has recently intensified governmental surveillance and official inquiries that I believe infringe on the constitutional rights of individuals.

Congress received so many complaints about unauthorized government data banks and information programs that the Subcommittee undertook a survey to discover what computerized and mechanized data banks government agencies maintain on people, especially about their personal habits, attitudes, and political behavior. We have also sought to learn what government-wide or nation-wide information systems have been created by integrating or sharing the separate data bases. Through our questionnaire, we have sought to learn what laws and regulations govern the creation, access and use of the major data banks in government.[7]

The replies we are receiving are astounding, not only for the information they are disclosing, but for the attitudes displayed toward the right of Congress and the American people to know what Government is doing.

In some cases, the departments were willing to tell the Subcommittee what they were doing, but classified it so no one else could know.[8] In one case, they were willing to tell all, but classified the legal authority on which they relied for their information power.[9]

---

7. For a sample of questionnaire sent to all agencies and departments with slight alterations, see Letter to Secretary of Defense Melvin Laird, July 20, 1970, *1971 Hearings* at 1182, and to Attorney General Mitchell, June 9, 1970. *Id.* at 1312.

8. *See, e.g.,* State Department response to questionnaire, concerning its "Lookout File." *See* Letter of Sept. 9, 1970 to Subcommittee Chairman from Assistant Secretary of Defense Robert Moot, and list of classified enclosures. *1971 Hearings* at 1186.

9. Navy Department response, Aug. 13, 1970, citing a Roosevelt Executive memorandum assigning responsibilities for intelligence activities. *Id.* at 1201.

Some reports are evasive and misleading. Some agencies take the attitude that the information belongs to them and that the last person who should see it is the individual whom it is about.[10] A few departments and agencies effectively deny the information by not responding until urged to do so.[11]

They reflect the attitude of the Army captain who knew Congress was investigating the Army data banks and issued a directive stating:

> The Army General Counsel has re-emphasized the long-standing policy of the Executive Branch of the Government ... that all files, records and information in the possession of the Executive Branch is privileged and is not releasable to any part of the Legislative Branch of the Government without specific direction of the President.[12]

So, on the basis of this study, and on the withholdings of information from the American people which the Subcommittee has experienced,[13] I have concluded that the claim of the Government departments to their own privacy is greatly overstated. The truth is that they have too much privacy in some of their information activities. They may cite the Freedom of Information Act[14] as authority for keeping files secret from the individual as well as from Congress. They then turn around and cite "inherent power"[15] or "housekeeping authority"[16] as a reason for maintaining data banks and computerized files on certain individuals; or they may cite the conclusions of independent Presidential factfinding commissions.[17]

---

10. Department of Transportation response. Testimony of Secretary Volpe. *Id.* at 720. Many other agencies will inform the individual of the general contents of his file, if he is denied some right, benefit or privilege and regulations permit a hearing or right of confrontation or cross-examination—but not before.

11. Department of Health, Education and Welfare, series of letters over a two year period on file with Subcommittee, and as of March, 1972, no response has been received containing substantive answers.

12. Directive, ICGP-G-S3, Jan. 9, 1971, *Release of Official Information to Legislative Branch of Government. 1971 Hearings,* at 1179.

13. Ervin, *Secrecy in a Free Society,* 213 NATION 454 (1971). *See generally Hearings on Executive Privilege Before the Subcomm. on Separation of Powers of the Senate Comm. on the Judiciary,* 92d Cong., 1st Sess. (1971). Testimony by Senator Tunney at 381 and William Rehnquist at 420.

14. 5 U.S.C. § 552 (1970).

15. *See, e.g., 1971 Hearings,* at 375, 431, 385. Testimony of Assistant Secretary of Defense Froehlke. *Id.* at 602, 599; testimony of Assistant Attorney General Rehnquist, note 13, *supra.*

16. *See, e.g.,* Justice Department response to Subcommittee questionnaire.

17. For Defense Department reliance on the findings of the National Advisory Commission on Civil Disorders (Kerner Commission), see testimony of Assistant Secretary of Defense

So far the survey results show a very wide-ranging use of such technology to process and store the information and to exchange it with other federal agencies, with state and local governments and, sometimes, with private agencies.

Most of this is done in connection with administration of Government's service programs. However, a number of these data banks and information programs may partake of the nature of large-scale blacklists. This is so because they may encompass masses of irrelevant, outdated or even incorrect investigative information based on personalities, behavior and beliefs. Unwisely applied or loosely supervised, they can operate to deprive a person of some basic right.

For instance, a Federal Communications Commission response[18] shows that the FCC uses computers to aid it in keeping track of political broadcast time, in monitoring and assigning spectrums, and in helping it make prompt checks on people who apply for licenses. The Commission reported that it also maintains a Check List, which now has about 10,900 names. This Check List, in the form of a computer print-out, is circulated to the various Bureaus within the Commission. It contains the names and addresses of organizations and individuals whose qualifications are believed to require close examination in the event they apply for a license. A name may be put on the list by Commission personnel for a variety of reasons, such as a refusal to pay an outstanding forfeiture, unlicensed operation, license

---

Froehlke, *1971 Hearings*, at 379; noting the Commission's finding that the "absence of accurate information, both before and during disorder, has created special control problems for police," and the recommendation that "Federal-State planning should ensure that Federal troops are prepared to provide aid to cities . . . . "

The Department also cited a report filed by Cyrus Vance following the Detroit 1967 disturbances. *1971 Hearings,* at 378.

For law enforcement reliance on the Kerner Commission and similar commissions, *see e.g.,* testimony of Richard Velde for the *Law Enforcement Assistance Administration. 1971, Hearings* at 608:

Several States are also developing with LEAA funds information systems related to civil disorders. Most of these systems have as their objective either tension detection and forecasting or providing support to tactical units. It should be noted that the Kerner Commission studied this problem carefully and recommended that the police develop adequate intelligence for tension-detecting as well as on-the-scene information for tactical units. Many of the systems LEAA supports in the civil disorders area arose out of the recommendations of the Kerner Commission and similar commissions established by the States.

For reliance on Warren Commission finding of information gaps, *see* response to Subcommittee questionnaries by the Secret Service, Nov. 21, 1969, reprinted at 115 CONG. REC. 39,114 (1969), and by the State Department Jan. 4 and Mar. 10, 1970; both responses in Subcommittee file.

18. Response to questionnaire, in Subcommittee files, Mar. 25, 1971.

suspension, the issuance of a bad check to the Commission or stopping payment on a fee check after failing a Commission examination.

In addition, this list incorporates the names and addresses of individuals and organizations appearing in several lists prepared by the Department of Justice, other Government agencies, and Congressional committees. For example, the list contains information from the "FBI Withhold List," which contains the names of individuals or organizations which are allegedly subversive, and from the Department of Justice's "Organized Crime and Racketeering List," which contains the names of individuals who are or have been subjects of investigation in connection with activities identified with organized crime. Also included in the list are names obtained from other Government sources, such as the Internal Revenue Service, the Central Intelligence Agency, and the House Committee on Internal Security. According to the Commission, the use of the data arose in 1964 because during the course of Senate Hearings chaired by Senator McClellan, it was discovered that a reputed racketeering boss in New Orleans, Louisiana, held a Commission license. In order that such licensing not take place in the future, the Commission established liaison with the responsible divisions within the Department of Justice to be kept current on persons who might have such affiliations.

The Civil Service Commission maintains a "security file" in electrically powered rotary cabinets containing 2,120,000 index cards.[19] According to the Commission, these bear lead information relating to possible questions of suitability involving loyalty and subversive activity. The lead information contained in these files has been developed from published hearings of Congressional committees, State legislative committees, public investigative bodies, reports of investigation, publications of subversive organizations, and various other newspapers and periodicals. This file is not new, but has been growing since World War II.

The Commission chairman reported:

> Investigative and intelligence officials of the various departments and agencies of the Federal Government make extensive official use of the file through their requests for searches relating to investigations they are conducting.

---

19. *Id.* Aug. 18, 1970.

In another "security investigations index" the Commission maintains 10,250,000 index cards filed alphabetically covering personnel investigations made by the Civil Service Commission and other agencies since 1939. Records in this index relate to incumbents of Federal positions, former employees, and applicants on whom investigations were made or are in process of being made.

Then, the Commission keeps an "investigative file" of approximately 625,000 file folders containing reports of investigation on cases investigated by the Commission. In addition, about 2,100,000 earlier investigative files are maintained at the Washington National Records Center in security storage. These are kept to avoid duplication of investigations or for updating previous investigations.

The Housing and Urban Development Department is considering automation of a departmental system which would integrate records now included in FHA's Sponsor Identification File, Department of Justice's Organized Crime and Rackets File, and HUD's Adverse Information File.[20] A data bank consisting of approximately 325,000 3x5 index cards has been prepared covering any individual or firm which was the subject of, or mentioned prominently in, any investigations dating from 1954 to the present. This includes all FBI investigations of housing matters as well.

In the area of law enforcement, the Bureau of Customs has installed a central automated data processing intelligence network which is a comprehensive data bank of suspect information available on a 24-hour-a-day basis to Customs terminals throughout the country.[21]

According to the Secretary of the Treasury:

These records include current information from our informer, fugitive and suspect lists that have been maintained throughout the Bureau's history as an enforcement tool and which have been available at all major ports of entry, though in much less accessible and usable form. With the coordinated efforts of the Agency Service's intelligence activities, steady growth of the suspect files is expected.

There is the "Lookout File" of the Passport Office and the Bureau of Security and Consular Affairs.[22] This computerized file illustrates the "good neighbor" policy agencies observe by exchanging information in order to keep individuals under surveillance for intelligence and law enforcement purposes. Maintained apart from the

20. *Id.* June 22, 1970.
21. *Id.* May 28, 1970.
22. *Id.* Jan. 4, 1970.

twenty million other passport files, its basic purpose is to assist in screening passport applicants to make certain they are citizens of the United States and that they are eligible to receive passports. Requests for entry into this system are received from component agencies of the Department, from other government agencies, or in the limited category of child custody, from an interested parent or guardian.

The Department assured the Subcommittee that data recorded in this "Lookout File" is not disseminated. Rather, it serves as a "flag" which, if a "hit" or suspect is recorded, is furnished to the original source of the lookout and consists of the name of the individual and the fact that he has applied for a passport. The individual is not told that he is in the file until the information is used adversely against him. Then, according to the report, "he is fully informed and given an opportunity to explain or rebut the information on which the adverse action is based."

Among some of the reasons listed for people being in the Lookout File are the following:

> If the individual's actions do not reflect to the credit of U.S. abroad;
> If he is wanted by a law enforcement agency in connection with criminal activity;
> If a court order restricting travel is outstanding or the individual is involved in a custody or desertion case;
> If he is a known or suspected Communist or subversive;
> If he is on the Organized Crime and Rackets List or is a suspected delinquent in military obligations.

The Defense Industrial Security Clearance Office is preparing to computerize its card files on over one and a half million private citizens who are employees of businesses doing classified contract work for the Federal Government.[23]

The Federal Deposit Insurance Corporation maintains information on people now associated with banks insured by the FDIC or who have been associated with such banks in the past.[24] It keeps a file on the names of individuals gained from newspapers and other public sources if they are characterized as having an unsatisfactory relationship with any insured bank or any closed insured bank. This also includes information supplied to the Corporation by other inves-

---

23. *Id.* Aug. 1970. *See also 1971 Hearings,* at 375, Froehlke testimony on this and other Defense Department records systems.
24. Response to questionnaire, Feb. 22, 1972. *See also* 12 U.S.C. § 1811 *et seq.* (1964), Amendments to Federal Deposit Insurance Act, requiring bank recording and reporting to Internal Revenue Service transactions, S. REP. 91-1139 and H.R. REP. 91-975.

tigative or regulatory agencies on persons connected with an insured bank.

The Army maintains the U.S. Army Investigative Records Repository (USAIRR) which contains about 7,000,000 files relating principally to security and criminal investigations of former and present members of the Army, civilian employees and employees of private contractors doing business with the Army. The other services maintain similar investigative files.[25]

There is a Defense Central Index of Investigation operated by the Army for the entire Defense Department. The Index is designed to locate any security or criminal investigative file for any Defense agency and will be computerized shortly. It contains identifying data such as name, date of birth and social security number on people who have ever been the subject of investigations.[26]

There are all the data banks and computers in the Department of Justice[27] for intelligence, for civil disturbance prevention; for "bad checks passers;" for organized crime surveillance; and for federal-state law enforcement cooperation through the computerized National Crime Information Center.

On the basis of our investigation of complaints reviewed by Congress,[28] I am convinced that people throughout the country are more fearful than ever before about those applications of computer technology and scientific information processing which may adversely affect their constitutional rights. Furthermore, my study of the Constitution convinces me that their fears are well founded.

First, they are concerned that through a computer error they may be denied basic fairness and due process of law with respect to benefits and privileges for which they have applied.

Secondly, they are concerned about illegal access and violation of confidentiality of personal information which is obtained about them by government or industry.

---

25. *See* note 23 *supra*.

26. Response to Subcommittee questionnaire, Aug. 1970. Also described in Froehlke testimony, note 23, *supra* and in Army Undersecretary Beal letter of Mar. 20, 1970, reprinted in *1971 Hearings, Part II* at 1051, and at 116 CONG. REC. 26327-51 (1970).

27. For descriptions and citations to supporting statutes and regulations, *see* response to Subcommittee questionnaires, *1971 Hearings, Part II* at 1312-68. *See also* discussion in testimony of Justice Department officials. *Id. Part I* at 597, 849.

28. For descriptions and summaries of some of these complaints and concerns, Remarks of Senator Ervin, 116 CONG. REC. 30,797, 41,751, 43,944 and 117 CONG. REC. S. 985 (daily ed. Feb. 8, 1971). In particular, note opening statements by Subcommittee Chairman each day of *1971 Hearings* outlining issues of concern for the day. Of interest here is a Dec., 1971 report, *A National Survey of the Public's Attitudes Toward Computers*, sponsored by the American Federation of Information Processing Societies and TIME MAGAZINE noting that:

These are actions which for any one individual or for entire groups may lead to a loss of the ability to exercise that "pursuit of happiness" which the Declaration of Independence declares is one of the unalienable rights of man.

These are actions which, by producing erroneous reports, may limit or deny a person's economic prospects and thereby impair that liberty which under the 5th and 14th amendments government may not impair without due process of law.

Arrest Records

This possibility is illustrated by a letter[29] I received from a man who describes the effect on his life of an incident which occurred when he was fifteen years of age. In connection with a locker theft, he was taken to the police station, finger-printed, questioned, and then he left, cleared of charges. He was not involved in any incident subsequently except a few minor traffic violations. He served 11 years in the armed services and held the highest security clearances. After gaining employment with a city government, he discovered that the youthful incident was, 15 years later, part of an FBI file and distributed to employers on request. He was asked to explain the incident for personnel records and to state why he withheld the information. Although he was unaware of the record, he believes the failure to list the incident was a factor in not gaining employment in several instances, and he was told he would have to institute court action to have the record expunged.

The problem he and millions of others face with respect to their records is illustrated by a regulation issued by the Attorney General last year restating the goal of the Federal Bureau of Investigation "to conduct the acquisition, collection, exchange, classification, and preservation of identification records . . . on a mutually beneficial

There is major concern about the use of large computerized information files. Thirty-eight percent of those surveyed believe computers represent a real threat to people's privacy as opposed to fifty-four percent who disagreed. Sixty-two percent are concerned that some large organizations keep information about millions of people. In addition, fifty-three percent believe computerized information files might be used to destroy individual freedoms; fifty-eight percent feel computers will be used in the future to keep people under surveillance; and forty-two percent believe there is no way to find out if information about you stored in a computer is accurate. In general, the public believes government should make increased usage of computers in a number of areas, that such usage will make government more effective, and that there will, and should be, increasing governmental involvement in the way computers are used.

29. Letter, identity withheld, in Subcommittee files with comment by the Director of the Federal Bureau of Investigation.

basis." [30] Among the agencies listed as eligible to receive and supply information were railroad police, banking institutions and insurance companies.

In Washington, D.C., a young man who was an innocent bystander during a campus demonstration was arrested by police and then released. Knowing that the FBI could distribute such records to employers, he hired a lawyer and spent large sums of money in a suit to have his arrest record expunged. The lower court denied his request, but the Court of Appeals ruled that, in the District of Columbia at least, arrest records should be expunged for innocent bystanders caught up in mass police arrests. [31]

In another case, a young man was arrested on probable cause and fingerprinted in California. When the police could not connect him with the case, he was released. He sought to have his arrest record expunged, or alternatively, to have strict limitations placed on its dissemination to prospective employers and others by the Federal Bureau of Investigation. While the U.S. District Court denied his request for expungement, it did say that his arrest record may not be revealed to prospective employers except in the case of any Federal agency when he seeks employment with that agency. However, it could be distributed for law enforcement purposes. Congress later restored this power to the F B I temporarily in an annual appropriation bill.

Judge Gesell's comments in this case of *Menard* v. *Mitchell*[32] are significant for the issue of arrest records, but also for the Army's computer surveillance program and for many other government in-

---

30. 28 C.F.R. § 0.85 (b); codifying rulings by the Attorney General pursuant to 28 U.S.C. § 534 which provides:

(a) The Attorney General shall—

(1) acquire, collect, classify, and preserve identification, crime and other records; and
exchange these records with, and for the official use of, authorized officials of the Federal Government, the States, cities, and penal and other institutions.

(b) The exchange of records authorized by subsection (a) (2) of this section is subject to cancellation if dissemination is made outside the receiving departments or related agencies.

(c) The Attorney General may appoint officials to perform the functions authorized by this section.

31. Morrow v. District of Columbia, 417 F.2d 728 (D.C. Cir. 1969). For a summary of case law on this subject, *see* Longton, *Maintenance and Dissemination of Records of Arrest Versus the Right to Privacy*, 17 WAYNE L. REV. 995 (1971).

32. Menard v. Mitchell, 430 F.2d 486 (D.C. Cir. 1970), *decision upon remand*, 328 F. Supp. 718 (D.D.C. 1971). The Court construed 28 U.S.C. § 534 narrowly to avoid the constitutional issues raised by *Menard* and found that:

telligence systems now being designed. He stated that while "conduct against the state may properly subject an individual to limitations upon his future freedom within tolerant limits, accusations not proven, charges made without supporting evidence when tested by the judicial process, ancient or juvenile transgressions long since expiated by responsible conduct, should not be indiscriminately broadcast under governmental auspices." He also said:

> The increasing complexity of our society and technological advances which facilitate massive accumulation and ready regurgitation of farflung data have presented more problems in this area, certainly problems not contemplated by the framers of the Constitution. These developments emphasize a pressing need to preserve and to redefine aspects of the right of privacy to insure the basic freedoms guaranteed by this democracy.

> A heavy burden is placed on all branches of Government to maintain a proper equilibrium between the acquisition of information and the necessity to safeguard privacy. Systematic recordation and dissemination of information about individual citizens is a form of surveillance and control which may easily inhibit freedom to speak, to work, and to move about in this land. If information available to Government is misused to publicize past incidents in the lives of its citizens the pressures for conformity will be irresistible. Initiative and individuality can be suffocated and a resulting dullness of mind and conduct will become the norm. We

---

It is abundantly clear that Congress never intended to, or in fact did, authorize dissemination of arrest records to any state or local agency for purposes of employment or licensing checks.

It found certain faults with the present system: (1) State and local agencies receive criminal record data for employment purposes whenever authorized by local enactment, and these vary state by state and locality by locality. (2) The Bureau cannot prevent improper dissemination and use of the material it supplies to hundreds of local agencies. There are no criminal or civil sanctions. Control of the data will be made more difficult and opportunities for improper use will increase with the development of centralized state information centers to be linked by computer to the Bureau. (3) The arrest record material is incomplete and hence often inaccurate, yet no procedure exists to enable individuals to obtain, correct or supplant the criminal record information used against them, nor indeed is there any assurance that the individual even knows his employment application is affected by an FBI fingerprint check.

The Court invited Congressional action, noting that:

with the increasing availability of fingerprints, technological developments, and the enormous increase in population, the system is out of effective control. The Bureau needs legislative guidance and there must be a national policy developed in this area which will have built into it adequate sanctions and administrative safeguards.

are far from having reached this condition today, but surely history teaches that inroads are most likely to occur during unsettled times like these where fear or the passions of the moment can lead to excesses.

There are many similar cases pending throughout the states. Present laws are not sufficient to assure that an individual will be judged on his merit and not by inaccurate arrest records distributed by a national law enforcement computer.[33]

Law Enforcement Intelligence Records

Such threats to privacy and liberty arise with special force in the area of intelligence records. The Subcommittee study reveals two serious problems which have acquired national urgency through the introduction of computer technology. First, the problem of safeguarding intelligence information from improper release by government it-

---

33. Congressional response to the District Court's invitation has taken several forms, among them, a bill, S. 2545, introduced, but not acted on, to authorize the Attorney General to exchange criminal record information with certain state and local agencies. Remarks by Senator Bible, S. 14558, 117 CONG. REC., (daily ed. Sept. 20, 1971); and an amendment to the Department of Justice Appropriation Act of 1972 temporarily restoring the power over arrest records limited by the *Menard* decision. 117 CONG. REC. S.20461 (daily ed. Dec. 3, 1971). House Judiciary Subcommittee No. 4 on Mar. 16 began hearings on H.R. 13315, a bill introduced by Rep. Edwards, "to provide for the dissemination and use of criminal arrest records in a manner that insures security and privacy."

A related, but more comprehensive bill, S.2546, was introduced by Senator Hruska on Sept. 20, 1971, 117 CONG. REC. (daily ed.) to insure the security and privacy of criminal justice information systems. This is termed the Attorney General's response to an amendment to the Omnibus Crime Control Act of 1970, 18 U.S.C. § § 351, 1752, 2516, 3731 (1964), requiring the Law Enforcement Assistance Administration to submit legislative recommendations to promote the integrity and accuracy of criminal justice data collection. LEAA demonstrated a prototype computerized system for exchange of criminal history information with the states, a project known as SEARCH — System for Electronic Analysis and Retrieval of Criminal Histories. In Dec. 1970, Project SEARCH was turned over to the FBI for the development of an operation system to be part of the National Crime Information System. The bill deals with criminal offender record information as well as criminal intelligence information.

A discussion of the philosophical, constitutional and legal issues and problems related to such a computerized system is found, with bibliographies, in *Security and Privacy Consideration* in *Criminal History Information Systems, Technical Rept. No. 2,* July, 1970, by Project SEARCH, California Crime Technological Research Foundation, funded by the Law Enforcement Assistance Administration, Department of Justice. Also pertinent is the testimony of LEAA officials on the use of information and intelligence systems by criminal justice agencies. *1971 Hearings,* on the National Crime Information Center. *Id.* at 914.

For a model state act proposed for criminal offender record information, *See generally Technical Memorandum No. 3,* May, 1971 by Project SEARCH.

As we have a highly mobile population, so we have a highly mobile criminal population, which requires that governments be able to share rapidly the information in their data banks in the interest of law enforcement. The problem is determining what agencies and what officials should control what information.

self, and secondly, the problem of confining its collection to appropriate areas and subjects.

Government has, and should have, power to collect information, even raw, unverified intelligence information, in fields in which government has a lawful, legitimate interest. But this great power imposes a solemn responsibility to see that no one is given access to that information, except the Government itself for some legitimate purpose. There could never, for instance, be justification for Government to disclose intelligence gathered about citizens pursuant to its powers, to other citizens for their own personal or financial aggrandizement. Nor should Government through disclosure of confidential documents aid and abet the writing of sensational articles in private journals operated for commercial profit.

Nevertheless, the Subcommittee received testimony and evidence about two cases which illustrate the misuse of confidential intelligence information for such purposes.

One involved a man in political life, the mayor of San Francisco, who was the subject of an article in Look Magazine purporting to establish that he associated with persons involved in organized crime. When the Mayor sued the magazine for libel, he undertook through subpoena power to learn the basis for such charges and where and how the authors obtained their information. He learned that they had received confidential information and documents from intelligence data banks. The information came from files and computer printouts of a number of major Federal, state and local government law enforcement agencies. They involved the U.S. Attorney General's Office, the Federal Bureau of Investigation, Internal Revenue Service, Federal Bureau of Narcotics, the Customs Bureau, the Immigration and Naturalization Service, the California Criminal Identification and Investigation Bureau, the California State Department of Justice, and the Intelligence Unit of the Los Angeles Police Department. By their own testimony for the case, the authors of the article admitted that they examined, obtained or borrowed originals or copies of such law enforcement records containing much raw unevaluated intelligence information on numerous people including the names of three U.S. Presidents, the state Governor, a number of Senators, and many private law-abiding citizens, not accused of any crime. These documents were obtainable despite the fact that many of them were stamped "Confidential" or

Property of U.S. Government. For official use only. May not be disseminated or contents disclosed without permission . . .

There is more about these and other disclosures in the hearing record but I believe the Mayor's testimony[34] illustrates many of the dangers to privacy in this age of large investigative networks and instant computerized dossiers. It also illustrates the lack of sufficient criminal, civil, or administrative sanctions against unwarranted sharing and disclosure of such confidential information. To my knowledge, no punitive action was taken except for a disciplinary personnel action filed against an agent of the Federal Bureau of Investigation, who was then allowed to retire.

The weakness of any applicable regulations is demonstrated by the report of the Bureau of Narcotics and Dangerous Drugs that its current disclosure order "would not cover the release of collateral intelligence information, information contained in dead files, or information on nondefendants, such as that disclosed in the Alioto testimony." The Bureau further stated that under the provisions of its new Agents Manual it is only a "breach of integrity" to make unauthorized disclosure of files which are restricted to official use.[35]

Misuse of Military Intelligence Records

Another case[36] illustrates how the Army's investigative intelligence services and files were put to private use to obtain the dismissal

---

34. *See 1971 Hearings* at 493-530, Testimony of Joseph Alioto, Mayor of San Francisco, and exhibits submitted. For response of Justice Department officials, see testimony of William Rehnquist, *id.* at 604, 878-88, and a series of memoranda from the Federal Bureau of Investigation, the Bureau of Narcotics and Dangerous Drugs, which memoranda were submitted by Assistant Attorney General Rehnquist with the caveat that:

> Under the traditional notions of separation of powers, it seems to me probable that the Department could justifiably decline to furnish portions of this information... *Id.* at 1371.

35. *1971 Hearings*, Part II at 1375. In his memorandum of Mar. 5, 1971, the Director of the Bureau of Narcotics and Dangerous Drugs noted " ... it is possible that the documents or information in these four exhibits could have been passed to the LOOK reporters by a BNDD employee." He cites BNDD Order 0-98, May 27, 1970 as the Bureau's current public information policy and as essentially a restatement of 28 C.F.R. Pt. 50, § 50.2, which covers the dissemination of most types of information for the Department. However, he states that the

> strongest applicable regulations in this matter are found in 28 C.F.R. Pt. 45, § 45.735: "No employee shall use for financial gain for himself or for another person, or make any other improper use of, whether by direct action on his part or by counsel, recommendation, or suggestion to another person, information which comes to the employee by reason of his status as a Department of Justice employee and which has not become part of the body of public information."

> Obviously, the disclosure of documents stamped "For official use only" would be contrary to this regulation if, in fact, the disclosures were made by Department of Justice employees.

36. For statement submitted by a Special Agent of Military Intelligence and related correspondence, *see 1971 Hearings*, Part II at 1451-1457.

of an employee of a private business. In this instance an Army intelligence agent whose routine duties involved security investigations and surveillance for the Army's civil disturbance prevention program described to the Subcommittee how he was ordered by his superiors to conduct an investigation of the bank loan records, police and court records of the private citizen and was told to give the resulting information to the employee's supervisor. He later learned that the investigation had been ordered by an intelligence officer as a personal favor for an official of the company. When the agent reported this to his superiors, he was told in a classified letter that the matter involved "national security." A year later, following his separation from the service, the agent reported the incident to the Inspector General of the Assistant Chief of Staff for the Pentagon, who began an investigation. All of his allegations were confirmed and firm disciplinary actions were taken against the guilty officers. It was too late, however, for the subject of the Army investigative report, who had already been dismissed.

These cases illustrate the concerns over political administrative and technical problems of access, confidentiality and purging of erroneous or outdated records in computer systems. But these are issues which have long concerned legislatures, bar associations and others.

The major reason for public apprehension about computer technology and information sciences is the use of them to acquire, process, analyze and store information about activities and matters which are protected by the First Amendment.

What people writing to Congress fear most is the uses to which this technology may be put by men of little understanding but great zeal. They know that, applied to unlawful or unwise programs, computers merely absorb the follies and foibles of misguided politically-minded administrators.

In Federal Government, the new technology, combined with extended Federal-state services and their spin-off information systems, have produced vast numbers of investigators, analysts, and programmers devoted to the study of people and society. With the zeal of dedicated civil servants, they are devoted to the building of data bases on the habits, attitudes and beliefs of law-abiding citizens. Much of what they gather is trivial; much of it goes far beyond the needs of government. Some of it is shared extensively and often unnecessarily by agencies who are components of these large information systems.

People seeking government jobs in some agencies are told to reply to personality tests asking:

I believe there is a God.

I believe in the second coming of Christ.
I believe in a life hereafter.
I am very religious (more than most people).
I go to church almost every week.
I am very strongly attracted by members of my own sex.
I love my father.
My sex life is satisfactory.
Once in a while I feel hate towards members of my family
    whom I usually love.
I wish I were not bothered by thoughts about sex.

When the Subcommittee held hearings on these practices, government officials explained that there was no right or wrong answer to the questions, that the responses were coded and analyzed by the computer.[37]

I asked whether they did not think such inquiries violated the privacy of the individual's thoughts about matters that were none of the business of government. The reply was that there was no Supreme Court decision holding that people who apply for federal employment have a constitutional right to privacy.

There was a Civil Service program telling employees to fill out computer punch cards stating their racial, ethnic or national origin along with their social security number.[38] In the land renowned for being the "melting pot" of the world, over 3 million individuals had to analyze their backgrounds and reduce them to one of four squares on an IBM card. If they protested that these matters were none of the business of government, they were blacklisted in their offices and harrassed with computer-produced orders to return the completed

---

37. *See generally Hearings on Psychological Tests and Constitutional Rights Before the Subcomm. on Constitutional Rights of the State Comm. on the Judiciary*, 89th Cong., 1st Sess. (1965) and *Hearings on S. 3779* on *Privacy and the Rights of Government Employees*, 89th Cong., 2d Sess. (1966).

38. *See 1966 Hearings, supra* note 37. In connection with a proposal introduced to protect the constitutional rights of employees of the executive branch and to prevent unwarranted governmental invasion of their privacy, *see* Senate remarks of Senator Ervin including discussion of need for law prohibiting requirements to reveal information on race, religion, national origin, personal family relationships, sexual attitudes and conduct and religious beliefs and practices in 112 CONG. REC. 16081, 18634 (1966), 113 CONG. REC. 4039, 10663, 27994 (1967), 114 CONG. REC. 11235, 17161, 19613 (1968), 115 CONG. REC. 2343, 117 CONG. REC. (daily ed. Apr. 1 and May 11, 1971). By such legislation, government may be prevented from intruding into protected First Amendment areas on subjects which should have nothing to do with the operation of a civil service merit system. By exclusion of such sensitive, subjective information from the computer systems, initially, government will be precluded from basing individual or general social judgments on outdated standards, changing mores, variants in ethnic, cultural or geographical backgrounds, or previous conditions of the individual's mind, heart, and personality. It will necessarily be confined to a consideration of current information relevant and pertinent to the problem at hand.

questionnaire. The resemblances between this program and those of totalitarian governments in our recent history were all too obvious.

The Census Bureau makes more use of computer technology for personal inquiries than anyone.[39] It conducts surveys for its own uses backed by the criminal and civil sanctions. One of these, the decennial census, asked people such questions as:

Marital Status: Now married, divorced, widowed,
separated, never married.
(If a woman) How many babies have you ever had,
not counting stillbirths?
Do you have a flush toilet?
Have you been married more than once?
Did your first marriage end because of death of
wife or husband?
What was your major activity 5 years ago?
What is your rent?
What is your monthly electric bill?
Did you work at any time last week?
Do you have a dishwasher? Built-in or portable?
How did you get to work last week? (Driver,
private auto; passenger, private auto; subway;
bus; taxi; walked only; other means).
How many bedrooms do you have?
Do you have a health condition or disability which
limits the amount of work you can do at a job?
How long have you had this condition or disability?

Under even heavier sanctions, the Census Bureau puts questionnaires to farmers, lawyers, owners of businesses, and others, selected at random, about the way they handle their business and finances.[40]

---

39. *See generally Hearings on S.1791 and Privacy, the Census and Federal Questionnaires Before the Subcomm. on Constitutional Rights of the Senate Judiciary Committee*, 91st Cong., 1st Sess. (1969) and hundreds of letters and complaints about coercive statistical questionnaires. Appendix also contains judicial, legal and constitutional research materials as well as examples of many social and economic questionnaires. *See also* Pipe and Russell, *Privacy: Establishing Restrictions on·Government Inquiry*, 18 AMER. UNIV. L. REV. 516 (1969). For a summary of the hearings, *see* Senate remarks of Senator Ervin, 115 CONG. REC. 17718 (1969). For possible political uses of such information acquired as economic and social indicators, *see* Report by House Government Operations Committee, Subcommittee on Government Information, on Department of Labor briefings on economic statistics; and 23 WESTERN POL. Q. 235 (1970). *See also* the finding and recommendations on privacy and confidentiality of the PRESIDENT'S COMMISSION ON FEDERAL STATISTICS (1971).

40. *See 1969 Hearings, supra* note 39,. testimony on behalf of the National Federation of Independent Business at 199, of attorney and farm owner William Van Tillburg at 74, W. Schliestett, businessman at 66, J. Cannon, attorney at 7,263.

The Census Bureau also makes surveys for many other depart-ments and agencies.[41] For example, they put out statistical question-naires which the Department of Health, Education and Welfare wanted to send to retired people asking:

- How often they call their parents;
- What they spend on presents for grandchildren;
- How many newspapers and magazines they buy a month;
- If they wear artificial dentures;
- "Taking things all together, would you say you're very happy, pretty happy, or not too happy these days?"
- And many other questions about things on which govern-has no business demanding answers.

These people are not told that their answers are voluntary, but are harrassed to reply and are given the impression they will be penalized if they do not answer.[42]

There are many other examples of inquiring social and economic data that are backed by the psychological, economic, or penal sanc-tion of government. Clearly, Government has great need for all kinds of information about people in order to govern efficiently and admin-ister the laws well; similarly, Congress must have large amounts of meaningful information in order to legislate wisely.

However, I believe these examples of governmental data collec-tion illustrate my contention that the First Amendment wraps up the principle of free speech, which includes the right to speak one's thoughts and opinions as well as the right to be free of governmental coercion to speak them.

There are other examples of government programs which, well-meaning in purpose, are fraught with danger for the very freedoms which were designed to make the minds and spirits of all Americans

---

41. *Id.* at 830. Table of Census surveys of population and households, conducted for other government agencies, with indication of penalties and compliance techniques. In many of these, the data is kept on tape or film by both the Census Bureau and the sponsoring agency, and the confidentiality rules of the sponsoring agency apply.

42. *Id.* at 251. Assistant Secretary of Commerce Chartener:

Assistant Secretary of Commerce Chartener: The wording deliberately has been rather subtle in its form. We never use the word "mandatory" on a questionnaire. Instead, people will be told that "your answer is required by law." In other cases, they may be told that a survey is authorized by law or it is important to your government or something of that sort. Now, the followup procedure is used not for purposes of coercion but rather in order to verify the correctness of an address.

Senator Ervin: Do you not agree with me that such a procedure is designed to implant in the mind of the recipient of these questionnaires the impression that he is required by law to answer them?

free, and which work to keep America a free society. A number of these would be impractical, if not impossible, without the assistance of computer technology and scientific data processing.

It is those First Amendment freedoms which are the most precious rights conferred upon us by our Constitution: the freedom to assemble peaceably with others and petition government for a redress of grievances; the freedom to worship according to the dictates of one's own conscience free of government note-taking; the freedom to think one's own thoughts regardless of whether they are pleasing to government or not; the freedom to speak what one believes whether his speech is pleasing to the government or not; the freedom to associate with others of like mind to further ideas or policies which one believes beneficial to our country, whether such association is pleasing to government or not.

The Secret Service

In the pursuit of its programs to protect high government officials from harm and federal buildings from damage,[43] the Secret

---

Mr. Chartener: If it is a mandatory questionnaire that would be the case. In other instances, the repeated mailings which may go up to five or may involve telephone calls or even a personal call are simply a means of emphasizing the importance that the Government feels in getting this response . . . .

The Department of Commerce opposed enactment of a simply-worded statute advising people that their responses to these statistical questionnaires were voluntary. *Id.* at 262.

Senator Ervin: Would the Department of Commerce and its Bureau of the Census be opposed to enactment of Federal statutes which would require that the Bureau of the Census advise every citizen on a questionnaire sent out by the Bureau that where it is not required by law, not mandatory, this is an effort to elicit information desired by the Government on a voluntary basis?

Mr. Chartener: Senator, I think we would oppose that. This is a matter of rather subtle psychology. I do not think, personally, and this is the position of the Department, that we ought to go out of our way to tell people they do not need to bother filling out this questionnaire . . . .

Senator Ervin: You think the statutes governing those questionnaires, which are mandatory and which are subject to the criminal penalty if not answered readily, are understandable by the average layman?

Mr. Chartener: I do not think any law is written to be readily understandable by the average layman. That is why we have lawyers.

But compare the testimony of the Secretary of the Department of Health, Education and Welfare in the *1971 Hearings* at 788, opposing legislation, but favoring administrative notice of voluntariness for that Department's forms.

43. 115 CONG. REC. 3356 (1969) and guidelines printed there. *See also* note 17, *supra,* correspondence and guidelines printed at 1541, *1971 Hearings,* Part II. *See* remarks of

Service has been pressured to create a computerized data bank. Their guidelines for inclusion of citizens in this data bank requested much legitimate information but also called for information on "professional gate crashers;" "civil disturbances;" "anti-American or anti-U.S. Government demonstrations in the United States or overseas;" pertaining to a threat, plan, or attempt by an individual or group to "embarrass persons protected by the Secret Service or any other high U.S. Government official at home or abroad;" "persons who insist upon personally contacting high government officials for the purpose of redress of imaginary grievances;" and "information on any person who makes oral or written statements about high government officials in the following categories: (1) threatening statements, (2) irrational statements, and (3) abusive statements."

Americans have always been proud of their First Amendment freedoms which enable them to speak their minds about the shortcomings of their elected officials. As one in political life, I have myself received letters I considered abusive. Similarly, I have uttered words which others have deemed abusive. While I am not a "professional gate crasher," I am a malcontent on many issues. I have written the President and other high government officials complaining of grievances which some may consider imaginary; and on occasion, I may also have "embarrassed" high government officials.

One man wrote me his concern about this program and commented:

> The Secret Service ought to go after my mother-in-law, too. On her last visit she said that the Vice President doesn't seem to have too many brains. She also said that Senator .... has a face like a carbuncle. Should I report this to the Secret Service?[44]

There is no doubt that the physical protection of the President and high government officials is a legitimate government purpose and all reasonable means must be taken in pursuit of it. Nevertheless, such broad and vaguely worded standards for investigating and adversely reporting Americans to their government on the basis of their utterances could, at one time or another, include most members of Congress and most politically aware citizens. It could cover heated words exchanged in political debate and discussion anywhere in the country. Yet civil and military officials throughout the Federal

---

Rep. Stanton, 118 CONG. REC. at H208 (daily ed. Jan. 24, 1972) [Complaints Against Secret Service].

44. Letter in Subcommittee files.

government and in some local law enforcement agencies were requested to report people coming to their attention who were thought to fit these criteria.

The Subcommittee has not received complete answers to our questionnaire on the subject of this computer and the national reporting system it serves. However, we have indications that other broad and zealous information programs, including the Army civil disturbance system,[45] are sharing or feeding on entries which, if not carefully evaluated, may produce serious consequences for the rights and privileges of citizens. Illustrating the misunderstandings and misinterpretations possible is the fact that military doctors have expressed to me their concern about an allegedly "secret" agreement between the Defense Department and the Secret Service which they were told was a recent one and which required reporting of all servicemen receiving administrative discharges. One psychiatrist writes of his concern for the confidentiality of medical records in such action:

> I see very little reason for this. My impression of the individuals whom I recommended for such a discharge was that these were immature individuals who were not able to adapt to the service for one reason or another. Not by any stretch of the imagination were these individuals unpatriotic or a threat to the security of the nation.[46]

When I asked the Secretary of the Navy about this, the Subcommittee was informed that a person is not reported to the Secret Service merely because he received an administrative discharge from the Navy or Marine Corps.[47] However, we were informed that Pursuant to Naval regulations issued under a secret 1965 Agreement,[48]

---

45. *See Department of the Army Civil Disturbance Information Collection Plan*, May 2, 1969, collection priorities and requirements and distribution list for government agencies. Printed in *1971 Hearings* at 1126, 1136. This plan also appears with remarks of Senator Bayh, 117 CONG. REC. 2290 (daily ed., Mar. 2, 1971).

46. Letters in Subcommittee files (identities withheld).

47. Letter of inquiry from Subcommittee Chairman, July 6, 1971, citing the large number of reasons for which a person can receive an administrative discharge, ranging from family hardship to national security grounds, the inadequate procedures and safeguards surrounding such discharges, and the threat to individual freedom from unrestricted reporting of law-abiding citizens, who may become subjects of official surveillance through no fault of their own or of the Secret Service.

48. This December 14, 1965 agreement between the Defense Department and the Secret Service was implemented within the Navy Department by SECNAV Instruction 5500.27, 18 March 1966, which contains a copy of the agreement. Administrative authority for this regulation is cited as Defense Dept. Directive 5030.34, dated 30 Dec. 1965; statutory authority for assistance to the Secret Service is cited as P.L. No. 90-331 (June 6, 1968) which provides for assistance to the Secret Service on request.

the Navy reports an average of 400 persons annually. We learned, for example, that among the many categories of people to be reported were not only servicemen but civilian employees of the Defense Department who were discharged on security or suitability grounds and who showed "evidence of emotional instability or irrational or suicidal behavior, expressed strong or violent sentiments against the United States," or who had "previous arrests, convictions, conduct or statements indicating a propensity for violence and antipathy for good order in Government."[49]

Military Spying

Another example of First Amendment information programs is the Army program for spying on Americans who exercised their First Amendment rights. Despite these rights, and despite the constitutional division of power between the federal and state governments, despite laws and decisions defining the legal role and duties of the Army, the Army was given the power to create an information system of data banks and computer programs which threatened to erode these restrictions on governmental power.[50]

Allegedly, for the purpose of predicting and preventing civil disturbances which might develop beyond the control of state and local officials, Army agents were sent throughout the country to keep surveillance over the way the civilian population expressed their sentiments about government policies. In churches, on campuses, in classrooms, in public meetings, they took notes, tape-recorded, and photographed people who dissented in thought, word or deed. This included clergymen, editors, public officials, and anyone who sympathized with the dissenters.

---

49. Appendix B of Agreement. Under Appendix A, identification data, photograph, physical description, date and place of birth, employment, marital status and identifying numbers are to be furnished, together with summaries or excerpts from DOD files as applicable to an individual or group reported.

In a related exchange of correspondence, the Subcommittee Chairman, in response to complaints, directed an inquiry to the Secretary of the Navy, on April 22, 1970 about a Navy directive which required that in any case where enlisted personnel were to be separated under other than honorable conditions within the continental United States, local civil police authorities were to be notified in advance of the name, race, sex and place and date of birth of the person, and of the time and place such separation is to be effected. This regulation seemed to serve no useful function since the Army and the Air Force functioned without one. On May 7, 1970, the Navy Department notified the Subcommittee that they concurred in this view and would delete the reporting requirement. (Correspondence in Subcommittee files.)

50. For legal and constitutional implications, as well as a comprehensive historical account, see testimony of Christopher Pyle, an attorney and former Captain in Army Intelligence. See 1971 Hearings at 147, and exhibits providing examples of nation-wide military surveillance.

With very few, if any, directives[51] to guide their activities, they monitored the membership and policies of peaceful organizations who were concerned with the war in Southeast Asia, the draft, racial and labor problems, and community welfare. Out of this surveillance the Army created blacklists of organizations and personalities which were circulated to many federal, state and local agencies, who were all requested to supplement the data provided. Not only descriptions of the contents of speeches and political comments were included, but irrelevant entries about personal finances, such as the fact that a militant leader's credit card was withdrawn. In some cases, a psychiatric diagnosis taken from Army or other medical records was included.

This information on individuals was programmed into at least four computers according to their political beliefs, or their memberships, or their geographic residence.[52]

The Army did not just collect and share this information. Analysts were assigned the task of evaluating and labeling these people on the basis of reports on their attitudes, remarks and activities. They were then coded for entry into computers or microfilm data banks.[53]

The Army attempts to justify its surveillance of civilians by asserting that it was collecting information to enable the President to predict when and where civilians might engage in domestic violence, and that the President was empowered to assign this task to it by the statutes conferring upon him the power to use the armed forces to suppress domestic violence.

I challenge the validity of this assertion.

Under our system, the power to investigate to determine whether civilians are about to violate federal laws is committed to

51. *See* Ervin, *Privacy and Governmental Investigations,* 1971 UNIV. ILL. L. FORUM 137 (1971) for an account of the various plans and their lack of relevance to the problem of putting down civil disturbances, and for analysis of the Defense and Justice Department's claims to constitutionality for the actions of the military. Texts of four "Plans," *1971 Hearings* at 1123, 1119, 1154, 1731; Memorandum at 1139, 1141, 1278-98, showing attempts by civilians to cut back on the program.

52. The bulk of investigative activity by the Army's own personnel occurred at the field level. Agents collected information and filed "spot reports," "agents reports," and "summaries of investigation." Most of this data was forwarded up the chain of command but record copies were kept in data centers at every level of command. Manual files were maintained at every level. At least four and possibly more computer systems were employed to store, analyse and retrieve the information collected. Many files on lawful citizens were microfilmed and integrated with other files on persons who were suspected of violations of security and espionage laws. These computer systems were located in the headquarters of the Intelligence Command (Fort Holabird), the Continental Army (Fort Monroe), the Third Army Corps (Fort Hood), and in the Pentagon. More than one computer data bank was maintained in some of these locations. (Subcommittee investigation).

53. Testimony of Ralph Stein on the difficulty of labeling young people on the basis of their speech, when a difference of one digit was the difference between a communist and a non-communist. *1971 Hearings* at 248, 260.

federal civil agencies, such as the FBI; and the power to investigate to determine whether civilians are about to violate state laws is reposed in state law enforcement officers.

If President Johnson believed he ought to have had information to enable him to predict when and where civilians might engage in future domestic violence, he ought to have called upon the FBI or appropriate state law enforcement officers for the information.

He had no power to convert the Army into a detective force and require it to spy on civilians.

This conclusion is made plain by the Constitution and every act of Congress relating to the subject. Sections 331, 332, 333 and 334 of Title 10 of the United States Code certainly did not confer any such power on the President. These statutes merely authorized him to use the armed forces to suppress domestic violence of the high degree specified in them, and conditioned their use for that purpose upon his issuing a proclamation immediately ordering the offenders "to disperse and retire peaceably to their abodes within a limited time."

The only other statute relevant to the subject is section 1385 of Title 18 of the Code, which prohibits the use of any part of the Army or Air Force "as a posse comitatus or otherwise to execute the law . . . except in cases and under circumstances expressly authorized by the Constitution or Act of Congress."

The legislative history of this statute is fully revealed in the opinion of United States District Judge Dooling in *Wrynn v. United States*, 200 F. Supp. 457 (E.D.N.Y. 1961). When the words of this statute are read in the light of its legislative history, it is obvious that the statute is not limited by the expression "as a posse comitatus or otherwise," but operates as a prohibition against the use of the Army to execute the laws without reference to whether it is employed as a posse comitatus or as a portion of the Army. Indeed, the statute embodies "the inherited antipathy of the American to the use of troops for civil purposes." [200 F. Supp. at 465].

President Johnson's use of the troops to spy on civilians, to build data banks and create computerized information systems, discloses that relevance of this statute to our day is sadly clear. Since neither the Constitution nor any Act of Congress expressly, or impliedly, authorized such use, the President was forbidden by section 1385 of Title 18 of the United States Code to use the Army to spy on civilians.

The Army's spying violated First Amendment freedoms of the civilians who became aware that they or the groups to which they belonged had been placed under surveillance. This is so because it undoubtedly stifled their willingness to exercise their freedom of speech, association and assembly.[54]

If any proof were needed of the logic and truth of this statement, it can be drawn from such testimony as the Subcommittee received from Dr. Jerome Wiesner who commented,

Many, many students are afraid to participate in political activities of various kinds which might attract them because of their concern about the consequences of having a record of such activities in a central file. They fear that at some future date, it might possibly cost them a job or at least make their clearance for a job more difficult to obtain.[55]

The Subcommittee has heard no testimony yet that the Army's information program was useful to anyone. The only result of the

---

54. *See* Brief for Respondents filed in Tatum v. Laird in the Supreme Court of the United States, No. 71-288, challenging the Army's surveillance program, and arguing that plaintiffs' claims are justiciable and ripe for adjudication; that the present inhibiting effect on the exercise of First Amendment rights creates a justiciable controversy; that the justiciability of their claims is enhanced because the military exceeded its constitutional and statutory authority and intruded into civilian affairs; that they have standing to adjudicate these claims for themselves and the claims of others similarly situated; and finally, that they argue that their case cannot be mooted by the Army's assertion that its domestic surveillance activity has been reduced. The appendix contains an interesting and landmark study of the chilling effect of overbroad governmental programs on First Amendment activity from the social science view.

All of the plaintiffs named have been subjects of political surveillance, and all are believed to be subjects of reports, files, or dossiers maintained by the Army.

In an amici brief filed by Senator Ervin on behalf of the Unitarian Universalist Association, the Council for Christian Social Action, United Church of Christ, the American Friends Service Committee and the National Council of Churches of Christ, the question posed for review is framed as follows:

Do individuals and organizations not affiliated with the armed services present a justiciable issue under the First, Fourth, Fifth and Ninth Amendments when they allege that their rights of free expression, privacy and association have been infringed by unauthorized, unnecessary and indiscriminate military investigation of their political activities and personal lives? Brief for Respondents as amicus curiae at 7, Laird v. Tatum, No. 71-288 (1971).

Essential though the freedoms are, they are not easily exercised in a climate of fear, discord, and dissension, especially when the ideas being expressed are those which are displeasing to government and unsettling to the majority of citizens. . . . It is as such a time that the First Amendment is most necessary, most in danger, and most difficult to exercise . . . . The First Amendment however, was made for the timid as well as for the brave. While government cannot instill courage in the meek, it may not take advantage of a climate of fear to undertake a program which has the effect of restricting the First Amendment only to the very courageous. Government action, such as military surveillance, seemingly innocuous in the abstract, has the very real effect of suppressing the exercise of the First Amendment. The coercive power of this government action lies in the national climate of fear and doubt, and in the very real, tangible apprehension of some unknown form of retribution by government on those whom it fears and therefore watches. That such apprehension exists in America today is manifest. *Id.* at 15.

testimony by the Defense Department was to confirm my belief that under the Constitution and under the laws, the Army had no business engaging in such data-gathering and that the scope and breadth of the surveillance was so broad as to be irrelevant to the purpose.

Congress has still to discover the complete truth about these Army computers. Apparently, even officials responsible for intelligence did not know of the existence of the computers for implementing the program. The Subcommittee has repeatedly requested the testimony of the Army Generals who would be most knowledgeable about the computers and what they contained. We have just as repeatedly been denied their testimony as well as delivery and declassification of pertinent documents demonstrating the scope and purpose of the program.[56] The Army said it would cut back on the data-gathering on law-abiding citizens and would defer to the Department of Justice. So I asked the Justice Department officials how many computers that Department had containing information on people who lawfully exercised their First Amendment freedoms.[57]

I had seen newspaper articles quoting the director of the Justice Department's Interdivisional Information Unit. He said there that the computer's list of thousands of names is not a register of "good guys" or "bad guys." "It is simply a list of who participated in demonstrations, rallies and the like." This would include non-violent people as well as violent, he said.[58] On the basis of these reports, I asked for the testimony of this official, but for some strange reason, he could not be located.

Despite questioning during the hearings and correspondence with the Justice Department, we have been unable to obtain an accurate description of the use of Justice Department computers for collecting, processing and analyzing information on lawful First Amendment activities of citizens. Nor have we been able to ascertain or obtain the standards followed by the Department in deciding what individuals should be the subjects in such files, or how they should be excluded from such files.

Legislative Remedies

There has been much discussion of the need for new laws granting access to individual records. I believe a person should have the

---

55. *1971 Hearings* at 765.
56. *See* exchange of correspondence on this subject. *Id.* Part II at 1046 A, 1180 Indices to letters.
57. *Id.* at 597, 849.
58. *Id.* at 616-22.

chance to expunge, update and correct his records. With the advent of systematic record-keeping, a man needs the chance which a businessman has to go into economic bankruptcy and obtain a discharge from his past.

I believe, however, that we must go beyond that relationship between the individual and his records. We must act to restore a healthy balance to the relationship between the citizen and his government, and necessarily between Congress and the Executive Branch. Mere access to and knowledge of his individual file is not enough. Remedial action must be addressed to the curbing of the power of government over the individual and to restricting its power to deny information about government programs. The claim to an inherent power to monitor, investigate and compile dossiers on law-abiding citizens on the off-chance that they might need to be investigated for a legitimate governmental purpose at some time in the future must also be opposed.

As a result of the Subcommittee's experience in playing hide-and-go-seek with the Federal Government's computers and with the people who plan and supervise them, I am convinced these computers have too much privacy today. The Congress, the press and the public should have available an *habeas corpus* action for entire computer systems and programs themselves. No department should be able to hide such broad-based data programs and information systems. If they are lawful, the American people then have a right to full knowledge about the operation of their government. If they are not lawful and relevant for some purpose, they should be exposed for what they are—attempts to intimidate citizens into silence and conformity.

First, we need to devise some judicial remedy for confronting and testing the nature, purpose, legality and constitutionality of governmental data banks and large-scale intelligence information systems which by their very existence may threaten the quality of our First Amendment freedoms or whose contents may affect economic prospects, reputations or rights. Now pending before the United States Supreme Court is just such a challenge to the Army surveillance program and the military data banks, including at least four computer systems for storing and processing information on American across the land. [*Tatum v. Laird*, no. 71-288 (1971) (argued March 27, 1972)] The lower court has denied standing to sue to plaintiffs who were subjects of surveillance and computer dossiers on grounds that they have not shown injury. [44 F.2d 947 (D.C. Cir. 1971)].

Congress must strengthen and enforce reporting requirements for computer systems. Not even in the audit of computers which the present law requires the General Services Administration to conduct each year is it possible for Congress, the press, and the public to get minimum information about all of the management uses of computers in government.

Secondly, I believe we must devise legal means of assuring the reporting of large government data banks to a central office established independently of the executive branch. This would require the filing of policy statements describing exactly what agencies feed a particular information system and who would receive or access data routinely from a particular data bank. These policy statements should be public records. In this way, people would have due notice of possible sharing of information by other agencies or state or local governments.

Thirdly, out of these directives, a graphic national information-flow chart would be designed and made available for public inspection. An individual concerned about his record could then go to the respective agencies and exercise his rights under the Freedom of Information Law to inspect his files.

Fourth, there is a need to fully implement the principle of open government implicit in the Freedom of Information Law by reducing the number of exemptions in it which the Executive Branch may use to deny or withhold information. This would make the judicial remedies it contains more meaningful.

Fifth, I believe there must be established a new independent agency for setting and enforcing strict standards in software and hardware for the assurance of security, confidentiality and privacy of records. These would be applied to all phases of gathering, processing and transmitting information about people by government computer systems. This would include such problems as interception of electronic transmissions and tapping of systems.

Sixth, Congress must enact specific prohibitions on unconstitutional or unwise practices which unfairly augment government's power to invade individual privacy. Examples of such legislation would be: (1) a ban on use of military resources to conduct unwarranted surveillance over civilians and to create and share data banks on them, and (2) a ban on unconstitutional means of coercing citizens into revealing personal information about themselves.[59] Such a bill is S. 2156 which would prohibit requirements on applicants and employees to submit to lie detectors in order to work.[60] Another bill is S. 1438, designed to protect federal employees and applicants from

---

59. S.1791, 91st Cong., 1st Sess. (1969).
60. Senate remarks of Senator Ervin, 117 CONG. REC. (daily ed. June 24, 1971.)

unwarranted demands for information about such matters as their race, national origin, religious beliefs and practices, sexual attitudes and conduct, and personal family relationships.[61] Another necessary protection would be a prohibition on distribution of arrest records to private companies and severe restrictions on their availability within government.[62]

Seventh, is the need for America to take a stand on whether or not every person is to be numbered from cradle to grave, and if so whether or not that number is to be the social security number. Until now, the idea of a universal standard identifier has been merely discussed in philosophical terms, but the need to reduce people to digits for the computer age has prompted wide government use of the number for identifying individuals in government files. Private industries, businesses and organizations have followed suit to the dismay of many people who have registered strong complaints against this practice with the Subcommittee. They were supported by the findings of a Social Security Task Force which reported in 1971 that:

> The increasing universality of the Social Security Number in computer data collection and exchange presents both substantial benefits and potential dangers to society; and that in order to maximize the benefits and minimize the dangers, there needs to be developed a national policy on computer data exchange and personal identification in America, including a consideration of what safeguards are needed to protect individuals' rights of privacy and due process.[63]

In outlining the areas in which state legislatures and the Congress must make important judgments, this Task Force stated:

> Defining the proper role of the Social Security Number in society requires that broad social judgments be made first about the desirability of large-scale computer recordkeeping in various settings; second, about the kinds of data necessary and appropriate to record about individuals within a given setting; third, about the safeguards needed to insure that the computer is being used within a given setting in ways that protect fundamental human rights; and fourth,

---

61. See S. Rep. 92-554 for legislative history (Now pending before the House Post Office and Civil Service Committee with House versions).

62. *1971 Hearings* at 782 (complaints read into the hearing record by the Chairman).

63. SOCIAL SECURITY NUMBER TASK FORCE REPORT to the Commissioner 17 (May, 1971).

about the desirability of *any* kind of universal identification system in terms of its psychological impact on the individual citizen.[64]

Summary

From the Subcommittee study of privacy and government data banks one conclusion is undeniable. This is that the extensive use of computerized systems to classify and analyze men's thoughts, speech, attitudes, and lawful First Amendment behavior raises serious questions of denial of substantive due process to our entire society. To try to condense the truth about what men believe and why they believe is a futile exercise which can lead to that tyranny over the mind against which Thomas Jefferson swore eternal hostility. Without grave dangers to our constitutional system, we cannot permit government to reduce the realities of our political life and the healthy traffic in our marketplace of ideas to marks on magnetic tapes and data on a microfilm.

Professor Robert Boguslaw[65] eloquently described the dangers posed by this "technology-screened power" when he wrote that "the specification of future and current system states within this orientation characteristically requires an insistence upon a uniformity of

---

64. *Id.* at 15.

It is clear that if the SSN became the single number around which all or most of an individual's interactions with society were structured, and if practices of the sort we have been discussing were to continue, the individual's opportunity to control the circumstances under which information about himself is collected and disclosed would be greatly circumscribed.

65. *See* BOGUSLAW, THE NEW UTOPIANS (1965), especially the chapter entitled *The Power of Systems and Systems of Power* at 181, 186, 190. I would dispute his observation of some years ago that people in the information-processing profession "are scientists and engineers—objective experts whose only concern is technical efficiency and scientific detachment." *Id.* at 198. It is indeed true, however, that:

to the extent that customers (and this may include government agencies or private industry) abdicate their power prerogatives because of ignorance of the details of system operation, *de facto* system decisions are made by equipment manufacturers or information-processing specialists. *Id.* at 198.

Implicit in the various issues raised during the Subcommittee Hearings is the wise observation of Professor Boguslaw that:

The paramount issues to be raised in connection with the design of our new computerized utopias are not technological—they are issues of values and the power through which these values become translated into action. *Id.* at 200.

In this case, I believe it is the constitutional value protected by the First Amendment.

perspective, a standardization of language, and a consensus of values that is characteristic of highly authoritarian social structures. Nonconforming perspectives, language, and values can be and, indeed, must be excluded as system elements."

He further points out certain engineering truths and certain human truths which face every politician, administrator, analyst and programmer who tries to use computers to convey either more or less than the straight facts about people. First is the truth that the strength of high-speed computers lies precisely in their capacity to process binary choice data rapidly. But to process these data, the world of reality must at some point in time be reduced to binary form. Second is the truth "that the range of possibilities is ultimately set by the circuitry of the computer, which places finite limits on alternatives for data storage and processing." Third is the truth "that the structure of the language used to communicate with the computer restricts alternatives." Then there is the truth "that the programmer himself, through the specific sets of data he uses in his solution to a programming problem and the specific techniques he uses for his solution, places a final set of restrictions on action alternatives available within a computer-based system."

It is in this sense that computer programmers, the designers of computer equipment, and the developers of computer languages possess power in our society.

These limitations of men as well as machines are what I remembered as I listened to the young Army analyst describing his assignment to condense truth for the Army data systems by assigning numbers to people on the basis of their speech and thoughts.[66]

On the shoulders of technology experts who are aware citizens rests the responsibility for guiding those politicians who seek computer-based solutions to political problems. At this point in our history, they, more than anyone, realize that computers have only those values which are designed and programmed into them.

If the attitude of the present Administration is any indication, Government will make increasing use of computer technology in pursuit of its current claim to an inherent power to investigate lawful activities and to label people on the basis of their thoughts. Municipal, state and federal agencies continue to plan, devise and build intelligence systems for many purposes. It devolves on those people involved in computer technology to make known the restrictions and the limitations of the machines as well as the alternatives for what is

---

66. *See* note 53 *supra.*

proposed. When the political managers ignore or abdicate their responsibility to assure the application of due process of law, they may have the final say over the constitutional uses of power.

What they say may not be popular with those who use their services, especially government departments. But I would suggest that when they advise on extending the power of government, they serve a higher law—the Constitution.

The technological forces which affect the quality of our freedoms come in many guises and under strange terminology. They are dreamers who would decry the advent of the computer as casting some sorcerer's shadow across an idyllic land. In their philosophical rejection or fear of this most intricate of machines, they would deny the spark of divinity which is the genius of man's mind; they would reject the progress of civilization itself. So there is no reason to condemn out of hand every governmental application of computers to the field of information processing or to systems study.

Our society has much to gain from computer technology. To assure against its political misuse, however, we need new laws restricting the power of government and implementing constitutional guarantees. We need increased political awareness of an independent nature by information specialists who understand the machines and the systems they constitute.

We do not, as some suggest, need new constitutional amendments to deal with these problems. The words of the original amendments will do, because they envelop our national concepts of personal freedom and I believe they can encompass anything which jeopardizes that freedom.

As Justice Oliver Wendell Holmes said:

A word is not a crystal, transparent and unchanged; it is the skin of a living thought and may vary greatly in color and content according to the circumstances and the time in which it is used.[67]

I believe, however, that Americans will have to work harder than ever before in our history so that the First Amendment remains a living thought in this computer age.

Otherwise, we may find the individual in our society represented not by a binary form, but by one digit.

And that will be "zero."

Otherwise, America may lose its cherished reputation as "the land of the Second Chance."

---

67. Towne v. Eisner, 245 U.S. 418, 425 (1918).

CRIME DATA CENTERS:
3

CRIME DATA CENTERS: The Use of Computers in Crime Detection and Prevention

NICHOLAS deB. KATZENBACH*
and RICHARD W. TOMC**

Crime and its effects rank among the foremost social and economic problems in this country. Crime against persons and property have shown a continuing and inexorable rise over the past decade,[1] while organized crime continues to flourish in its traditional occupations of narcotics, gambling and prostitution, and more recently in legitimate business and labor racketeering.[2] *White-collar* crime has grown increasingly sophisticated in the areas of securities thefts, embezzlement and political corruption. The human and dollar cost of crime to American society is inestimable.

At the same time, the social patterns of crime have become increasingly complex. Street crime has been linked to the problems of racial discrimination and ghetto poverty. The traditional legal definitions of crime have been greatly strained by attempting their application to the recent disorders on campuses, in prisons and at mass protest demonstrations, while the laws regulating drug use and sexual conduct have been challenged as intrusions on private morality. Too often lacking key resources of manpower, training and equipment, law enforcement authorities face the added problem of growing public suspicion aroused by recent investigations of police corruption and brutality.

New Law Enforcement Tools. New responses to the problems of modern crime are nonetheless developing. Public willingness to fund

*Vice-President and General Counsel of I.B.M.; former Under Secretary of State; former Attorney General of the United States.
**L.L.B. Harvard University; Attorney, Legal Department, I.B.M.
    1. *See generally* UNIFORM CRIME REPORTS - 1970, United States Government Printing Office (1971).
    2. *See* TASK FORCE REPORT: ORGANIZED CRIME OF THE PRESIDENT'S COMMISSION OF LAW ENFORCEMENT AND THE ADMINISTRATION OF JUSTICE 1-5 (1967).

police manpower and training efforts and to participate on civilian review boards may demonstrate a reviving community support and confidence in the police. New civilian grievance mechanisms have resulted in higher professional conduct among policemen. Some evidence suggests that law enforcement is becoming an attractive career alternative to the college-educated young.[3]

One of the most significant and promising developments in modern law enforcement is the application of new technologies to the deterrence and detection of crime. Just as the introduction of patrol cars and two-way radios revolutionized law enforcement a generation ago, high-intensity street lighting, citizen emergency call boxes, police-alert alarm systems, and remote-control TV and photographic surveillance are capable of dramatically reducing the incidence of crime,[4] especially in traditionally high-crime areas.

The Evolution of Crime Data Networks. Perhaps the most significant development in crime technology during the past decade has been the use of computer data banks to store, classify and retrieve vital information on criminal suspects and stolen property. The most extensive use of such a system is the National Crime Information Center (NCIC) operated by the Federal Bureau of Investigation.[5] The FBI's system contains records of all cars reported stolen for more than 24 hours, all persons wanted for extraditable offenses, stolen guns, and stolen property valued at over $1000, and provides state and local police forces with immediate access to its computerized files.[6]

State police forces have introduced similar systems. The New York State Indentification and Intelligence System (NYIIS) provides its state and local law enforcement agencies with data on individuals with arrest and conviction records, as well as information on wanted persons, gun registrations and narcotics addicts.[7] California operates a state-wide computer network which provides its police with data on wanted persons, firearms and stolen property.[8] Both states operate

---

3. N.Y. Times 35, col. 5 (July 22, 1971).

4. *See* TIME MAGAZINE 46 (May 10, 1971); N.Y. Times 58, col. 4 (Apr. 11, 1971); The Daily Argus, Mt. Vernon, N.Y. (Apr. 9, 1971); Buffalo Courier Express (Mar. 28, 1971).

5. *See* MILLER, THE ASSAULT ON PRIVACY: COMPUTERS, DATA BANKS AND DOSSIERS 147-48 (1971) [hereinafter cited as MILLER].

6. *See* PRESIDENT'S COMMISSION ON LAW ENFORCEMENT AND THE ADMINISTRATION OF JUSTICE, TASK FORCE REPORT: SCIENCE AND TECHNOLOGY 72 (1967) [hereinafter cited as TASK FORCE REPORT: SCIENCE AND TECHNOLOGY]. *See generally* THE INSTITUTE FOR DEFENSE ANALYSIS, TASK FORCE REPORT: SCIENCE AND TECHNOLOGY (1967).

7. *See* TASK FORCE REPORT: SCIENCE AND TECHNOLOGY note 6, *supra* at 69; MILLER, note 5, *supra* at 148-49.

8. N.Y. Times 24, col. 3 (May 19, 1970). *See also* Project, *The Computerization of Government Files: What Impact on the Individual?* 15 U.C.L.A. L. REV. 1371 (1968).

supplemental systems which compile information on stolen and wanted motor vehicles.[9]

Local crime data systems are more prolific. The Police Information System (PINS) of Alameda County, California provides computerized access to wanted persons files and is linked to the state's system for information on stolen vehicles.[10] Kansas City's Automated Law Enforcement Response Team (ALERT) is a computerized system containing information on wanted persons, criminal suspects and persons with criminal records, as well as the license numbers of cars owned by wanted persons and stolen vehicles.[11] New York, Chicago, and St. Louis and other cities have computer systems with files on crimes, wanted persons, stolen cars and other property.[12]

Many of these systems have access to the FBI's National Crime Information Center which reportedly exchanges information with state and local police forces in every state except Alaska.[13] Regional sharing of crime information among state and local agencies has also been stimulated by federal grants to local law enforcement agencies under the Omnibus Crime Control and Safe Streets Act of 1968.[14]

In 1967, the President's Commission on Law Enforcement and the Administration of Justice studied and proposed a national criminal information network which envisioned a country-wide computer information complex containing the nation's crime data.[15] Linked to state and local police agencies, the system would have an immediate inquiry-response capability, able to give individual police organizations crucial crime data in a matter of minutes. In addition to criminal records, the system would include vehicle and firearms registrations, crime reports and missing persons reports.

The Commission's proposal has become a near-reality. By evolutionary steps, American law enforcement is developing a computer and telecommunications network linking local and state police departments with the FBI's National Crime Information Center and with each other.[16] If the trend continues, there will soon be a national crime file, readily accessible to local police, which will contain comprehensive criminal information, including police and court records, gun and vehicle registrations, and reports on stolen property.

9. TASK FORCE REPORT: SCIENCE AND TECHNOLOGY, note 6, *supra* at 69.
10. *Id.*
11. COMPUTERS AND THE LAW 111 [American Bar Assoc. Standing Comm. on Law and Technology (2d ed. 1969)]. *See generally* Satchell, *Intelligence Network Here*, Kansas City Times (Jan. 22, 1971).
12. TASK FORCE REPORT: SCIENCE AND TECHNOLOGY, note 6, *supra* at 69.
13. MILLER, note 5, *supra* at 147.
14. 42 U.S.C. § 3701 *et seq. See also* N.Y. Times 93, col. 1 (Sept. 24, 1970).
15. TASK FORCE REPORT: SCIENCE AND TECHNOLOGY, note 6, *supra* at 68-79.
16. *See* MILLER, note 5, *supra* 148-51.

Advantages of a National Crime Data Network. Crime information networks make vital information immediately available to a broad range of law enforcement officials. Reports on a stolen car, a gun registration, a criminal record, or a physical description can all be stored and retrieved as needed by a policeman encountering a criminal suspect, even far from the scene of the crime. By making immediate criminal identification possible, the crime data system eliminates much of the fleeing criminal's traditional anonymity, and increases the chance of his speedy apprehension.

Two persistent criticisms of law enforcement in recent years have been the harassment suspects suffer by street frisks and questioning, and the unduly long periods of detention after apprehension.[17] With the use of terminal access devices in police cars, criminal identification can be made within seconds after encountering the suspect. When a suspect must be detained, the need to hold him while crucial data is received can also be minimized. Instant suspect identification could reduce the need for *aggressive patrolling* which has frequently caused strained relations between the police and the community.

A chief advantage of the crime data networks is the reduced need for duplicative police work. Once a person's criminal record is established, or that a particular motor vehicle has been stolen, the need for other police agencies to independently verify those facts is eliminated.[18] Faster criminal identification and shorter interrogation and detention periods can free police manpower for more crucial assignments.

In addition to its prime function of criminal identification, a crime data network affords extensive data on the types, location and disposition of crimes which could become an extraordinarily effective tool in understanding the complex social patterns of crime and violence. By being permitted limited access to the crime system's data on stolen vehicles and other property, used car and appliance dealers could be required to warrant to purchasers that merchandise has not been stolen. Individual crime records can provide the courts invaluable assistance in the sentencing process, and correctional institutions in parole matters.

Problems and Possible Controls. The major problems of the developing crime data networks are ones of controlling the accuracy,

---

17. *Cf.* Terry v. Ohio, 392 U.S. 1, 19 (1968); Davis v. Mississippi, 394 U.S. 721 (1969).
18. *See Hearings on Federal Data Banks, Computers and the Bill of Rights Before Subcomm. on Constitutional Rights of the Senate Comm. on the Judiciary* 1772, 92d Cong., 1st Sess. (1971) [hereinafter cited as *Senate Hearings*].

accessibility, scope and uses of crime information.[19] Much of the basic data in such systems consists of local police reports, arrest records, rap sheets, and court records which are often inaccurate and incomplete. Not only does unverified or questionable information risk the false apprehension of innocent parties, but, absorbed on a large scale, could undermine the credibility of the system itself. Incomplete information—recording a person's indictment without his subsequent acquittal, for instance, or failing to withdraw an outdated warrant— could subject innocent parties to continued police pick-ups and interrogations.[20]

While the accurancy and completeness of police and court records can never be completely assured because of the inevitable time lag between the police or court action and the computer record of the activity, local law enforcement agencies should nonetheless be encouraged to develop improved record-keeping techniques, perhaps as a condition of obtaining access to the centralized files or of receiving federal funding for their systems. Participating agencies might be required within a designated period of time to provide the judicial disposition of all reported warrants, arrests and indictments or, alternatively, exclude altogether information on which an administrative or judicial determination is pending. Upon proof of identity and payment of a reasonable fee, persons whose files are in the system could be given the right to review their dossiers and challenge inaccurate data.

Crime records in a centralized data network may be subjected to tampering or accidental destruction. By bribing officials who have access to the data bank or through unauthorized intrusions by wiretapping or electronic eavesdropping devices, *data saboteurs* could intentionally destroy or obfuscate the computer files on particular criminals or purposely introduce false information on innocent parties into the system. Poorly trained computer operators or ill-designed systems might inadvertently *dump* vital data records.

These dangers can be minimized by some of the many computer security devices and procedures which are now commercially available. Each authorized user could, for example, be required to carry a machine-readable identification card in addition to furnishing a special number or code word known only to him as a condition of obtaining access to the data bank. Access to more sensitive data could be conditioned on dual identification systems which require full identification

19. *See generally* Karst, *The Files: Legal Controls Over the Accuracy of Stored Personal Data,* 31 LAW AND CONTEMP. PROB. 342 (1966); Project, *The Computerization of Government Files: What Impact on the Individual?* 15 U.C.L.A.L. REV. 1371 (1968).

20. *See, e.g.,* Menard v. Mitchell, 430 F.2d 486 (D.C. Cir. 1970), *remanded,* 328 F.Supp. 718 (D.D.C. 1971).

of two or more qualified access personnel before data is released. The system could be designed to audit each access by user, terminal and requested information, identifying each procedural violation for further investigation. Remote access transmissions of data could be electronically scrambled or coded to thwart would-be wiretappers. Terminals and the data bank environment can be physically safeguarded by locks, guards and alarm systems and anti-dumping devices can be installed.

Proliferation of unusable or undesirable information—data on criminals who have died, for instance, or information on juvenile offenders which is clearly outdated—could conceivably choke the system with irrelevant detail and processing expenses. Information on persons who have committed no criminal offenses, but who are "suspected" of radical political activity or seemingly immoral or antisocial behavior could also creep into the system.[21]

The scope of individual data maintained in crime data systems has generally been limited to matter of public record—police records, gun and motor vehicle registrations. Careful consideration ought to be given to the problems of expanding this scope. Recording conduct not directly related to crime such as an individual's political associations, his credit rating or employment history, for instance, could create a potential for personal or political repression.[22] Procedures for discarding outdated information on persons who have died, for instance, or on former juvenile offenders who have been *clean* for a prescribed number of years should be studied.

Uses of crime data networks for other than legitimate police work is also a difficulty. Lists of gun or vehicle registrants might be sold for advertising and marketing purposes. Banks and corporations might use the system to run private security checks on their employees and customers. Blackmailers and extortionists could find a ready price for some information within the system. The curious peeping toms of the computer age could conceivably check whether there are files on their neighbors or business associates.[23]

Careful study should be given to the problem of the system's commercial uses. While permitting banks and private employers to

---

21. *See generally Senate Hearings*, note 18 *supra*.

22. *See, e.g.*, Tatum v. Laird, 444 F.2d 947 (1971), *cert. granted*, No. 71-288 (1971).

23. *See* Miller, *Personal Privacy in the Computer Age: The Challenge of a New Technology in an Information-Oriented Society*, 67 MICH. L. REV. 1089 (1969); *Symposium: Computers, Data Banks, and Individual Privacy*, 53 MINN. L. REV. 211 (1968); Note, *Privacy and Efficient Government: Proposals for a National Data Center*, 82 HARV. L. REV. 400 (1968); *Hearings on Computer Privacy Before Subcomm. on Administrative Practice and Procedure of the Senate Comm. on the Judiciary*, 90th Cong., 2d Sess. (1968); *Hearings on the Computer and Invasion of Privacy Before a Subcomm. of the House Comm. on Government Operations*, 89th Cong., 2d Sess. (1966).

run checks on loan or job applicants might indeed expedite the credit-granting and hiring processes, it is also true that some persons who have a minor blotch on their records might be forever trapped in a *data-prison* of denied credit and foreclosed job opportunities. There is also the problem that as data is released from the primary police system, it becomes more and more difficult to control, update and verify.[24] Selling network data for advertising purposes has little to recommend it, and would lend itself to an even greater daily aggravation in the form of reams of junk mail which already beleaguer post office and consumer alike. To counter the problems of extortion and blackmail, authorized users of the data system should be specially educated in informational security and ethical responsibility.

Apart from regular internal checks to ensure compliance with data network regulations, other branches of the federal government might be given special audit powers. The Bureau of the Budget or the Census Bureau for instance, with experience in regulating statistical data might be an appropriate representative of the Executive. Congressional Committees could stimulate public sensitivity to the issues of *information privacy* by conducting ongoing hearings on the effect of crime data systems on individual civil liberties.[25]

Public Records versus Intelligence Reports. Information within existing crime data systems has been largely confined to matters of public record. The National Crime Information Center and its state and local counterparts have so far compiled only that information which has always been available to law enforcement agencies— criminal records, gun and vehicle registrations. The application of computer technology to this kind of information has had the simple but far-reaching effect of broadly and quickly disseminating pre-existing crime information.

Quite different from this type of data is what might be characterized as intelligence information collected by some federal law enforcement agencies, and, to a lesser extent, by state and local police forces. This kind of information is generally not drawn from public records, but is the product of the surveillance and investigation of suspected members of organized crime, *white-collar* criminals, corrupt public officials, and persons whose conduct threatens national securi-

---

24. *See, e.g., Senate Hearings,* note 18, *supra* at 492, 510 and 1372 (testimony, exhibits and disclosures re: San Francisco Mayor Joseph Alioto).

25. *See, e.g., Senate Hearings,* note 18 *supra; Hearings on Data Processing Management in the Federal Government Before a Subcomm. of the House Comm. on Government Operations,* 90th Cong., 1st Sess. (1967); *Hearings on Invasions of Privacy (Government Agencies) Before the Subcomm. on Administrative Practice and Procedure of the Senate Comm. on the Judiciary,* 89th Cong., 1st Sess. (1965-1966).

ty. Intelligence information is a wide-ranging collection of facts—employment records, bank statements, tax returns, telephone bills, reports of personal associations—which may provide the basis for major criminal prosecutions.[26]

Although arguments can be made that the collection of intelligence information is potentially more threatening to individual civil liberties than are matters of public record, it is difficult to support the proposition that intelligence information should not be collected at all. Without it, law enforcement authorities would be without the informational basis for prosecuting many elusive, high-ranking and sophisticated criminal suspects. Nor can it be feasibly proposed that certain kinds of data should not be compiled because it is virtually impossible to determine in advance what information may eventually be relevant in a criminal investigation or prosecution.

As a general proposition, the fewer the people who have access to intelligence information, the greater the degree of control which can be exerted over its use. Commercial access to intelligence information—by employers and credit information agencies, for example—risks mutual back-scratching by industry and government at the expense of personal privacy. Free access by local police forces to intelligence dossiers entails the possibility that vital data will leak to the subject under investigation, thus undercutting its primary value of confidentiality.

These and other questions relating to intelligence information deserve close study. Should government agencies be permitted access to intelligence information in order to determine the suitability of a political appointee? Of a government contractor? Who should be given the power to review the practices of intelligence-gathering agencies to assure their compliance with appropriate standards? What sanctions should be imposed when there are violations? Should intelligence dossiers be compiled on persons other than suspected criminals or those posing a threat to national security? What interface should there be between intelligence-gathering organizations and crime data networks?

Conclusion. We have the technological capacity to handle efficiently and cheaply masses of information about people. That this technology is potentially important to the criminal justice system is clear enough. Given the public pressures which presently exist to improve that system, it is very nearly inevitable that it will increasingly be used.

---

26. *See* Appendix to Brief for Petitioners, Tatum v. Laird, 444 F.2d 947 (1971).

Obviously its use presents problems of its abuse. The more information collected, stored, preserved and made available for any purpose, the greater the possibility it is available for many purposes—legitimate or illegitimate—depending on the standards accepted and the controls involved. Concepts of public interest and public morality are necessarily involved. Law enforcement officials must think far more rigorously than has been their wont as to what information is collected, who has access to it, for what purposes, and how this system is given integrity. Civil libertarians have to think on the same problems. A debate cast in terms of improved law enforcement *versus* privacy is pretty sterile once the emotion is dissipated.

Both sides of the current controversy have resorted to legitimate, although sometimes exaggerated, argumentation. Neither side has as yet made sufficient effort to deal with the realities. The blunt truth is that views are becoming polarized through failure to ask the most important questions *now*, to design systems which can provide effective controls and safeguards and standards which can improve the quality of law enforcement in terms of *both* efficiency and decency. That opportunity is open today. It may not be open tomorrow.

We believe that improved methods for collection, storage, comparison and retrieval of information are important for improved efficiency in law enforcement—and that in many instances this improved efficiency can eliminate or moderate abuses of the police power. But if this is to be accomplished debate must concentrate on process and procedures, and not be satisfied with generalities of highly emotional content.

SURVEILLANCE:
The Social Science Perspective

4

FRANK ASKIN*

I. INTRODUCTORY REMARKS

Mr. Justice Brennan succinctly stated the legal implications of governmental actions which *chill* the exercise of First Amendment rights in his concurring opinion in *Lamont* v. *Postmaster-General*[1]: "[I]nhibition as well as prohibition against the exercise of First Amendment rights is a power denied to government."[2]

This statement has in turn called forth disclaimers and qualifications by several courts in cases in which litigants have attempted to make *chill* the legal basis for enjoining a governmental program. The District of Columbia Circuit said it was not persuaded that every litigant who "shivers in court" asserts a justiciable controversy or that every "official breath of cold air" requires judicial intervention.[3] Another court noted that "the very existence of this court may 'chill' some who would speak or act more freely if there were no accounting before us for trespassers against others."[4]

The surveillance cases pose the constitutional issue most sharply. These are the suits, now proliferating throughout the country, which attack one or another agency of government for monitoring and recording the political activities and associations of radicals and other social dissidents. They include suits against the United States Army

---

*Professor of Law, Rutgers University, School of Law, Newark. The author is counsel for plaintiffs in Tatum v. Laird, 444F.2d 947 (D.C. Cir), *cert granted, – U.S. – (1971), argued* March 27, 1972, challenging the constitutionality of the Army's domestic intelligence program. He is also counsel for plaintiffs in the suit challenging the constitutionality of political surveillance by state and local police in New Jersey, Anderson v. Sills, 56 N.J. 210, 265 A.2d 678 (1970), *rev'g* 106 N.J. Super. 545 (Ch. Div. 1969), now in pretrial proceedings on remand *sub nom.* Anderson v. Kugler, and in the suit challenging the F.B.I.'s surveillance operations, as revealed in the Media, Pennsylvania, documents, Kenyatta v. Hoover, Civ. Act. No. 2595, (E.D. P.a.).

1. 381 U.S. 301 (1965).
2. *Id.* at 307.
3. National Students Association v. Hershey, 412 F.2d 1103, 1114 (D.C. Cir., 1969).
4. Anderson v. Sills, 56 N.J. 210, 226, 265 A.2d 678 (1970).

over its domestic intelligence program,[5] suits against the F.B.I.'s internal security operations[6] and suits against state and local police agencies seeking to enjoin a large variety of operations by mini-Red-squads.[7]

The allegations in all of these suits are essentially the same. In addition to claiming generally that such surveillance invades the Plaintiffs' privacy, it is alleged that police agencies which monitor constitutionally protected political activities and keep files and dossiers on persons and organizations engaged in wuch protected activity, cause an unconstitutional chilling effect upon the willingness of citizens to exercise their First Amendment rights of political protest.[8]

Plaintiffs in these cases insist that diminution of First Amendment rights caused by such programs is sufficient injury to entitle a proper party to injunctive relief in a class suit. They contend that the class does not have to wait until someone has been prosecuted or deprived of a job as the direct result of such surveillance in order to structure a legal challenge to the program.[9] Courts and lawyers are thus faced with the need to sharpen and more closely define the developing law with respect to the chilling effect in order to determine its applicability to the surveillance situation.[10]

When is there a chilling effect and how much chill is necessary in order to invoke a judicial remedy? Neither question has ever been directly answered by the United States Supreme Court. In many cases, the Court has referred to the existence of chill as a factor—often the prime factor—in support of its holding of unconstitu-

---

5. Tatum v. Laird, 444 F.2d 947 (D.C. Cir.), *cert. granted*; 408 U.S. 1 (1972), *argued,* March 27, 1972; ACLU v. Westmoreland, 70 Civ. 3191 (N.D. Ill., 1970), *appeal argued sub nom.* ACLU v. Laird, 71-1159 (7th Cir., 1972).

6. Kenyatta v. Hoover, Civ. Act. No. 2595 (E.D. Pa. 1971); Fifth Avenue Peace Parade Committee v. Hoover, 70 Civ. 2646 (S.D.N.Y.) 1970).

7. Anderson v. Sills, *supra* note 4; Yaffe v. Powers, 40 U.S.L.W. 2494 (1st Cir. Jan. 26, 1972), *rev'g* 71-514-J (D. Mass. June 13, 1971) and remanding for class action determination and discovery proceedings; Aronson v. Giarusso, 436 F.2d 955 (5th Cir. 1971); Holmes v. Church, 70 Civ. 5691 (S.D.N.Y. 1970); Vietnam Veterans Against the War v. Nassau County Police Dep't. (E.D.N.Y., 1971, not reported); Avirgan v. Rizzo, 70 Civ. 477 (E.D. Pa. 1970).

8. See generally Askin, *Police Dossiers and Emerging Principles of First Amendment Adjudication,* 22 STAN. L. REV. 196 (1970).

9. The law supporting this proposition was summed up in National Students Association v. Hersey, *supra* note 3:

[A] plaintiff need not invariably wait until he has been successfully prosecuted, dismissed, denied a license, or otherwise directly subjected to the force of a law or policy before he may challenge it in court (at 1110).

10. *See generally* Note, *The Chilling Effect in Constitutional Law,* 69 COLUM. L. REV. 808 (1969).

tionality.[11] However, very few of these cases offer actual proof of deterrence of the exercise of First Amendment rights.[12] In most decisions, the Court *assumed* that chill would result from the government program or regulation being considered. In at least one case, the Court cited sociological studies to support its assumption.[13]

However, last term the Court upheld, five to four, a program challenged as violative of the First Amendment because the majority was not convinced it *need result* in a chilling effect.[14] In this case, plaintiffs had a full evidentiary hearing and the opportunity to produce evidence of chill, but none was offered.

In *Tatum* v. *Laird*,[15] the ACLU-sponsored suit challenging the Army's domestic intelligence system, the Court of Appeals, after holding, two to one, that plaintiffs' complaint stated a justiciable controversy, remanded the case for a trial to determine, *inter alia*, whether "the existence of any overbroad aspects of the intelligence gathering system . . . have or might have an inhibiting effect on appellants or others similarly situated."[16] The dissent disparaged the plaintiffs' allegations of chill founded on "amorphous fears" and "indefinite claims of highly visionary apprehensions . . . based in abstractions which cannot be comprehended, or are beyond human experience or understanding . . . ."[17]

The government in its petition for certiorari granted by the Supreme Court, is echoing this dissent by Judge MacKinnon. In the case waiting decision by the high court the government argues that a claim of chill from surveillance activities is too hypothetical to present a justiciable controversy. Plaintiffs take the position that chill is a real phenomenon which, even if not judicially noticeable in a case such as this, is empirically demonstrable. Thus, after .citing the numerous decisions in which the Court has assumed deterrence of First Amendment rights as a result of government regulation or intrusion into

---

11. *See* Lamont v. Postmaster-General, *supra* note 1; Talley v. California, 362 U.S. 60 (1960). *See also* Baird v. State Bar of Arizona, 401 U.S. 1 (1971); Keyishian v. Board of Regents, 385 U.S. 589 (1967); Elfbrandt v. Russell, 384 U.S. 11 (1966); DeGregory v. Attorney-General, 383 U.S. 825 (1966); Baggett v. Bullitt, 377 U.S. 360 (1964); Gibson v. Florida Legislative Investigation Committee, 372 U.S. 539 (1963); NAACP v. Button, 371 U.S. 415 (1963); Shelton v. Tucker, 364 U.S. 479 (1960); Speiser v. Randall, 357 U.S. 513 (1958); Sweezy v. New Hampshire, 354 U.S. 248 (1957). Cf. Dombrowski v. Pfister, 380 U.S. 479 (1965); Zwickler v. Koota, 389 U.S. 241 (1967).

12. *But see* Shelton v. Tucker, *supra* note 11, at 486, one of the few cases in which the Court indicates there was actual evidence of specific deterrence.

13. Keyishian v. Board of Regents, *supra* note 11, at 607 n.12.

14. Law Students Civil Rights Research Council v. Wadmond, 401 U.S. 154, 167 (1971).

15. *See* note 4, *supra*.

16. *Id.* at 959.

17. *Id.* at 961.

constitutionally protected areas, the plaintiffs' brief takes the alternative position that they are at least entitled to an opportunity to prove chill.

In support of this position, plaintiffs' brief includes a lengthy Appendix, prepared in consultation with social scientists, giving a scientific definition of chill and detailing the psychological and sociological evidence which indicates that such a phenomenon does actually take place as a result of a surveillance program such as the Army's.[18] The brief has three distinct purposes: 1) to demonstrate that the Court has been on sound ground in past cases in assuming chill as a result of certain governmental programs enroaching upon the First Amendment, 2) to demonstrate that chill is not, as the government argues, an abstract and visionary notion, but rather an empirically verifiable phenomenon, and 3) to demonstrate the need for the opportunity to prove the existence of the chilling effect.

The Appendix, reprinted below, establishes a rationale for the "chilling effect" grounded in social psychology. It should be significant in determining the legal parameters of government surveillance.

II. APPENDIX*

A. *Introduction to the Social Science Data*

The sociological, political, and psychological processes which result in a chilling effect on political action are receiving renewed attention in the social sciences. The reappearance of chill as a social issue is one good indicator that certain repressive social forces which have been present intermittently throughout the long history of this nation threaten once again to rise into dominance. An atmosphere of public fear prevailed during the witch hunts of Salem, the repressions of the Alien and Sedition Acts, the silencing of critics of slavery through the firing of teachers and ministers in the pre-Civil War South, the Red

---

18. The Supreme Court has often looked to social science data when deciding consititutional questions. *See, e.g.,* Powell v. Texas, 392 U.S. 514 (1968); Robinson v. California, 370 U.S. 660, 670-71 (1962); Brown v. Board of Education, 347 U.S. 483, 494 n.11 (1954); Mueller v. Oregon, 208 U.S. 412, 419 n.1 (1908).

*Plaintiffs' Counsel gratefully acknowledges the assistance of the following persons in the preparation of this appendix:

scare of post-World War I, the early and more recent tactics against union organizing activity, the anti-Japanese measures during World War II, and the anti-Communist fervor of the McCarthy era.[1]

Democratic politics is predicated on the belief that people can reason, grow and change. Anxious men are rarely free men. Those tormented by the thought that it may have been an exercise of freedom that cost them their jobs, deferments, civil rights or liberties—but who never know for sure—are not likely to develop the strengths political democracy needs. Surveillance serves to chill thought and to discourage the risks of freedom.

By chilling effect we refer to any diminution in or inhibition of the expression of legitimate political behavior in response to governmental practices. It is, in the instant case, the diminution and inhibition of political behavior as a result of military surveillance of legitimate political activity.

By surveillance we do not mean limited record-keeping of the conventional type necessary for the functioning of a specific organiza-

---

Michael Baker, doctoral candidate, Department of Sociology, Columbia University; and Assistant Director, Project on Computer Data Banks; Dr. Sally Hillsman Baker, Assistant Professor of Sociology, City University of New York, Queens College; Astrida Butners, doctoral candidate, Department of Sociology, Columbia University; and Research Associate, Center for Policy Research; Dr. Robert Engler, Professor of Political Science, Graduate Division, City University of New York; Dr. William Goode, Professor of Sociology, Columbia University; and President, American Sociological Association; Dr. Leonard Krasner, Professor of Psychology, State University of New York at Stony Brook; Robert Laufer, Lecturer in Sociology, State University of New York at Albany; Dr. Hannah Levin, Professor of Psychology, Livingston College, Rutgers University; Dr. Milton Mankoff, Assistant Professor of Sociology, City University of New York, Queens College; Dr. Harold Proshansky, Dean of the Graduate Division, City University of New York; Dr. H. H. Wilson, Professor of Politics, Princeton University; Dr. P. G. Zimbardo, Professor of Psychology, Stanford University; Sandra Abramson, graduate student, City University of New York; and Norman Buntaine, law school student member of the Constitutional Litigation Clinic, Rutgers School of Law at Newark.

1. For some pertinent sources from a very extensive literature, see: Z. Chafee, FREE SPEECH IN THE UNITED STATES, (1942); M. Starkey, THE DEVIL IN MASSACHUSETTS (1961); John C. Miller, CRISIS IN FREEDOM: THE ALIEN AND SEDITION ACTS James M. Smith, FREEDOM'S FETTERS: THE ALIEN AND SEDITION LAWS AND AMERICAN CIVIL LIBERTIES (1956); R. Nye, FETTERED FREEDOM (1964); C. Eaton, FREEDOM OF THOUGHT IN THE OLD SOUTH (1951); Robert K. Murray, RED SCARE: A STUDY OF NATIONAL HYSTERIA, 1919-1920 (1955); M. Grodzins, AMERICANS BETRAYED: POLITICS AND THE JAPANESE EVACUATION E. Bontecou, THE FEDERAL LOYALTY-SECURITY PROGRAM (1953); John L. O'Brian, NATIONAL SECURITY AND INDIVIDUAL FREEDOM (1955); Fred J. Cook, THE NIGHTMARE DECADE W. Gellhorn, SECURITY, LOYALTY AND SCIENCE (1950); J. Faulk, FEAR ON TRIAL (1964); D. Trumbo, ADDITIONAL DIALOGUE and J. Cogley, REPORT ON BLACKLISTING.

tion or institution. Surveillance in *Webster's Dictionary* is defined as "a watch kept over a person, especially a suspect." In common usage, surveillance implies that some actor or entity (in the instant suit, the military) subjects to scrutiny another actor or entity because the probability exists that the person surveilled is doing something contrary to established practice. Criminal suspects are kept under surveillance, while industrial workers, for example, are only supervised. Supervision involves also the notion of keeping watch over a performance, but does not intimate that the performance is illegitimate in some way. Similarly, newspaper investigations involve only reportorial functions, and carry no such negative connotations.

By legitimate political behavior we mean behavior which does not deviate from accepted legal norms. These norms or standards of action are the result of past experiences and historical solutions to the problems of democratic participation.[2] Surveillance implies in the public's mind that a judgment has been made by a governmental unit that the behavior surveilled is not within the range of legitimate political behavior.

The application of surveillance stigmatizes, i.e., it labels as deviant and illegitimate the behavior of those involved in protected political expression. The deviant label has grave consequences for the individual so designated.[3] Chill occurs as a result of this stigmatization.

The charge that protected behavior is chilled by military surveillance is supported by a great deal of data extracted from psychological investigations. The occurrence of chill is a recognized and normal response to threatening social situations, which people have learned to categorize as threatening because of their own or other people's past experiences in similar situations. This is a case of social learning called avoidance behavior which is acquired directly or vicariously.[4] Among the several factors which facilitate the response of chill to surveillance are, in the terms used by psychologists: the power or authority of the surveillance agent; evaluation apprehension (the anxiety which occurs to someone whose behavior is being judged); the probabilistic nature of perception; the uncertainty and ambiguity of the surveillance situation; and the phenomonological experience of the person being surveilled, as to his anonymity or deindividuation.

---

2. *See generally* H. Eckstein, DIVISION AND COHESION IN DEMOCRACY (1966); POLITICAL CULTURE AND POLITICAL DEVELOPMENT (L. Pye and S. Verba eds. 1965); A. de Tocqueville, DEMOCRACY IN AMERICA (1969); and A. Lindsay, THE MODERN DEMOCRATIC STATE (1947).

3. E. Schur, LABELING DEVIANT BEHAVIOR: ITS SOCIOLOGICAL IMPLICATIONS 7-36 (1971). *See also* E. Goffman, STIGMA: THE MANAGEMENT OF SPOILED IDENTITY (1963).

4. A. Bondura, PRINCIPLES OF BEHAVIOR MODIFICATION (1969).

These psychological principles which describe human behavior are tied together by the nature of the human perceptive process itself: people must first define a situation before they respond to it. This definition is reached by individuals as they unite all the discrete elements of the situation into their respective meaningful categories. Individuals categorize different objects, events, and people into classes and proceed to respond to them as a function of their classification rather than as a function of their uniqueness.[5]

In categorizing apparently different stimuli (e.g. political meetings, knowledge of surveillance by the military, and sanctions in the past which have stemmed from these situations) into the same class—"a threatening situation"—individuals have chosen certain aspects of the situation which are critical or relevant and have discarded others which are irrelevant. This class is named ("a threatening situation") and then provides direction for the individual's activities so that he knows in advance what are the appropriate and inappropriate actions for him to take.[6] Surveillance is one class of events under which the individual categorizes particular events as potentially threatening and then functions appropriately in terms of his own well-being, to avoid or minimize the perceived possible negative consequences.

B. *Chill: Theoretical and Empirical Bases*

The very act of the government's surveillance of an individual or group engaged in dissent tends to define the activities of the individual or group as being in some sense illegitimate. Surveillance, in American society, is traditionally reserved for those individuals and groups which in some way are presumed to be engaged in illegitimate activities. This traditional American use of surveillance is in contrast to its use in totalitarian societies, where surveillance is an intrinsic control device used by the government power elite to maintain the governmental structure.[7]

Critical literature about Eastern Europe, the U.S.S.R. and Nazi Germany demonstrates the caution, passivity and terror of citizens who have been taught that dissent is dangerous. In these foreign non-democratic political systems, comments, telephone calls, mail, writings, associations and actions are watched. There are conse-

---

5. J. Bruner, J. Goodnow and G. Austin, A STUDY OF THINKING (1956).
6. *Id.*
7. C. Friedrich and Z. Brzezinski, TOTALITARIAN DICTATORSHIP AND AUTOCRACY (2d. Ed. 1965). *See also* W. Kornhauser, THE POLITICS OF MASS SOCIETY (1959). A. Sakharov, PROGRESS, COEXISTENCE AND INTELLECTUAL FREEDOM (1968); and H. Arendt, THE ORIGINS OF TOTALITARIANISM (1951).

quences for "wrong" sentiment and behavior. Citizens learn by grim example to police themselves rather than to test the system and thereby invoke punishment for being "unreliable."

The general popular assumption is that surveillance means control, concurrence and the ultimate "retooling" of thought. As Hannah Arendt has written,

> In a system of ubiquitous spying, where everbody may be a police agent and each individual feels himself under constant surveillance; under circumstances, moreover, where careers are extremely insecure and where the most spectacular ascents and falls have become everyday occurrences, every word becomes equivocal and subject to retrospective interpretation.[8]

Similarly, in the United States, a public which is aware of the existence of a governmental surveillance program will consciously or unconsciously limit or alter the scope of expression of its political beliefs, both in the present and the future. Surveillance by the government of a particular group can have a real and measurable effect on that group, as well as repercussions on the quality of political expression throughout all of society.

There are, in general, two processes which result in chill. In the first, an individual knows about (or perceives that such is the case without direct knowledge) surveillance and the accompanying record-keeping activities which are directed at groups engaged in legitimate political activity. As a result he, along with others, redefines the *legitimate* political activities as *illegitimate* and is therefore reluctant to act on his political beliefs. He has been "prevented" from taking part himself and in turn becomes intolerant of the activity. He is now himself part of the mechanism of this redefinition.

In the second process, the individual knows about (or perceives) surveillance and record-keeping directed against legitimate political groups. He also knows that records are sometimes misused. As a result he modifies his form of political expression because he is afraid of the consequences of a record of his presence being kept and later misused or misinterpreted. Both processes can occur simultaneously.

Psychological literature recognizes four categories of responses which, in the surveillance situation, cause chill:

1) individuals perceive and categorize surveillance situations as threatening, on the basis of their needs, past experiences, and expectations;

---

8. Arendt, *supra* note 7, at 431.

2) individuals respond to surveillance situations in such a way as they conceive appropriate to this categorization;

3) individuals learn to avoid threatening situations based on the principles of discrimination, avoidance, generalization, vicarious learning, and aversive conditioning; and lastly,

4) the social psychological factors of power and authority, evaluation apprehension, uncertainty and ambiguity, and anonymity and deindividuation influence how the individual perceives, categorizes, and responds to the stimuli.

Herbert Hyman has asked the following question[9] in his research: what difference between the phenomena experienced by citizens in England and America respectively, in their political environments, could account for the more widespread intolerance of political deviation on the part of Americans in the 1950s, than was the experience in England during the same time? He concluded that the contributing factor was that Americans experienced a far greater amount of official investigative activity (such as security checks and publicly visible surveillance of non-conformists) than did the English. Such activity in the United States led to a widespread activation of intolerant attitudes on the part of citizens. This led to citizen oppression of other citizens who were labeled as non-conformists. Also, the surveillance practices had created an atmosphere of fear among the sub-groups which had been so labeled by the investigative activities.

Another classic exploratory study[10] of the psychological effects of surveillance attempted to evaluate the impact of governmental loyalty and security inquiries. Marie Jahoda and S.W. Cook questioned in depth 70 professionals in federal positions and 15 faculty members in universities, all in the Washington, D.C. area. The investigators felt that the impact of security measures depended upon how people perceived the measures as well as on the actual measures that were taken. In fact, their underlying proposition was that the "social psychological consequences of a social policy can, but need not, coincide with the purposes for which the policy was designed."[11]

Jahoda and Cook found that people responded to the entire situation as defined by the prevalent atmosphere or climate of

9. Hyman, *England and America: Climate of Tolerance and Intolerance*, esp. at 298, in THE RADICAL RIGHT (D. Bell ed. 1963). Herbert H. Hyman is Professor of Sociology at Wesleyan University in Middletown, Connecticut.

10. Johoda and Cook, *Security Measures and Freedom of Thought*, 61 YALE L. J. 296-333 (1952).

11. *Id.* at 298.

thought, rather than perceiving and responding only to the specific official and unofficial security measures which were taken. In responding to the global situation, people began to adhere or to fear that they must adhere to more specific and concrete codes of behavior than they had traditionally observed. After this occurred, people often internalized the newly accepted standard or code. They perceived it as one to which they voluntarily complied rather than as one which was forced upon them as a consequence of the pervasiveness of a climate of thought. Examples of the behaviors which changed as a result of the foregoing process were: 1) severing of membership in organizations on the Attorney General's list and cancelling of subscriptions to literature sent by these organizations; 2) refusing to sign petitions without proof of a bona fide sponsorship; 3) refraining from joining an organization *not* on the Attorney General's list for fear it might turn out to be a communist front or might perhaps later develop in a radical direction; and 4) being cautious in political conversations with strangers.

The authors stressed that respondents were often unable to distinguish between "founded" and "unfounded" fears and allegations because of the climate of thought which prevailed. This resulted in the stigmatization of anyone who was investigated, either officially or unofficially. The penalties which the respondents felt were incurred by those being investigated included personal agony, damage to physical health, legal expenses, mental agony, and loss of reputation. Respondents also perceived that a subsequent clearance of any charges made by the government did not provide relief, because 1) fears continued to exist that an investigative file would be reopened; 2) suspicions of others were not erased by a mere clearance of the charges (in fact, files *were* reopened based on this continuing suspicion); and 3) those under scrutiny were judged on the basis of the past, not the present, and therefore knew that their present activity might well come under scrutiny in the future. People know that the climate of the times will change many times within the span of one life. The investigators concluded that:

> [T]he hazards of *being investigated*—even if one is subsequently cleared—are so great that individuals are induced to limit their behavior by avoiding (or trying to avoid) anything that might conceivably arouse anyone's suspicion and thus lead to charges and an investigation.[12]

---

12. *Id.* at 318.

It must be stressed, as did Jahoda and Cook, that an individual does not respond to a specific administrative measure or event but instead perceives that specific event as an integral part of related activities, a class of events, and thus responds to these interrelated measures. The specific events of government security measures taken in the 1950s were categorized by individuals as psychologically salient elements of the category "surveillance," particularly with respect to people's perceptions of the government measures. From the responses reported, we have an indication of the type of responses an individual makes under conditions of surveillance. These responses determine the individual's perception of what actions may be appropriate or inappropriate in *other* situations. By being aware of the operation of a system which is categorized as surveillance, and in responding to the total situation or climate of thought, respondents in the study (as is evidenced by their own limiting of activities) were in fact chilled.

The experiences which people have with the political process are key factors which determine the psychological preconditions needed for a democratic or participative political system. Since the key to political democracy is not that citizens be always active (i.e., acting politically) but that they be "potentially active,"[13] the public's reactions to various political experiences, such as surveillance, are of the utmost importance. The potentially active public is deterred from participating because the surveillance of the politically active public effectively neutralizes the participative incentive which might have appealed to the potential actor. The dynamic of potential activity is in this way eliminated, and the psychological precondition needed for a participative political system is absent.

An individual's political behavior, as well as his social behavior, contains an historical dimension. For example, as the result of past political experiences in which dissenting political activity was severely sanctioned, German and Italian adults today feel greatly limited in their freedom of political communication. The empirical finding[14] is that they feel more restricted than do Americans and British in discussing political and governmental affairs. The habits and feelings developed during these earlier periods have persisted into the present, "despite the formal freedoms of the contemporary German and Italian political systems."[15]

---

13. G. Almond and S. Verba, THE CIVIC CULTURE: POLITICAL ATTITUDES AND DEMOCRACY IN FIVE NATIONS 481 (1963).
14. *Id.*
15. *Id.* at 119. *See also* D. Brogan, CITIZENSHIP TODAY: ENGLAND, FRANCE, THE UNITED STATES (1960); L. Milbraith, POLITICAL PARTICIPATION: HOW AND WHY DO PEOPLE GET INVOLVED IN POLITICS (1965).

Evidence that governmental policies or practices affect the scope of political expression should be taken very seriously, since these findings from Germany and Italy strongly suggest that negative sanctions, when applied to political activity, have a chilling effect not only on current levels of expression and participation but also have long-term inhibiting effects that may last from 20 to 30 years or more.

There is evidence that intelligence gathering units are acutely aware of their ability to stigmatize a group and inhibit their political expression by engaging in surveillance.[16] Because surveillance is practiced secretly and the information it produces is kept secret, no citizen involved in political dissent can ever be certain that he is or is not under scrutiny—once he becomes aware that some people in his situation are. This condition of uncertainty gives rise to anxiety and to the suppression of his normal political responses.[17]

Just as important, if not more so, those who are not already involved in political activity are more likely to be reluctant to participate politically. The sociological literature in deviant behavior amply documents the extent to which individuals avoid assuming stigmatized roles.[18] A frightening aspect of this situation is that individuals or groups who are only curious bystanders can also be stigmatized,[19] by being indiscriminately included in the lists of those present at the activity surveilled.

The phenomenon of chill is well described in the psychological literature as a special case of learning, called avoidance learning or aversive conditioning.[20] As a result of undergoing either direct or vicarious experiences, an individual's behavior comes to be regulated by stimuli that were present in the situation that preceded the responses. A very simple example of this principle of conditioning or learning is where a person stops when seeing a red light because of having seen what can happen if he does not stop (negative reinforcement), and likewise learns to proceed when seeing a green light. The

---

16. *See, e.g.,* Wall, *Special Agent for the FBI,* 12 NEW YORK REVIEW OF BOOKS, no. 1, at 12-18. *See Hearings on Privacy and the Rights of Federal Employees Before the Subcomm. on Manpower and Civil Service of the House Comm. on Post Office and Civil Service,* 90th Cong., 2d Sess. (June 1968). *See also* the FBI Media, Pennsylvania, document which encourages agents to make their presence known to members of the New Left in order to generate paranoia among them by fostering the belief that "there is an FBI agent behind every mailbox" in Donner, *The Theory and Practice of American Political Intelligence,* NEW YORK REVIEW OF BOOKS, 27 (April 22, 1971). This last quotation on paranoia has been widely publicized; *see e.g.,* NEW YORK TIMES, Mar. 25, 1971, at 1, 33.

17. Bandura, *supra* note 4.

18. M. Clinard, SOCIOLOGY OF DEVIANT BEHAVIOR 1-48 (1968). *See also* Schur, *supra* note 3.

19. Goffman, *supra* note 3.

20. Bandura, *supra* note 4.

red light tells him to avoid crossing the street when the stimulus is present. In the surveillance situation at a peaceful demonstration, the actor's observation or belief that a military agent is present, watching his behavior, perhaps photographing and taking notes, is a stimulus to avoid the situation. He has learned either directly or vicariously (through the numerous media sources) that this surveillance has been and is taking place, and can lead to further investigation, permanent police records, and other negative consequences which would endanger his reputation, friendships, and livelihood.

The surveillance agent need not be recognized or obvious. Bandura[21] discusses how symbols, words, or knowledge can act as a stimulus and control behavior just as effectively as the external stimulus of a red light. Plaintiffs know that surveillance of political dissent meetings is being conducted, and their responses are controlled by this knowledge just as effectively as if there were men on guard in military uniform at the door.

Another principle of learning important to the surveillance situation and described by Bandura is the generalization of learning. This principle, demonstrated in many psychological experiments,[22] explains how a situation that one learns to avoid need not be identical to a prior situation where one has witnessed aversive consequences to himself or to someone else. Bandura concluded from these findings that where negative sanctions are applied to a wide range of social responses in diverse settings, one finds a large number of behaviors inhibited.[23] The surveillance case described in this lawsuit is such a situation.

Avoidance of a perceived dangerous situation can maintain effective control over behavior for a long period of time. This inhibitory control seems to be effective because the person who avoids a threatening situation feels relieved as a result of having avoided it. This feeling is reinforcing and strengthens the person's tendency to avoid future similar situations.[24]

---

21. *Id.*

22. *See* Desiderato, *The Relation of Repetitions in the Speech of Young Children to Certain Measures of Language Maturity and Situational Factors: Part I*, 4 JOURNAL OF SPEECH DISORDERS 303-318 (1964); Hoffman and Flishler, *Stimulus Factors in Aversive Controls: the Generalization of Conditioned Suppression*, 4 JOURNAL OF EXPERIMENTAL ANALYSIS OF BEHAVIOR 371-378 (1961); and Honig and Slivka, *Stimulus Generalization of the Effects of Punishment*, 7 JOURNAL OF EXPERIMENTAL ANALYSIS OF BEHAVIOR 21-25 (1964).

23. Bandura, *supra* note 4.

24. Bandura, *Influences of Models' Reinforcement and Contingencies on the Acquisition of Imitative Responses*, 1 JOURNAL OF PERSONALITY AND SOCIAL PSYCHOLOGY 589-595 (1965).

Other studies by Kanfer[25] on verbal behavior (speech) show that human subjects learn to inhibit speech by observing the negative consequences to others of specific speech behavior. People learn to internalize the information they gain from observing others, and are guided in subsequent situations by the anticipations of rewards and punishments. Also, people do not have to be aware of surveillance, or of their changed responses (such as inhibition of speech behavior), for a chill to have occurred. Krasner describes how people can change or decrease their verbal behavior without being aware of this change.[26]

Jerome Bruner has shown[27] that past experiences, needs, and expectations influence perception. In addition to perceiving situations in a particular way as a result of those influences, individuals confronted with stimuli which require a response will interpret the stimuli so as to make the appropriate response.[28] In ambiguous or complex situations individuals will attempt to structure the relevant situation or event in such a way that it is understandable.[29]

Actual surveillance of an individual or group at a particular event, political or otherwise, is not an essential element for chill to occur. With public knowledge that surveillance of political activities has occurred and is continuing to occur, the individual's perception of the actual event has been influenced. Based on the expectation that surveillance might be going on, people exhibit the same verbal inhibitions as if they were certain through direct knowledge that a surveillance agent were present.

The need to protect oneself from being investigated, when coupled with the public knowledge that surveillance occurs at certain types of political meetings, can lead to the perception that it is occurring or will occur at a specific meeting in question. People will then respond to the meeting based not on what the actual social situation is, but on what past reality has taught them to expect it to be.[30]

When people are surveilled by the military at a demonstration and have no knowledge of the consequences of this surveillance, or of

---

25. Kanfer, *Vicarious Human Reinforcement: a Glimpse Into the Black Box*, in RESEARCH IN BEHAVIOR EDUCATION 244-267 (L. Krasmer and L. Ullman eds. 1964).

26. Krasner, *Verbal Operant Conditioning and Awareness*, in RESEARCH IN VERBAL BEHAVIOR AND SOME NEUROPHYSIOLOGICAL IMPLICATIONS (K. Salzinger and S. Salzinger eds. 1967).

27. J. Bruner, *Social Psychology and Perception*, in READINGS IN SOCIAL PSYCHOLOGY (E. Maccoby, T. Newcomb and E. Hartley eds. 1958).

28. F. Bartlett, REMEMBERING: A STUDY IN EXPERIMENTAL AND SOCIAL PSYCHOLOGY (1932).

29. Cohen, Stotland and Wolfe, *An Experimental Investigation of Need for Cognition*, 41 JOURNAL OF ABNORMAL AND SOCIAL PSYCHOLOGY 291-297 (1955).

30. Bandura, *supra* note 4, at 300.

what behaviors are targeted specifically, or of who is being surveilled in particular, or of why the surveillance is being conducted in the first place, then the absence of predictability in the situation gives rise to uncertainty and anxiety. In fact, the results of studies of uncertainty and predictability have shown that individuals have a desire for predictability about a forthcoming unpleasant event, even if this knowledge will not keep the event from occurring. Not only is the predictability preferable, but it also arouses less anxiety.[31] People tend to avoid these surveilled political events because they would have little or no control over the consequences of their behavior if they attended.

Another factor influencing both the individual's perception of political activities and his behavioral response to them is what is called in psychological literature "evaluation apprehension." This apprehension is an active anxiety that subjects feel when they are being evaluated. It leads the individuals to behave in a manner that will win a positive evaluation from the person who is judging him. In the situation discussed in this case, that would be the surveillance agent. Rosenberg[32] found that evaluation apprehension could be reduced by assuring the subject that his "public spiritedness" or "patriotism" would not be open to assessment or evaluative judgment. In this way, a more accurate self representation could be obtained. Rosenberg also learned that if the experimenter has some *power* over the subject, he will bias his responses so as to appear in conformity with most others.

The psychological consequence of concern over social evaluation (induced through awareness that one's behavior is under surveillance) is the arousal of anxiety. This anxiety raises the threshold for expression of all behaviors which could be judged as non-normative, deviant, atypical, or politically dissident. The overt consequences of such an internal state of "evaluation apprehension" are:

1) a likely avoidance of such evaluative situations;

2) a limitation or modification of the public speech or actions of the individual who is in such situations, so as to render the speech or action "acceptable" to the sponsors of the surveillance; and,

---

31. Lanzetta and Driscoll, *Preference for Information About an Uncertain but Unavoidable Outcome,* 3 JOURNAL OF PERSONALITY AND SOCIAL PSYCHOLOGY 96-102 (1966). *See also* Pervin, *The Need to Predict and Control Under Conditions of Threat,* 31 JOURNAL OF PERSONALITY 570-587 (1963).

32. Rosenberg, *The Conditions and Consequences of Evaluation Appreciation,* in ARTIFACT IN BEHAVIORAL RESEARCH 279-349 (R. Rosenthal and R. Rosnow eds. 1969).

3) an arousal of feelings of shame and worthlessness by the individual who avoids such situations, if he is committed to those beliefs relevant to the situation. If he is not yet committed to the beliefs, he is likely to come to view those beliefs as illegitimate, as a direct consequence of the surveillance.[33]

Government surveillance agents can be used to enforce individual compliance to certain norms or standards of behavior. By observing and surveilling the individual or group in a situation where dissenting political speech is being displayed, the surveilling agents, who are authority figures, act as a pressure toward compliance with their own norms.[34] Kiesler and Kiesler have shown that an individual may re-evaluate not only his overt behavior because of the pressure produced by observation (surveillance), but also will reexamine his beliefs.[35] Thus, surveillance may interfere not only with verbal and other opinion-related behavior, but may also act as a method of thought control.[36]

In an experimental situation, Milgram[37] illustrated the ability of legitimate authority figures to enforce compliance, when he was able to get subjects to administer what they believed to be painful shocks

---

33. *Cf.* L. Festinger, A THEORY OF COGNITIVE DISSONANCE (1957) and Zimbardo, *The Cognitive Control of Motivation,* in 17 THE NEBRASKA SYMPOSIUM ON MOTIVATION 237-307 (W. Arnold and D. Levine eds. 1969).

34. C. Kiesler and S. Kiesler, CONFORMITY (1969). In an editorial column entitled *Big Brother is Coming* (New York Times, Nov. 14, 1971, §4 at 13) Russell Baker writes:

> The object of unconcealed surveillance is not to get the goods on its man, but to plant fear of the state in his marrow, to keep his mind sensitive to the powers that the corporate state can bring to bear, if it chooses, upon him whose existence annoys it.

35. Kiesler, *supra* note 31, at 86.

36. Jerome B. Wiesner (*infra* note 88 and accompanying text) has warned that the interconnecting communications hardware and new sophisticated techniques for data analysis may one day make it possible:

> to stimulate patterns of behavior for individuals and social groups and attempt to predict or anticipate their behavior with the purpose of maintaining better surveillance. . . . In a way this was what the Army was doing when it selected antiwar organizers, speakers and demonstrators for particular attention.

Hearings on Federal Data Banks, Computers and the Bill of Rights before the SUB-COMMITTEE ON CONSTITUTIONAL RIGHTS OF THE SENATE COMMITTEE ON THE JUDICIARY, 92nd Cong., 1st Sess. at 764 (Feb.-Mar. 1971)[hereinafter cited as *Ervin Hearings*].

37. Milgram, *Some Conditions of Obedience and Disobedience to Authority,* 18 HUMAN RELATIONS 259-276 (1965).

to other people at the instruction of a perceived legitimate authority. In commenting on the amount of compliance an authority figure could command, he states:

[I]t is the extreme willingness of adults to go to almost any lengths on the command of an authority that constitutes the chief finding of this study ... relatively few people have the resources needed to resist authority.[38]

The military, being the agent of authority as well as the agent of surveillance, provokes the individual's fear of subsequent negative consequences. The individual's response is the result of a belief that if he complies with the powerful agent (rather than resisting the latter's attempt to influence him), he can maximize his gains and minimize his losses in relation to the agent's ability to punish.[39] Berkowitz states that "anticipated punishment is a negative incentive which often causes the person to suppress actions that might bring about the noxious consequences."[40] Furthermore, the individual may attempt to hide his own opinions because they differ from those of the agents of power.[41]

Another body of psychological data which has a bearing on the chilling effects of surveillance comes from research on anonymity and deindividuation. Anonymity is provided by situations in which an individual perceives that his thoughts, speech, action and judgments cannot be identified by others as belonging to him. Deindividuation is the process by which individuals attempt to become anonymous or indistinguishable from others. When an individual is surveilled he loses his anonymity and attempts to deindividuate himself.

Deutsch and Gerard[42] have found that people experience less influence to conform to social norms when they are able to express their judgments anonymously, rather than when someone knows the source of the judgments. Similarly, Cantril[43] found a discrepancy between what one will say secretly in voting on a controversial issue

---

38. Milgram, *The Compulsion to Do Evil*, PATTERN OF PREJUDICE 5 (Nov.-Dec. 1967).

39. Berkowitz, *Social Motivation*, in 3 THE HANDBOOK OF SOCIAL PSYCHOLOGY (G. Lindzey and E. Aronson ed. 1969).

40. *Id.* at 73.

41. Ring and Kelley, *A Comparison of Augmentation and Reduction as Modes of Influence*, 66 JOURNAL OF ABNORMAL AND SOCIAL PSYCHOLOGY 95-102 (1963).

42. Deutsch and Gerard, *A Study of Normative and Informational Social Influences Upon Individual Judgment*, 51 JOURNAL OF ABNORMAL AND SOCIAL PSYCHOLOGY 629-636 (1955).

43. H. Cantril, GAUGING PUBLIC OPINION (1944).

and what one will say when one is identified. Zimbardo,[44] using soldiers from the Belgian army as subjects, has shown that conditions which led the soldiers to feel more conspicuous resulted in the inhibition of their overt responses, as compared to subjects who felt inconspicuous in the situations. In another study using New York University coeds, subjects who were made to feel that they were readily "individuated," distinguishable, or conspicuous because they were under the surveillance of the experimenters, were significantly more inhibited in their interpersonal responsiveness than were individuals who felt that they were secure from identification.[45]

C. Contemporary Awareness

Today in the United States there is mounting concern over the government's widespread surveillance activities. Ample empirical evidence from numerous sources shows that the American public is consciously aware of these activities and especially of those involved in this suit. The congressional hearings held by Senator Sam J. Ervin in February and March, 1971[46], indicate the visibility of public concern over the system of military surveillance of citizen political activities.

The proliferation of books dealing with the "privacy debate" cannot be listed to any advantage individually, but the fact that they have been widely disseminated to the public, along with the attendant scholarly and popular magazine articles,[47] and with other media sources such as television topical coverages,[48] newspaper items, and editorials, should serve to put this Court on notice that the public *is* generally cognizant of the fact that systems of surveillance by government do exist.

---

44. Zimbardo, *supra* note 33.

45. *Id.*

46. *See Ervin Hearings, supra* note 36. *See also* 116 Cong. Rec. 30797 (1970) for an earlier report by this Sub-committee on the extent of security and investigative files held by the Civil Service Commission and used interchangeably with other federal agencies.

47. For an extended bibliographical listing, see the materials in A. Westin, PRIVACY AND FREEDOM (1967). *See also* Arthur R. Miller, THE ASSAULT ON PRIVACY: COMPUTERS, DATA BANKS AND DOSSIERS (1971). For more specific activities of the House Internal Security Committee HISC, see the disclosures by Representative Robert Drinan in 117 Cong. Rec. 3210 (daily ed. April 29, 1971), where he says that HISC holds 754,000 files on individuals and groups, which are available to any Congressman upon request with absolutely no ban on publication of any file so acquired.

48. A CBS-TV network documentary, entitled "Under Surveillance", was broadcast Dec. 23, 1971, and was seen by millions of viewers. It dealt with the government's investigation of political dissidents in Philadelphia, and concluded that the surveillance was "political surveillance in the sense that it is directed mostly at those who disagree with the government. But in private and public files there are dossiers on most of the rest of us as well."

The ABC-TV network broadcast a one hour documentary on surveillance on Jan. 8, 1972, entitled "Assault on Privacy". It, too, was seen by millions of viewers and concluded:

In addition to this material there is other evidence of the public's consciousness of surveillance and record-keeping. Since this society is one which sociologically could be termed "organizational," interactions between individuals and organizations most often involve recorded transactions. As a result, individuals have become oriented very early in life to making or maintaining a "good record," or sometimes to avoid if possible making any record at all (as is clearly the point with police records).[49]

The knowledge of what is now occurring[50] and the manner in which people today perceive the situation is strikingly similar to that which was reported by Jahoda and Cook[51] in 1952. When conceptualizing the contemporary events as belonging to the class of stimuli "surveillance," individuals also conceptualize the relationship between what surveillance is and other classes of events related to it, particularly the sanctions and penalties to which it may lead. As Jahoda and Cook stressed, the sanctions and penalties may not be officially administered, but still are the direct results of indirect administrative measures. Individuals modify their behaviors in accordance with their perceptions of the possible negative outcomes.

Recognizing this, noted historian Henry Steele Commager has adivsed that this nation must concern itself for its welfare, and has warned that "we may be witnessing, even now, a dissolution of the fabric of freedom that may portend the dissolution of the Republic."[52]

Clearly, some sectors of the public are responding to this threat, in part through a growing awareness of the dangers involved. This

---

Our rights, our freedoms, our constitutional guarantees, the result of human thought and centuries of struggle, must be protected whether threatened by overzealous law enforcers or by mechanical brain . . . . But today in the United States of America there is a clear and present danger that they can prevail over us.

49. *See generally* ON RECORD: FILES AND DOSSIERS IN AMERICAN LIFE (S. Wheeler ed. 1965).

50. The *scope* of what is occurring is a factor of the public's knowledge. Today, the FBI, the Secret Service, the House Internal Security Committee, the Bureau of Customs, the Passport Division, the Internal Revenue Service, the Intelligence Division of the Post Office, the Immigration and Naturalization Service, the Department of Justice, the National Science Foundation, the Housing and Urban Development Department, the Department of Health, Education and Welfare, and numerous State and local agencies conduct extensive intelligence operations which affect the lives of millions. HISC, to cite a specific example of the use to which such information may be put, has published a list of "radical" campus speakers and their affiliations presumably as a warning to innocent universities. But U.S. District Judge Gerard A. Gesell, District of Columbia, has barred its publication or distribution because of the inescapable conclusion that the report sought to inhibit free speech. *See* New York Times, Oct. 29, 1970, at 1. Arthur Miller has estimated that the average American may be the subject of anywhere from ten to twenty dossiers. *See Ervin Hearings, supra* note 36 at 9.

51. *See supra* notes 10-12.

52. LOOK, July 14, 1970.

awareness has been documented in several relevant surveys, and the simple statistical results are very revealing. For example, one 1970 national sample survey on public reactions to computer uses[53] reports that 53% of the sample believed that computerized information files might be used to destroy individual freedoms, and 58% felt that computers will be used in the future to keep people under surveillance. Thirty-eight per cent believed that computers represent a real threat to personal privacy. Ninety-one per cent of those questioned felt that computers were used to compile information files on U.S. citizens, and 54% believed that these files were maintained for surveillance of activist or radical groups. People also indicated their general concern (62%) over the types of informaton being kept, and 45% said that political activity records should not be kept.

Another survey[54] measured 56% of the respondents as being opposed to the creation of any primary national data bank. Forty-three per cent of respondents felt that already the government knew too much about their personal lives. Representative David R. Obey of Wisconsin has reported[55] that of nearly 10,000 constituents who responded to his questionnaire, 56% strongly feel that surveillance of the political activities of private citizens and public officials by military intelligence personnel should not be allowed to continue. This very lawsuit reflects precisely this public consciousness and sentiment.

This evidence is supported by another statement of concern which has manifested itself in the executive realm. A concise statement found in the Report of the White House Conference on Youth reads:

> There is a feeling among youth of an abrogation and diminution of civil rights in the United States, particularly with reference to . . . surveillances by various government agencies of the activities of politicians, political candidates, and politically active citizens, and those considered radical (whether to the left or the right of the political spectrum).[56]

In addition, the Conference indicated its concern over "a chilling effect that has resulted in a feeling of fear and intimidation among

---

53. A National Survey of the Public's Attitudes Toward Computers, November 1971 (published by and available from the American Federation of Information Processing Societies, Inc. (AFIPS) and Time, Inc.).

54. *A Survey of Public Attitudes Toward Technology*, SIXTH ANNUAL REPORT OF THE HARVARD UNIVERSITY PROGRAM ON TECHNOLOGY AND SOCIETY (Dec. 1970).

55. 117 CONG. REC. 111,080 (daily ed. Oct. 20, 1971).

56. REPORT OF THE WHITE HOUSE CONFERENCE ON YOUTH 169 (1970).

the youth, minorities, and a significant number of people in this nation and members of both houses of the United States Congress."[57] The chilling effect arises, according to the Conference Report, because of "political surveillance of citizens who express themselves by engaging in protesting public policies."[58]

At a recent labor union conference in Washington, D.C., on various aspects of privacy, a hundred participants were surveyed and the results have a significant bearing on the issues at hand.[59] Almost half of the respondents felt that the Administration wanted to suppress dissent, while another 40% felt that the Administration's aim was to discourage dissent. The respondents clearly evidenced concern about the atmosphere in which political dissent can take place.[60] The participants opposed surveillance measures by law enforcement agencies in general, and especially by the Army.[61] Of the participants, 74% were opposed to the collection of political intelligence by Army Intelligence.[62]

The respondents opposed permitting the law enforcement agencies, on their own discretion, to collect and maintain files on groups which might engage in criminal acts of violence. However, a majority supported such efforts if a court issuing a warrant had judicially recognized that a group might engage in criminal acts.[63] In essence, the respondents felt that the maintenance and collection of investigative files was a legitimate aspect of the law enforcement agency if the scope of the files were limited by direct court mandate. Almost all the respondents supported the maintenance of records by law enforcement agencies about persons convicted of criminal offenses.[64]

These data indicate that opposition to collection of information on a discretionary basis is not directed to the maintenance of materials needed for organizational functioning, as long as the need is perceived as meeting a legitimate function (as the court warrant served to certify legitimacy, for example). In terms of their personal experiences with surveillance, 26% asserted that they had been photographed at political meetings or rallies, and a significant minority (16%) felt that some governmental file had been opened on their political activities. Finally, 76% would oppose law enforcement of-

---

57. *Id.* at 171.
58. *Id.*
59. Conference Report of the Transportation Institute of the AFL-CIO, Fall 1970 (published by and available from the AFL-CIO).
60. *Id.* at 7.
61. *Id.* at 3
62. *Id.*
63. *Id.* at 2.
64. *Id.*

ficers photographing people attending public protest meetings and rallies.[65]

Morris Janowitz has testified recently[66] about the cause of this consciousness by the public about military surveillance systems:

> ... the scope and intensity of surveillance of civilian institutions and groups is unprecedented in American society. [467]
> ... it is again my reasoned judgment that [this activity by the military] raises issues about civil liberties and freedom of speech. It chills people. ... [469]

The public has also become aware of the unauthorized distribution of information obtained through surveillance. An example of public knowledge of misuse of information collected can be found in New York State Controller Arthur Levitt's public statement[67] that the State's Identification and Intelligence System permitted unauthorized military personnel to search its records, and gave almost unlimited access to its confidential files to any state employee in any of its 3600 user agencies.

In New York City, Investigation Commissioner Robert K. Ruskin recently suspended, with much public notoriety, a police detective on charges that he had sold confidential information from police files to banks, airlines, detective agencies and other companies.[68] Similarly, in an affidavit Police Commissioner Patrick V. Murphy of New York City acknowledged that his department had passed information, gathered by undercover police agents, about the political and protest activities of applicants for admission to the Bar to the Committee on Character and Fitness of the First and Second Judicial Departments of the Appellate Division of the State Supreme Court.[69]

Even the Justice Department in this instant case has conceded that abuses occurred in connection with the military surveillance system. Assistant Attorney General (now Mr. Justice) Rehnquist, testifying in his former capacity as an Assistant Attorney General, indicated

---

65. *Id.* at 6.
66. *See* the Transcript of Proceedings Before Hon. Richard B. Austin in A.C.L.U. et al. v. Westmoreland (N.D. ILL. Dec. 29, 1970). *See also* Janowitz, THE PROFESSIONAL SOLDIER (1960); THE ROLE OF THE MILITARY IN THE POLITICAL DEVELOPMENT OF NEW NATIONS (1964); and THE NEW MILITARY (1967). Janowitz is Chairman of the Department of Sociology at the University of Chicago.
67. New York Times, Dec. 13, 1971, at 15.
68. New York Times, May 21, 1970, at 1. For related developments, see New York Times, Nov. 23, 1970, at 17.
69. New York Times, Jan. 19, 1972, at 41.

that it would indeed be "surprising if there were not isolated examples of abuses of this investigative function."[70] The misuses which Mr. Rehnquist admitted included collection of information not legitimately related to law enforcement authority, and unauthorized dissemination of information in the surveillance files.

Mayor Joseph L. Alioto of San Francisco has publicly charged that certain confidential information, which formed the basis of a 1969 *Look* magazine article, had come illegally from the data files of six Federal agencies and two California police departments.[71]

Most recently, the Internal Revenue Service has acknowledged (under pressure of public charges by a former FBI agent) that it has a special investigative unit which collects information on political dissidents for special investigation of their returns.[72] As was nationally publicized by a story on the front page of the *New York Times*,

> ... the IRS investigators explained they had assembled files on "antiwar people and draft-card burners and black militants." They said they were preparing to open investigations on all of them, but were just getting started and were not sure where they were going. ... [73]

Moreover, Mr. Johnnie Walker, Commissioner of Internal Revenue, said "that he did not know much about the special IRS unit's operations because the existence of the unit came to his attention only about a week ago. ... "[74]

There is apparently no question but that interagency use of data in one agency's files is a common practice which is not even remotely regarded by user agencies as a form of abuse and misuse. Nevertheless, it is *exactly* that in the eyes of the public. In reflection of this attitude, Representative Robert Drinan of Massachusetts has disclosed that the staff of the House Internal Security Committee has obtained from IRS the tax returns of citizens whose political activities they are reviewing and recording.[75]

The fear of misuse of information contained in files has provoked various protective moves by different groups. In academia, for

---

70. *See Ervin Hearings, supra* note 36, at 602. *See also* Newark Evening News, Mar. 9, 1971, at 1.

71. *Ervin Hearings, supra* note 36, at 492-530. *See also* New York Times, Mar. 4, 1971, at 22.

72. New York Times, Jan. 13, 1972, at 1. *See also* 12 New York Review of Books, *supra* note 16.

73. New York Times, Jan. 13, 1972, at 20.

74. *Id.*

75. *See* Drinan, *supra* note 47.

example, some years ago Dean Carl W. Ackerman of the Columbia University School of Journalism announced he would no longer cooperate with federal, state or police investigators seeking information on students, except upon written request and on advice of counsel:

> Students are "tried" secretly without their knowledge and without an opportunity of explaining or defending their records before employment by any governmental agency.[76]

It is now an accepted principle of academic freedom that no lists of membership of campus organizations should be kept by college authorities. Some schools allow graduating students the right to examine personal records and remove references to clubs and other activities.[77]

D. *Impact of Awareness*

The effects of surveillance in academia on political expression have been extensively documented. A classic sociological study, *The Academic Mind*,[78] examined the effect of the measures taken against academics during the McCarthy era on their feelings, subjective experiences, and expectations. The authors constructed an index of apprehension, which consisted of two sets of items—one pertaining to worry about security, the other pertaining to precautionary behavior.[79] The index clearly showed that certain portions of the social science community had been affected.

Herbert Kelman states that *The Academic Mind* illustrates how, by increasing the level of apprehension, the overt behavior of dissenters is inhibited.[80] He notes that those subjected to the pressures of the McCarthy years tended to "disengage themselves from legitimate activities and associations"[81] because these associations were regarded with suspicion by others.

---

76. New York Times, April 4, 1953, at 1.

77. *See Ervin Hearings, supra* note 36, at 996 (University of Minnesota, Recommendations Derived from the Admissions and Records Experience), 999 (University of Minnesota, Files Policy), 999 (University of Minnesota, Recommendation on Administrative Accountability), and 1002 (University of Minnesota, Policies of the Student Counseling Bureau Regarding the Release of Information About Students).

78. P. Lazarsfield and W. Thielens, THE ACADEMIC MIND (1958).

79. *Id.* at 74.

80. H. Kelman, A TIME TO SPEAK: ON HUMAN VALUES AND SOCIAL RESEARCH 287 (1968). Herbert Kelman is Cabot Professor, Department of Social Relations, Harvard University.

81. *Id.* at 288.

An analogous situation exists today. The University of Minnesota is a case in point.[82] Military Intelligence began a systematic surveillance of campus activities and personnel in 1967 and this surveillance became publicly known. The fear of being surveilled, according to Malcolm Moos,[83] President of the University of Minnesota, hung like "a deadly mist"[84] over the campus community.

A necessary consequence of this high level of apprehension is the resulting change in the political actor's orientation to political phenomena. The University of Minnesota's administration is gravely worried about the effect which this surveillance has had on the quality of academic and political expression on the campus. Eugene Eidenberg,[85] assistant Vice President for Administration at the University, stressed in his report on military surveillance to President Moos that some faculty members who might privately dissent may well refuse to express this dissent publicly, for fear that the item might be recorded and later used against them.[86]

It is this fear, this apprehension created by the knowledge that extensive surveillance has occurred, which changes the quality of orientation of the actor to his political behavior. This indiscriminate surveillance "detracts from the democratic fabric of our society, destroys mutual trust, and chills"[87] the political behavior of those on *any* campus.

The apprehension is widespread through all levels of academia. In recent testimony, Jerome B. Wiesner has said that

> ... many, many students are afraid to participate in political activities of various kinds which might attract them because of their concern about the consequences of having a record of such activities appear in a central file. They fear that at some future date, it might possibly cost them a job or at least make their clearance for a job more difficult to obtain. . . .[88]

---

82. *Ervin Hearings, supra* note 36, at 531-569, 900-1021.

83. Moos was also formerly a political science advisor to President Eisenhower.

84. *Ervin Hearings, supra* note 36, at 535.

85. Eidenberg is also a professor of political science at the University of Minnesota.

86. *Ervin Hearings, supra* note 36, at 551.

87. *Id.* at 992.

88. *Ervin Hearings, supra* note 36, at 765. Wiesner is provost elect at the Massachusetts Institute of Technology, and in the past was President Kennedy's science advisor. Moos and Wiesner reiterated this same point in a recent article by Kosson, *Students Fear U.S. Snooping,* NEWS AMERICAN (Mar. 12, 1971). *See also* R. Flacks, YOUTH AND SOCIAL CHANGE 2 (1971), where he cites the fear by students that "joining anything 'might jeopardize the government job I'm planning to get' " or the "fear that taking any kind of stand on any issue might get you into trouble."

Whether the intelligence gathering unit intends in a specific situation to stigmatize the political actor is irrelevant. The actor's fear is based on reality. Wiesner and Moos note that "they are real fears and that they frequently have caused students to back away from activities which attract them."[89] The activities to which they refer are not violent, planned confrontations or demonstrations, but rather include those activities clearly within the bounds of what have traditionally been defined as *legitimate* political and/or academic behavior (i.e., participation in seminars or political study groups, where participants might subject governmental policies to criticism). The evidence of fear indicates that the process of redefinition has already begun to occur, so that what has been legitimate in the past is now tainted with illegitimacy because of governmental surveillance, and political participation is affected.

Blacks and other minorities have had direct experiences with surveillance. The close watch kept over Dr. Martin Luther King by the FBI and the military while he was alive, even when he was buried, and when the Poor People marched after his death—these and other similar instances have fed what some observes see as a profound fear today among Blacks of surveillance.[90]

Military surveillance of legitimate political behavior creates an apprehension on the part of actual or potential actors which arises from (1) the question of the legitimacy or illegitimacy of engaging in this behavior, and (2) the fear of misuse of the information gathered. The disengagement, both behavioral and psychological, which Kelman identified in the context of the 1950's, is occurring today. Evidence cited indicates that many Americans have redefined as illegitimate or stigmatizing what is, and remains by present democratic political norms, legitimate political expression and behavior.

Even certain decisions of federally elected officials seem to be affected by the various surveillance and record-keeping systems that

---

89. Kossen, *supra* note 88.

90. One account of such reactions was offered by a former member of the Army's Counterintelligence Analysis Branch. He was discussing domestic military surveillance on a TV program called "Black Talk" while before an entirely Black audience:

The first person to get up asked me about the existence of a plan for the genocidal extinction of Blacks through the use of military forces. I was about to dismiss my questioner's fears, perhaps casually, when I realized that his question had electrified the entire audience. After trying to convince him that I believe that we had no Hitlers in our military and government, the rest of the audience began expressing their fears. These people believe that the Army must have a terribly malevolent intent in collecting this information and there was no dissuading them . . . .

Ervin Hearings, supra note 36, at 257-258, 275.

abound, and by the fear of misuse which arises. Many members of Congress admit privately that the dossiers maintained by the FBI and other national security agencies are a principal factor in the reluctance of their colleagues to challenge the practices and budgets of the FBI and the House Internal Security Committee (HISC). Representative Drinan, a member of HISC, has confirmed on public record that such dossiers on Congressmen do exist.[91]

Representative Abner J. Mikva of Illinois, who was himself (as was brought out in public disclosure) the subject of a political intelligence file developed by the Army, agrees with Senator Ervin that "[t]he objection to this program is not that a U.S. Senator may have been subjected to surveillance, or that a special file was or was not kept on him.... The harm comes rather when the ordinary citizen feels he cannot engage in political activity without becoming a 'person of interest,' without having his name and photo placed in a file colloquially, if not officially, labeled 'subversive'."[92] But Representative Mikva continued:

> ... who can say that in future months or future congresses there will be none who will have second thoughts about a vote on military affairs? Who can be certain that his judgment will not be swayed, perhaps even unconsciously, by the belief that he is being watched? Even the possibility of surveillance raises the specter of subtle political interference. The scenario might go something like this. Those who speak out strongly in oppostion to the policies of those in power are subjected to precautionary surveillance by the military. Constituents learn that their elected representative is under Army surveillance. The inference is made, either explicitly or implicitly, that he must be doing something wrong, or at least questionable, and that suspicion will be evident in the next election results. After all, who wants to be represented by a man who is so disreputable that the Army feels that the national security requires that his activities be monitored ... it is entirely likely that some elected officials will exercise greater caution than they otherwise would in speaking their minds in order to be sure that their political future is not imperiled by a military spy.[93]

The knowledge of the consequences of surveillance leads to these "second thoughts," these unconsciously altered judgments, this "greater caution" that threatens to reduce social and political dia-

---

91. 117 CONG. REC. H3,210 (daily ed. April 29, 1971).
92. *Ervin Hearings, supra* note 36, at 89.
93. *Id.* at 137.

logue. The public's fear of surveillance is rooted in the knowledge of the costly impact it has had on the communities of scientists, entertainment figures, labor groups and workers, and Blacks, among others.

Because science has become an instrument of national policy, scientists have learned either to be cautious about their political associations, or to accept being watched as potential loyalty or security risks. A study by Walter Gellhorn[94] of the untoward consequences of McCarthyism on scientists reported that the system of political and speech accountability had been misused to such an extent "that the atmosphere of suspicion surrounding scientists in government was an effective deterrent to procurement and use of their services."[95] Fewer scientists enlisted in public service because they felt compelled to avoid the uncertain situation where intelligence information could be misused against them.

> In the field of science, the crudities of the loyalty program discourage efforts to draw into public service the live-minded and experienced men whose talents are needed in many agencies. The distress occasioned by an unwarranted inquisition by a loyalty board is felt by a wide circle of friends and fellow-workers. Especially in the case of scientists there is a realization that even after a man has been exonerated following a hearing, he may still be subjected to a renewal of the charges and a dusting off of the same evidence if the winds of politics continue to blow strongly. . . . What [eight of America's great scientists] said publicly has been echoed privately by scientific men of every level of eminence.[96]

Political surveillance in the past has ruined careers and haunted the lives of many in the entertainment world. Private groups and public legislative bodies combined their investigative techniques against an industry which (they accused) tolerated political deviants. Under the threat of denunciation and boycott, the entirety of the entertainment industry in the late 1940's altered its usual course of conduct, and purged its own house of those suspected of unorthodoxy. Blacklists of all who would not cooperate with legislative inquiries were established, and many entertainers went underground or left the country. Others broke relations with their families and

---

94. W. Gellhorn, SECURITY, LOYALTY AND SCIENCE (1950). Walter Gellhorn is Professor at the Columbia University School of Law.
95. *Id.* at 158.
96. *Id.* at 157-158.

friends.[97] Many survived, but only by naming names and pledging to stay clear of politics. Actress Judy Holliday, testifying before the McCarran Committee in 1952 about her support of Henry Wallace for President in 1948, summed up the "greater caution" which investigated subjects feel: "I don't say 'yes' to anything now except cancer, polio, and cerebral palsy, and things like that."[98]

Surveillance was a recognized fact of life also in early union activities. Company tactics, including labor spies and informers whose authority derived from the standing threat of industry-wide blacklisting, and harassment by police and citizen front groups have in the past been employed to intimidate union organizers and other potential union members in the textile, mining and other industries. Companies threatened to close plants, to lay off workers, and even to move main plants if workers supported any "outside" agitation for unionization.[99] Use of the surveillance technique in this situation labeled unionists as a deviant group *per se*, and discouraged (and retarded) the growth of associations which today are regarded as unquestionably legitimate.

E. *Conclusions*

The foregoing materials demonstrate that people today are indeed chilled in their political participation, in their speech, in their associations, and in their right to petition for redress of grievances, and that this chill results in large part from the system of military surveillance of legitimate civilian political activities.

To suggest, as the government does, that Plaintiffs' allegations of chill are "imaginary and speculative" is to blind oneself to truth and to deny the reality of what "all others can see and understand." *Bailey v. Drexel Furniture Company*, 259 U.S. 20, 37 (1922).

The societal consequence of surveillance was well described by Judge Learned Hand during the McCarthy era:

God knows, there is risk in refusing to act till the facts are all in; but is there not greater risk in abandoning the conditions of all rational inquiry? Risk for risk, for myself I had

---

97. *See* the relevant literature in note 1, *supra*.

98. New York Post, Sept. 24, 1952, at 30.

99. Abundant documentation can be found in the Senate La Follette hearings and the more recent investigations of labor-management relations by Congress and by the National Labor Relations Board. The NLRB has interpreted corporate surveillance of worker activity in union elections and collective bargaining as intimidating and therefore the cause of injury. *See, e.g.*, National Labor Relations Board v. Friedman-Harry Marks Clothing Co., 301 U.S. 58 (1937).

rather take my chance that some traitors will escape detection than spread abroad a spirit of general suspicion and distrust, which accepts rumor and gossip in place of undismayed and unintimidated inquiry. I believe that that community is already in process of dissolution where each man begins to eye his neighbor as a possible enemy, where nonconformity with the accepted creed, political as well as religious, is a mark of disaffection; where denunciation, without specification or backing, takes the place of evidence; where orthodoxy chokes freedom of dissent; where faith in the eventual supremacy of reason has become so timid that we dare not enter our convictions in the open lists, to win or lose. Such fears as these are a solvent which can eat out the cement that binds the stones together; they may in the end subject us to a despotism as evil as any we dread; and they can be allayed only in so far as we refuse to proceed on suspicion and trust one another until we have tangible ground for misgiving. The mutual confidence on which all else depends can be maintained only by an open mind and a brave reliance upon free discussion. I did not say that these will suffice; who knows but we may be on a slope which leads down to aboriginal savagery. But of this I am sure: if we are to escape, we must not yield a foot upon demanding a fair field and an honest race to all ideas.[100]

---

100. L. Hand, THE SPIRIT OF LIBERTY 216 (3d. ed. 1960).

RECORD PRIVACY AS A MARGINAL PROBLEM: The Limits of Consciousness and Concern

5

MICHAEL A. BAKER*

In this essay I would like to place what are broadly called *record privacy* problems in the context of organizational routines and everyday personal experiences, arguing that the manner in which record keeping is embedded in the "background" of most individual and organizational existence has real rather than trivial implications for how we deal with confidentiality and due process problems which involve personal records. Specifically, I will suggest that those who control record systems typically find that privacy protections are something on the order of a nuisance organizationally and that often attention to the individual's rights is not *built into* record-keeping practices. As a result, there is a strain in the direction of ignoring civil liberties protections and we cannot look to the managers of organizations for new protections for the citizen. Second, I will suggest that what we can expect in the way of self-protective action on the part of the individual citizen is severely limited by the fact that record-keeping practices are of relatively low visibility to and salience for the individual in the course of his everyday round of affairs.

Let us begin with some scene-setting. We live in a world in which organizations are the principal consumers of recorded knowledge about individuals and in which they principally determine what is gathered and how these data will be used and shared. Theoretically, the individual can refuse to share information about himself with organizations, but there are three important conditions operating to reduce individual control in this area: (A) Much of what an organization (e.g., a police department or a market research body) wants to know about citizens or potential customers is available totally without their cooperation: (B) For the individual to refuse to cooperate in a record-keeping process often means giving up whatever that record keeping is in support

* A.B. Union College; Instructor in Sociology, Brooklyn College. Mr. Baker served as the Assistant Director of the National Academy of Sciences' Project on Computer Databanks and, with Alan F. Westin, co-authored its final report. (DATABANKS IN A FREE SOCIETY, Quadrangle Books, New York, 1972). *Mr. Baker has revised and expanded this paper.*

of—rather considerable deprivation where, say, welfare or medical care is concerned or where a job is at stake. The similarity of record-keeping practices among organizations of the same type makes it difficult in many cases to "shop around" for goods or services offered with what the individual regards as an appropriate level of intrusion into his or her personal life; (C) Where an individual is in a position to control certain aspects of the record-keeping process, it is usually only through the ability to marshall the support of one or more other organizations. Part of the meaning of living in an organizational society is that in the relationships between the organization and customer, the citizen or client there is implied a set of relations with other organizations (such as the courts) whose aid the individual may invoke. That this is the individual's principal source of power as far as record privacy is concerned means that the ownership and control of record identities is, for the most part, firmly in the hands of organizations. It is an important truism that the individual, *qua* individual, has little real power.

We must keep in mind that significant aspects of the privacy-and-records problem are built into the record-keeping process. Invasions of privacy are rarely accidental and do not usually reflect a "breakdown" of organizational practices in any sense. Instead, they grow out of such processes. Important also is the place of civil liberties concerns in the consciousness of organizations and individuals. In some of what appear to be the more hackneyed statements about the conditions for a free society, civil liberties protections are described as the underpinning for a decent human existence. Rather than being ends in themselves, constitutionally protected liberties are an important set of means. As such they may exist in the background of political life, for the most part taken for granted. By way of noting that there is something of real importance in such a description, however, I suggest that the *background* character of civil liberties concerns produces some of the most important features of what we have come to call the *privacy and records* problem.

Record Privacy as a Nuisance. In some form, privacy, confidentiality and due process issues are important within most organizations, and a degree of organizational awareness exists with respect to them. In most cases, however, a manager's orientation to record privacy issues does not reflect an abstract commitment to civil liberties protections; it is tied instead to concrete features of the organizational environment in which he works. The kind of awareness one encounters in record-keeping organizations is the practical concern of managers for the implications of civil liberties claims and challenges. This concern is typically embedded in a complex of operating procedures and cost considerations which virtually insures that only minimal attention will be paid to individual privacy needs.

Having to take into account the privacy rights of those on whom they store and use records is something akin to a nuisance for many organizations. There are several reasons why this frequently turns out to be the case. First, record keeping is a means for most organizations and in some respects goes on in the background of the organization's daily activities. Resolving civil liberties problems in the interests of individuals may at some points require managers to attend to aspects of their record processing to which little time and attention would otherwise be given. In many organizations, for instance, management has little systematic knowledge concerning the accuracy of personal records. The organization "gets by" with a level of accuracy acceptable in light of its own goals and comes to recognize that an accuracy *problem* exists only when its own operations are disturbed in some way. As has been evident so often in the case of credit or law enforcement files, there may be a considerable gap between an organization's practices and a level of accuracy which civil liberties spokesmen or record-subjects themselves find acceptable.

Second, many organizations are by their very nature manipulative of clients, customers, citizens, research subjects, students, suspects, etc. Whether their goal is therapy, education, law-and-order or marketing, they are more or less oriented to the individual as an object rather than as a citizen-with-rights. This is especially true for large organizations which *batch process* clients or citizens through a series of operations designed to transform them into fully "acceptable" members of society or to keep them manageable during a period of custody. Providing civil liberties for such people may be seen as *technically* unnecessary. Erving Goffman, in his work on total institutions notes that in many respects processing people is like processing things; certain minimum conditions have to be met (*e.g.*, the temperature of the "warehouse") if the "material" is to be kept in good shape to be worked upon. But unlike non-human objects, he notes:

> Persons are almost always considered to be ends in themselves, according to the broad moral principle of a total institution's environing society. Almost always, then, we find that some technically unnecessary standards of handling must be maintained with human materials. The maintenance of what we call "humane" standards comes to be defined as part of the "responsibility" of the institution, and presumably is one of the things the institution guarantees the inmate in exchange for his liberty.[1]

There is built into the structure of some people-processing organiza-

---

1. ERVING GOFFMAN, ASYLUMS 76 (1961).

tions, then, "constant conflict between humane standards on the one hand, and institutional efficiency on the other."[2]

Finally, for some organizations the protection of individual privacy may mean a loss of highly cherished autonomy, since recognizing such rights implies that the individual may invoke the aid of courts, legislatures, guardian groups and other organizations when his expectations as to data gathering, sharing, access and use are not met. Prior to the passage of fair credit reporting acts at the state and federal level, for instance, individuals had virtually no relationship with the commercial organizations which compiled credit, pre-employment and pre-insurance reports on them. Individuals were quite literally the *objects* of a report and little more. Passage of these laws has given individuals covered in the files of consumer reporting firms a formal relationship with these organizations, backed up by regulatory agencies and the courts. Whether individual citizens will indeed be able to help themselves under such laws remains to be seen; but, in every case, the commercial interests involved fought hard against this new legislation in part to avoid increased state or federal controls over their activities.

The significance of these features of organizational processing for the record privacy question is that we cannot expect from organizations a high level of awareness and concern about civil liberties problems unless coincidental internal needs make for privacy protections or external legal or economic pressures place privacy protections among the courses of action it is in the interests of the organization to pursue.

Record-Keeping As Invisible. Like many processes which are means rather than ends, much of the record keeping which affects individuals goes on in the background of social life and for this reason is of low visibility to the individuals concerned. On a given person there may be upwards of 100 files maintained in various organizations. These range in visibility from those in which data gathering, use and sharing go on completely behind closed doors (*e.g.*, intelligence files) to those files of which the individual has some knowledge about content and use but little, if any, knowledge about the data sharing which goes on from his file (as in the case of a bank which routinely shares customer account experience information with local credit bureaus). In very few settings is the individual fully knowledgeable about the content, use and sharing of "his" record, and in almost all cases there are some aspects of the record process which the individual would find it difficult to observe even upon making a special effort (e.g., who works on the files; what is the liklihood of an error in my record; in how many locations is the information duplicated once I give it to the organization?). For instance, one of the central problems in attempts to control and update arrest record circulation is that a single arrest may generate records in

2. *Id.*

many locations as the arresting agency establishes its own set of records on the event and passes on fingerprint and arrest information to other organizations such as the FBI, state identification agencies or the courts. "It is virtually impossible for any person to know what happens to his criminal record. For example, one study made by the Oakland Police Department revealed that as many as 40 separate documents of an arrest record, with a minimum of 71 copies are routinely made."[3] To fully communicate the plethora of records and record transactions in which the individual citizen is involved or by which he is affected, detailed examples would need to be drawn from perhaps twenty different areas of information about the individual, including credit, physical and emotional health, vital statistics, military service, voting, employment and religious activity. Further complicating the problems of public knowledge about record-keeping practices is the fact that people are often in no position to know very much about the computer systems which are increasingly used to store and process records about them. Sometimes the fact of computerization—to say nothing of the details of its impact on civil liberties—is not even visible.[4]

The low visibility of record-keeping processes does not always arise out of the intentions of managers to hide what they are doing. In some cases the individual could learn a great deal about the files and data sharing which affect him *if* he had the time and the knowledge of where to look and whom to ask. But as the history of the privacy and records debate makes plain, there are many record-keeping operations intentionally carried on with as low a profile as possible. Much of the informal exchange of personal information which characterizes the "information buddy system" in fields such as law enforcement and personnel administration is accomplished with the understanding that the record subject will have no knowledge of the occurrence or content of the transaction. As another example, the commercial reporting industry managed to keep its activities out of the public eye for better than fifty years of its growth, until the privacy debate of the 1960's focused attention on this important piece of the record-keeping world.

The civil liberties import of the general lack of visibility which characterizes record-keeping processes has been displayed over and over again in the course of the privacy and records debate of the 1960's and early 1970's. Whether by happenstance or managerial intention, individuals did indeed have their rights abridged without their knowledge. And most of those who came forward to tell their story of being hurt

---

3. *Hearings on National Penitentiaries Before the Subcommittee on National Penitentiaries of the Senate Committee on the Judiciary,* 92d Cong. 2d Sess. (1972) (statements by Aryeh Neier and John Shattuck, at 14-15).

4. For a full study of the impact of computer technology on civil liberties in record systems, see A.F. WESTIN & M.A. BAKER, DATA BANKS IN A FREE SOCIETY (New York, Quadrangle Books, 1972).

through record-keeping policies or errors reported that they did not at first know about the data gathering and use which was the source of their trouble and that they had not been concerned in a general way about privacy problems prior to their difficulties.

As important as the sheer *visibility* of record processes is, the matter of how *salient* they are to the individual while he is in the course of some transaction with an organization is perhaps even more critical. Civil liberties problems in record systems are often generated at points in our lives when, compared to other events taking place simultaneously, they must occupy relatively low positions on our list of priorities as to what is deserving of worry and attention.

Arrested on an armed robbery charge, a New York City youth discovered a rather important record error: an acquaintence had given this young man's name and address on two occasions when arrested in order to avoid having a police record himself. The name and fingerprints were forwarded to the appropriate agency, but since neither youth had a record at that time, there was no way for this piece of duplicity to be uncovered. When the court requested the youth's record for arraignment on the robbery charge, a garbled return was forthcoming from the identification agency, since there was a match on name and address (and, by unhappy coincidence, on some other items such as height, race and age), but no match on fingerprints. But garbled record or not, the *possibility* that this youth had been arrested twice before was enough to convince the court that the charges being made against him by a storeowner were plausible. The young man claimed that he had never been arrested before (true) and that he had had no part whatsoever in the robbery (also true). A very high bail was set.

What is important in this example is that the young man came to know of his record problem at a point of crisis and it was pointed out to him that there were procedures by which he could go about getting his record straightened out. But given the problem of dealing with the armed robbery charge (and of surviving the experience of incarceration at Riker's Island awaiting trial), the record problem receded into the background of his concerns. Further, while he had a lawyer for the more important function of dealing with this indictment, he did not have assistance afterwards for dealing with the rather complicated process of getting records expunged and corrected. The state had come through with a lawyer for the important event, but had left him with a nagging record problem which he was in no position to solve without devoting a great deal of time and energy to it.

More mundane examples point to the same feature of the record privacy problem. While the individual may challenge the record when something in it seems to be barring him from some right or privilege, he is far less likely to question practices which are not of immediate import. In the process of getting medical care, insurance, or credit an individual may feel reluctant to inquire about the meaning of the waiver he signs authorizing the physician or firm to seek more information about him. Even if curious or worried about what exactly he is giving up by signing, his more or less dependent position may encourage him not to risk challenging questions. Problems of confidentiality are often problems for the future in just this way. Some vague worry about future uses of the record may surface in the course of a record transaction, only to be submerged by more important uncertainties of the moment.

There are of course situations in which worry about the future of a record affects present behavior considerably, as for instance the case of the pre-law student who might want to be officially active in a radical political group on campus, but who is *chilled* from this course of action by the prospect of having future trouble with the gatekeepers of the profession. But, as I think became quite clear during the McCarthy period, people find it hard to mold their lives around each and every record possibility of the future. The old records which surfaced to harm so many during the 1950's reflect in part the fact that politically active citizens in the 1920's and 1930's were not in a position to act with high consciousness of their future record profiles.

Overall, many record-keeping tasks have the character of an errand—frequent enough to annoy us and claim a good deal of our time, but so trivial, given the larger events for which they represent a means, as to warrant little of our concerned attention.[5]

A related problem arises when the *meaning of* recorded information is not clear because we are not in a position to know what criteria are being used in decisions about us. The civil liberties implication here, of course, is that knowledge about how information is used is critical to most privacy and confidentiality complaints. Underlying our ideas about what data should be collected and shared are fears about the eventual use of such information. In addition to the more obvious kinds of problems, such as discrimination on the basis of age, sex or race, are situations in which the content of a record system appears to "make sense" as far as its functions are concerned, but where in fact the information on file has a very different relationship to a decision about us than we imagine. The manager of a branch bank, for instance, may be told that he must keep employee costs down. At the same time, he knows that there are very few opportunities for promotion within the bank for the employees he supervises. He does not want to lose his trained tellers and other personnel, so instead of telling them why he

---

5. Martin Wenglinsky discusses the concept of errands as a special type of social activity in the forthcoming book, INTO THE ORDINARY (A. Birnbaum & E. Sagarin, Eds., 1973).

cannot give them very much in the way of a raise, and why he cannot promote them, he refers with great manipulative skill to their record, suggesting that "if you had a little bit more on the education side, I might be able to help you." For some employees, this is a logical explanation, given their notions as to how one gets ahead in the world and the fact that they are not in a position to see that those very few who *are* promoted have no more education than they do. As a result, they may orient themselves to improving their record identities in ways that are really quite irrelevant as far as advancement is concerned. In other settings, such as a university, the same technique of using what are thought to be "sensible" criteria as a screen is employed to hide the real reasons for not granting tenure to a faculty member. Even where individuals see through such an organizational ruse, it remains a powerful technique because it is difficult to demonstrate in the appropriate forums for appeal that this tactic is being employed.

There is in the privacy area a small but interesting body of public opinion literature. One of the clear pictures emerging from this material is that, even where record processes are visible to the citizen, he often has no clear idea what his formal constitutional liberties are. Popular concepts of individual rights often correspond poorly to the civil libertarian's view of what constitutional guarantees are available. Where interaction with private organizations is concerned, for example, an individual's claim that a certain kind of decent treatment is "rightfully" his may have in fact little basis in law or tradition. At the same time, where he has contact with government organizations, there may be constitutional protections which a citizen could, but often does not, claim. In fact, the task of convincing people that they should vigorously pursue their rights has frequently fallen to civil liberties organizations and often involves, as a first step, informing the public as to what these rights are.

A further problem is that citizens differ in their experience of situations which might raise the issue of some constitutional protection. Often it is difficult for citizens to sympathize with those in the society whose rights may be in jeopardy, and this blocks recognition of how a given official practice might threaten their own rights. Those who are not politically active, for example, may have little sympathy for the first amendment claims to protection of groups seeking to express themselves and convince others in the political arena. An almost classic civil liberties dilemma arises when a legislature moves with public support in ways that threaten the liberties of some segment of the population—with little apparent worry on the part of the general public that the damaging legislation might be turned against themselves at some future time.

It is quite clear I think that at a number of points in American history a national referendum might well have failed to approve the Bill of Rights. That consciousness of civil liberties is neither sharp nor self-protective in *anticipatory* ways, represents still another respect in which record privacy problems remain on the margin of everyday existence.

On the more specific matter of privacy, many commentators have noted that in law this is one of our least clearly articulated rights. In the public mind, it is a concept that is less clear still, and as a result, it is difficult to measure through public opinion research the strength of the set of values we have come to label *privacy*. Under the simplest kind of questioning, virtually everyone declares himself for privacy; the Friends-of-Big-Brother Association is a trifle short of admitted members in contemporary America. But this generalized allegiance to privacy, confidentiality and due process protections dissolves into a complicated set of opinions as the focus of questioning becomes more specific and the balance between individual liberties and the practical needs of organizations is introduced as an issue. Striking a balance between such interests *is* complicated, to be sure, but most individuals do not appear to have the kind of strong consciousness of their own civil liberties interests which might serve as a resource for beginning to deal with record privacy problems.[6] While there may be some room to expand this consciousness, it seems more likely that civil liberties issues in general and privacy issues in particular will remain matters of strong conscious concern to only a minority of citizens.

This is an organizational society in which the presentation of self through records is commonplace. But it is not a world in which individuals are thoroughly comfortable with and knowledgeable concerning the record errands which are part of their daily rounds of existence. We cannot assume that individuals are entirely document wise, especially where the individual is not quite sure what decision criteria are being used as services, rights and benefits are allocated. Sometimes the gulf between individual capacities and the requirements for informed citizenship is very wide indeed. In his study of record keeping in a West Coast social welfare agency, Don Zimmerman recounts an instance where an old woman became an object of amusement to social workers who were well built into the world of documents-as-proof. She reported that she could not find the citizenship papers required as proof of age but that she did recall having copied down her age and the date on a piece of paper at one time. She handed

---

6. For a discussion of the public opinion literature in this area see Westin & Baker, *op. cit.*, Appendix B.

over a rumpled paper with that information written upon it—a "document" not official but no less authentic from her perspective. It was of course not acceptable, and the story, when related to fellow workers, was greeted with great amusement.[7]

Lest we think that such misunderstanding of formal record-keeping processes is a problem only of the poor and less educated, remember that several decades of credit bureau activity took place before middle class critics—who had been the objects of much of this commercial reporting—discovered the existence of their local credit bureau and even national giants like Retail Credit Company of Atlanta, and began the process of dragging this industry into the critical glare of journalistic and congressional exposure and into a modicum of public accountability. In many cases, differences in knowledge between citizens of different socioeconomic status probably mean very little as far as their respective levels of control over record privacy problems are concerned. Born high or low, the individual may not have the time or other resources for controlling those records most important for his or her own life.

That both record keeping and civil liberties occupy only the margins of individual consciousness would not matter at all if records were at most points accurate reflections of our qualities and activities. Under fire for their record-keeping practices, organizational managers are fond of the defense that individuals "make their own records" and "have nothing to fear if they have behaved appropriately" with respect to credit, educational, citizenship and other responsibilities. But we know all too well at this point in the history of the privacy and records debate that record keeping is by no means a *neutral* process. Though used in the background, the manner in which the record is constructed, its completeness and accuracy and its particular relationship to information gathered on a face-to-face basis can affect the outcome of decision processes markedly.

The Problem of Remedies. With this reminder, we come to the question of remedies. Drawing together the ideas that people are not generally knowledgeable about the record-keeping practices of organizations with which they deal and that they may not have a sense of either what their own rights are or when these are being trod upon, we derive a picture of the individual as a poor candidate for self-protection where record privacy problems are concerned. As things currently stand for most record-keeping situations, the range of corrective action we can expect on the part of the individual himself is quite limited. In my view, we can for the most part expect this built-in predicament to

---

7. D. Zimmerman, Paperwork and People Work: A Study of a Public Assistance Agency, 1966 (unpublished Ph.D. dissertation, Department of Sociology, University of California at Los Angeles).

remain for the future as well. We may be able to engage in some productive consciousness-raising aimed at record privacy problems. But if our goal is to establish the individual's control over his own record identity we will have to realize that we are dealing in most cases with a zero-sum game as far as the resources of the individual are concerned. Given the amount of complex and detailed information about record-keeping which the individual would be required to absorb if he were to genuinely *take charge* of records about himself, it does not seem likely that we can expect self-protective vigilance from more than a few dedicated citizens who will apportion to record privacy matters some substantial part of their resources. As Wenglinsky notes in his discussion of this as a broader issue, "solutions" to problems of citizens or consumers often come at their own expense, rather than out of some reallocation of institutional resources:

> . . . just as caveat emptor was a doctrine which placed the burden on the consumer beyond his ability to challenge the offers of the powerful, so contemporary law and usage places a burden on the errand-runner far beyond his ability to contend with the powerful who manipulate and create the errands. Indeed, so ingrained is the legitimacy of unequal resources between seller and consumer, that legislation supposes that fairness in the relationship is achieved through giving extra errands to the consumer. In unit pricing, for example, as in much legislation of the New Deal variety, the consumer is given information that allows comparison shopping only if he adds more time, effort and skill in computation to the errands of the supermarket. It is as if the resources for errands on the part of the consumer are inexhaustibly elastic and can be drawn upon without compensation.[8]

In the tradition of *informed consent*, it is possible that we can build in some real choice for the individual with respect to what information about him is gathered, used and shared. But we have to beware of establishing remedies which turn out to be fictional because they require daily acts of minor heroism on the part if the individual, as he challenges clerks, managers and officials on record-keeping matters and works to grasp the significance for his interests of each record-related choice he is given. There are a number of situations in which it is probably impossible to create the conditions under which genuinely free individual choices can occur. "Requesting" the cooperation of a public housing tenant in government sponsored evaluation research, for instance, or asking a welfare applicant to "voluntarily" supply his

---

8. Wenglinsky, *supra* note 5.

Social Security number for more efficient record processing, do not seem to be the kind of measures which reflect real life in this organizational society.

Several suggestions have been made for remedies which embody the notion that organizations will keep each citizen continuously informed of the content and use of his record and allow him to approve all record transactions for which he has not given previous consent. Aside from the immense logistical problems such remedies would entail for record-keeping organizations (of some concern where the public purse would shoulder this burden), it is not at all clear that, used on a wide scale, such programs would solve very many serious record privacy problems without creating problems of even greater moment for the citizen. This is especially true if the *only* source of protection would be the vigilance of the individual himself. The resources required for monitoring hundreds of record transactions each year would be quite considerable.

Neither record-keeping nor civil liberties concerns are likely to move from the background of individual daily existence into the forefront of attention. This means that we must look beyond the individual himself for creative solutions, and beyond the kind of arrangements that will involve substantial commitments of time and energy on the part of individuals already overburdened with adapting to the needs of the organizations which process or serve them. Along these lines, it is clear that while allowing the individual access to his own record should be the rule in all but a very few instances, the most important aspect of this access process will be the procedures for challenges to and correction of the individual's record. If such remedies are to be of real significance, they have to be *structured into* the record process so as to prove almost effortless for the individual. Similarly, the destruction of records after appropriate periods of time really needs to be an automatic weeding process, rather than one which waits upon requests from individuals. Further, enforcement for record privacy protections has to be a matter of routine that lies for the most part outside the individual's responsibility, since court challenges and even regulatory proceedings are out of reach for most individuals psychologically, financially and in terms of their time and energy.

Wherever it does prove possible to increase the level of individual consciousness about record privacy problems, public reactions may serve as a resource out of which some policy can be derived as to what information organizations are *allowed* to gather and use in their decision-making about individuals. Access by individuals to their own records may bring practices to light which were not previously matters of common knowledge and may generate the public concern and political pressure necessary for support of legislation and court action.

We have learned over the years that however much organizations foster the appearance of necessity and rationality with respect to their information needs, these needs remain quite negotiable. Organizations rarely fail or even falter because of restrictions on data gathering, storage, sharing or use. Direct regulation of the content of record systems is perhaps the most difficult route to take in handling record privacy problems, since organizations resist strongly intrusions upon their autonomy in this area and since it is often difficult to demonstrate either the relevance or the irrelevance of personal information for a particular decision. But there are occasions on which the approach of challenging information needs may still prove fruitful. For instance, it would seem that we now have enough formal research and other information about the effect of arrest and conviction records on employment and licensing decisions to begin to make some clear decisions about where the use of such records should be forbidden in the interest of protecting individual liberties.

Finally, record privacy problems are often a reflection of an organization's *attitude* towards its record subjects. If such attitudes change (which in most cases would entail a change in the actual operating goals of the organization), we may see some record privacy problems disappear or become amenable to genuine individual control. Barring this, however, solutions to record privacy problems are going to have to come from outside the record-keeping organization itself, and be accomplished primarily for, not by, the individual—a paternalism which, while perhaps not welcome, does reflect the individual's position in this society and his existential relationship to everyday record-keeping processes.

6 | POLICE SURVEILLANCE OF POLITICAL DISSIDENTS

DONALD R. DAVIS*

An Overview. Physical surveillance[1] of political dissidents has increased as a routine practice among all echelons of law enforcement agencies.[2] The gathering of political intelligence[3] is viewed as a necessary response to the active and often militant dissent from various governmental policies. It affords information which enables the government to monitor the overt and covert activities of the dissidents, to identify the leaders of activist groups and to react swiftly

---

*Staff member, *Columbia Human Rights Law Review.*

1. *See* WESTIN, PRIVACY AND FREEDOM 69-89 (1967) for a discussion of the various modes of physical surveillance and at 90-132 for a discussion of the uses to which such devices and techniques are put.

2. *See* Donner, *The Theory and Practice of American Political Surveillance,* monograph reprinted from THE NEW YORK TIMES REVIEW OF BOOKS 27 (April 22, 1971) [hereinafter Donner]; Lundy, *The Invisible Police,* THE NATION 629-32 (Dec. 8, 1969); N.Y. Times 1, col. 4 (Feb. 29, 1972); N.Y. Times 1, col. 5 (Jan. 19, 1972). Another indicator of increasing government surveillance is the increasing number of suits being brought to enjoin the practice. *See, e.g.,* Tatum v. Laird, 444 F.2d 947 (D.C. Cir. 1971), *cert. granted,* No. 71-288 (1971); Anderson v. Sills, 106 N.J. Super. 545 (Ch. Div.(1969), *rev'd and remanded,* 56 N.J. 210, 265 A.2d 678 (1970); and Holmes v. Church, 70 Civ. 5691 (S.D.N.Y., June 10, 1971). Surveillance of dissidents, moreover, has not been confined to orthodox enforcement agencies; it has been practiced by numerous branches of government, most notably the United States Army. *See* Pyle, CONUS *Intelligence: The Army Watches Civilian Politics,* WASHINGTON MONTHLY 4 (Jan. 1970); Pyle, CONUS *Revisited: The Army Covers Up,* WASHINGTON MONTHLY 49 (July, 1970); Hentoff, *The Secret Companions,* EVERGREEN 55 (Sept., 1970). But the most important source of information is the *Hearings on Federal Data Banks, Computers and the Bill of Rights Before the Subcomm. on Constitutional Rights of the Senate Comm. on the Judiciary,* 92d Cong., 1st Sess. (1971) [hereinafter *Senate Hearings*]

3. Political intelligence is a term used to describe "a body of techniques for collecting political information about a 'subject' (physical surveillance, photography, electronic eavesdropping, informers—planted or recruited 'in place'—and other deceptive or clandestine practices), the product of these activities (files and dossiers), and a set of political assumptions (the intelligence mind)." Donner, at note 1.

and decisively to insure the national security.[4] Certainly, data collection is a necessary and proper aspect of police work, and it inures to the public good—if, in the process, individual rights are not sacrificed.

It is clear that the widespread advocacy of minority or politically unpopular causes has resulted in a multiplicity of new surveillance targets.[5] Often, individuals engaged in dissent have become subjects of police scrutiny,[6] despite the legality of their conduct. The collection, storage and dissemination of such information by government agencies can and has worked hardship upon them.[7] With rising frequency, the surveillance activities of the police have been used for the secondary purpose of harassment of the "dissident."[8] Harassment may come in the form of notification regarding the collection of data, dissemination of such data (at present or at a later date) to disparate enforcement agencies or other organizations or continuation of surveillance and investigation for the purpose of monitoring the individual and augmenting existing dossiers.[9]

Incidents of governmental encroachment upon the First Amendment rights of free speech and association have steadily increased in recent years[10] despite the fact that most private organizations and

4. Donner, section III. With respect to the problems which the phrase "national security" involves, see Comment, *Privacy and Political Freedom: Applications of the Fourth Amendment to National Security Investigations*, 17 U.C.L.A. L. REV. 1205 (1970); Note, *Eavesdropping at the Government's Discretion—First Amendment Implications of the National Security Eavesdropping Power*, 56 CORNELL L.Q. 161 (1970); Schwartz, *The Legitimation of Electronic Eavesdropping: The Politics of Law and Order*, 67 MICH. L. REV. 455 (1968).

5. Donner, section I. *See also* N.Y. Times 1, col. 4 (Feb. 29, 1972); N.Y. Times 41, col. 5 (Jan 19, 1972); Transcript of ABC broadcast, *Assault on Privacy*, (Jan. 8, 1972) [hereinafter ABC Transcript]; Transcript of CBS broadcast, *Under Surveillance*, (Dec. 23, 1971) [hereinafter CBS Transcript].

6. *See* Aronson v. Giarusso. 436 F.2d 955 (1971); Anderson v. Sills, 106 N.J. Super. 545 (Ch. Div. 1969), *rev'd and remanded*, 56 N.J. 210, 265 A.2d 678 (1970); Avirgan v. Rizzo, 70 Civ. 477 (E.D. Pa. 1970) (settled); Handschu v. Murphy, 71 Civ. 2203 (S.D.N.Y. 1971). *See generally* Donner; ABC Transcript; CBS Transcript.

7. *See, e.g.,* Holmes v. Church, 70 Civ. 5691 (S.D.N.Y. June 10, 1971); Fifth Avenue Peace Parade Committee v. Hoover, 70 Civ. 2646 (S.D.N.Y. 1971). *See also* Appendix to Petitioner's Brief for Certiorari, Tatum v. Laird, 444 F.2d 947 (D.C. Cir. 1971), *cert. granted*, No. 71-288 (1971); SKINNER, BEYOND FREEDOM AND DIGNITY (1971); Fried; *Privacy*, 77 YALE L.J. 475 (1968); 117 CONG. REC. 985-87 (Feb. 8, 1971) (remarks of Senator Sam J. Ervin); 116 CONG. REC. 21418-20 (Dec. 29, 1970)(remarks of Senator Sam J. Ervin); *id.* at 41751-52 (Dec. 16, 1970) (remarks of Senator Sam J. Ervin); *id.* at 2632-51 (July 29, 1970) (remarks and materials inserted by Senator Sam J. Ervin). *See also* N.Y. Times 2.§4 (Mar. 5, 1972).

8. *See* National Student Association v. Hershey, 412 F.2d 1103 (D.C. Cir. 1969); DuBois Clubs v. Clark, 389 U.S. 309 (1967); Ervin, *Privacy and Government Investigations*, 1971 U. ILL. L. FORUM 137 (1971); Comment, *Warrantless Electronic Surveillance of Dissident Domestic Organizations Under the National Security Exception*, 5 VALP. U. L. REV. 651, 664 (1971); Donner, sections VIII, IX, X, XI and XII.

9. *Id.*

10. *See, e.g.,* Holmes v. Church, 70 Civ. 5691 (S.D.N.Y. June 10, 1971); Kenyatta v. Hoover, 71 Civ.–'(E.D. Pa., Complaint filed Oct. 27, 1971). *See also* N.Y. Times 53 (June 23, 1971); N.Y. Times 1, Col. 4 (Feb. 29, 1972); ABC Transcript; CBS Transcript.

individuals neither advocate nor precipitate criminal or subversive action.[11] Indeed, many such groups or individuals maintain a politically neutral stance, believing that they will thereby avoid conflict with police or other government agents. But all too frequently this belief is erroneous, especially if the group or individual supports minority or unpopular causes which are potential political issues.[12]

The conflict between the right to dissent and the need for order presents the difficult problem of designing standards and safeguards that are sufficient to permit society to function in the manner established by the Constitution.

It is only the indiscriminate use of political surveillance which endangers both the law abiding citizen and the lawbreaker and which poses significant constitutional problems.[13]

Therefore, it is necessary to draw a line between warranted and unwarranted surveillance regardless of how difficult such a distinction may be if we are to insure that information channeled into dissident data banks is both necessary and appropriate.[14] Anything less would invite more serious infringements upon basic constitutional guarantees.

The Proposal in Brief. It is submitted that the government surveillance activities of recent date are beyond their constitutional authority, and that the procedural safeguards of the Fourth Amendment would not unduly hamper law enforcement but would do much to insure the privacy and the free exercise of First Amendment rights

---

11. *See* notes 6 and 7 *supra. See generally Senate Hearings,* note 2 *supra;* Brief for Respondents as Amicus Curiae, for Certiorari, Tatum v. Laird No. F1-288 (1971).

12. *Id.*

13. *See* Ervin, *Privacy and Government Investigations,* 1971 U. ILL L. FORUM 137 (1971). Donner, sections I and II; Lundy, *The Invisible Police,* THE NATION 629-632 (Dec. 8, 1969); N.Y. Times 27, col. 1 (June 5, 1969) (surveillance of the late Dr. Martin Luther King). *Cf.* United States v. Sinclair, Criminal No. 44375 (E.D. Mich., Jan. 25, 1971) (surveillance of the White Panther Party leaders); United States v. Smith 321 F.Supp. 424 (C.D. Cal. 1971) (surveillance of members of the Black Panther Party). *See also Senate Hearings,* note 2 *supra* at 1119, 1123, 1154, 1427, 1429 and 1500. In cases such as *Sinclair* and *Smith* where defendant's actions drew the attention of the government, the surveillance was particularly intense and resulted in the question of whether the Attorney General, as an agent of the President, had the power to authorize warrantless eavesdropping on dissident domestic organizations under the guise of protecting the national security. *Sinclair* and *Smith* were held in the negative. For a discussion of this issue, see Comment, *Warrantless Electronic Surveillance of Dissident Domestic Organizations under the National Security Exception,* 5 VALP. U. L. REV. 651 (1971).

14. The primary consideration in determining whether data gathered is necessary and appropriate is the purpose for which it is collected. Information collected by the federal government on dissidents is used not for indictment or prosecution but for monitoring the actions, speech and associations of the dissident. To ascertain the truth of this statement, it is necessary to weigh the relatively few actions brought by the government against the huge number of files maintained. The concern here expressed is in respect to the dissident monitored but not prosecuted; the dissident prosecuted will have the exclusionary rule among other safeguards which are unavailable to those not prosecuted.

of dissidents and other parties. The interests of the Fourth Amendment and privacy are the same—securing to the individual control over the communication of information which concerns himself where such control has not been forfeited by action giving rise to probable cause. This identity of interests requires that procedural determinations under the Fourth Amendment be made in terms of balancing the individual right to privacy against the public interest in surveillance. The burden would be on the government to show sufficient grounds to obtain a warrant and the warrant requirement would attach automatically in any "search" with the reasonableness of the government action turning on the privacy questions involved. Relief for unreasonable or unwarranted surveillance may be injunctive, or damages, and must take into account the problem of deferred reckoning with information stored and later disseminated. The legislature must, in addition, establish policy and guidelines for the conduct of surveillance and the maintenance of individual privacy. It should also permit access to court for those whose privacy is illegally invaded by providing court costs and attorneys' fees and even punitive damages for injury to First and Fourth Amendment rights. Lastly, government agents who through willful or grossly negligent acts do injury to these rights should not be kept immune from these sanctions.

Part I: Present Surveillance Practices

The competing interests of order and dissent often lead to excesses of behavior when individuals attempt to influence governmental policies. The fundamental element of both interests is the collection, assimilation, collation, storage and dissemination of information to effect and further their ends.[15] In order to carry out goals of communicating critical information and discrediting the opposition, a knowledge of the opponent and his arguments is required, and the more extensive and precise that information, the better. These factors invite acts of surveillance in behalf of both interests.[16] However, the tremendous disparity in the ability to gather, maintain and use information gives the government consider-

---

15. Information here is meant to be a generic term, inclusive of evidence and political intelligence (as defined in note 3 *supra*). *See* note 139 *infra*.

16. An example of counter-intelligence gathering by political dissidents is the seizure of the "Media FBI documents," which were forcefully taken from a small FBI office in Media, Pennsylvania. Of the more than 1,000 documents stolen, fourteen were given to elected officials, the Washington Post, The New York Times and the Los Angeles Times which clearly established that the FBI concentrates much of its investigative effort on college dissenters and black students groups. *See* Donner, Section I.

able advantage in any confrontation with the subjects of its surveillance activities. A real danger lies in this differential: there is no check on the government's surveillance; it is free to conduct surveillance within limits determined solely by its own discretion.[17] This situation has fostered a practice of information gathering so extensive as to impute the ability to control dissent to the government.[18] Dissidents, in response, are forced to employ more controversial and more demonstrable methods of disseminating their beliefs.

This paper will attempt to explore both the standards by which political surveillance may be conducted, and the safeguards available to those who choose to make their political beliefs public.

A. Increasing Surveillance—Data Collection and Dissemination

The political surveillance activities of government intelligence agencies have increased dramatically as these agencies have felt a need to anticipate and control civil disorders.[19] This response has not been confined to the federal government but has been manifested in state, county and municipal governments as well.[20] To be sure, however, the federal government is a leading proponent of political surveillance, engaging some twenty agencies in intelligence gathering. Among the most committed are:

The FBI with an estimated 2,000 agents on political investigative assignment in charge of thousands of undercover informers;

---

17. *See* Note, *Eavesdropping at the Government's Discretion–First Amendment Implications of the National Security Eavesdropping Power,* 56 CORNELL L. Q. 161 (1970); Theoharis, *The "National Security" Justification for Electronic Eavesdropping: An Elusive Exception,* 14 WAYNE L. REV. 749 (1968). *See also* Memorandum from President Roosevelt to Attorney General Jackson, May 21, 1940 and Memorandum from President Johnson to the Heads of Executive Departments and Agencies, June 30, 1965 cited as Appendices I and II, United States v. White, 401 U.S. 745, 766-68 (1971) (Douglas, J., dissenting).

18. *See* Comment, *Warrantless Electronic Surveillance of Dissident Domestic Organizations under the National Security Exception,* 5 VALP. U.L. REV. 651, 664 (1971); Donner, section III.

19. *Id. See* Complaint, Kenyatta v. Hoover, 71 Civ. –, Appendices A-K (E.D. Pa., Complaint filed Oct. 27, 1971) for the kind of information the FBI gathers in its general investigative efforts. Included are informants' reports, information obtained from Bell Telephone, duplicate bank statements, Xerox copies of checks, FBI agent exchange reports, and memoranda from the FBI itself.

20. *See Report for Action, The Governor's Select Commission on Civil Disorder, State of New Jersey* (February, 1968); *Report of the National Advisory Commission on Civil Disorders,* Bantam Books (1968); *Rights in Conflict, The Official Report to the National Commission on the Causes and Prevention of Violence,* Signet Books (1968) which encourage enforcement agencies at all levels to create and maintain intelligence groups.

The Army, which concededly had at one time 1,200 agents in the field together with a huge staff operating a data bank of 25 million "personalities";

The CIA;

The Internal Revenue Service (for several weeks in 1970 its agents requested access to the circulation records of public libraries in a number of cities in order to learn the names of borrowers of books on explosives and "other militant and subversive" subjects, a practice which it defended as "just a continual building of information");

The Intelligence Division of the Post Office;

The Secret Service (where names of 50,000 "persons of interest" are on file);

The Customs Bureau of the Treasury Department;

The Civil Service Commission (15 million names of "subversive activity" suspects);

The Immigration and Naturalization Service;

The Navy, Air Force, and Coast Guard;

The Task Force Division of the State Department;

The Department of Justice Community Relations Service which feeds information into its computerized interdivisional intelligence and information unit;

The civil rights and poverty projects sponsored by the Department of Health, Education and Welfare and the Office of Economic Opportunity. The Executive Department agencies cooperate with and are supplemented by the Congressional Anti-Subversive Committees.[21]

On the state and local levels, the proliferation of intelligence units is remarkable. The State of New Jersey, for example, was recently taken to task for its surveillance of political dissidents in *Anderson v. Sills*,[22] which had resulted from the distribution of a memorandum entitled "Civil Disorders—the Role of Local, County and State Government" to all the municipal and county police departments within the state by the State Attorney General. The memorandum dealt with aspects of civil disorder, including tactics of

---

21. Donner, section II. *See also* Ervin, *The Final Answer: The People in Control,* TRIAL MAGAZINE 14 (March/April, 1971) in which it is noted the number of federal agencies carrying on surveillance activities.

22. Anderson v. Sills, 106 N.J. Super. 545 (Ch. Div. 1969), *rev'd and remanded,* 56 N.J. 210, 265 A.2d 678 (1970).

advance planning, cooperation between municipalities, assistance from the state police and the national guard, the steps necessary to proclaiming an emergency, and the control of false information. The plaintiffs in *Sills* were concerned with the portion of the memorandum entitled "Potential Problems," which read as follows:

> Our state police have been working closely with local police in various communities throughout the state in a continuing effort to keep abreast of potential civil disorder problems. In that respect, therefore we are already familiar generally with the basic problems in these communities. However, these problems change and we should never become over-confident to the end that we lose sight of the cause, as well as the effect of civil disturbances. The state police central security unit has distributed security summary reports (Form 421) and security incidents reports (Form 420) . . . to each police department. It is necessary that these reports be used routinely to inform the state police of the situation in your community. We urge you to see that this vital intelligence is communicated to this central bureau for evaluation and dissemination.[23]

The pervasive scope of the New Jersey state police intelligence gathering system is apparent from the examination of the memorandum in which it is presented.[24] It is also indicative of the kind of response provoked by civil disorders on both the federal and state levels.[25] Response at the local level is similar; county and municipal intelligence groups are common elements in a police department.[26]

23. Memorandum from Attorney General Sills to all Municipal and County Officials of New Jersey, April 23, 1968 at 19.

24. *See* Appendix A in Anderson v. Sills, 106 N.J. Super. 545, 558 (Ch. Div. 1969). It is instructive to examine Forms 420 and 421 as they detail the *information* in which the state is interested. Form 420 (Security Incident Report) in paragraph 9, refers to a civil disturbance, riot, rally, protest, demonstration, march and confrontation as being illustrative of the incidents in which the central agency is concerned. Paragraphs 4, 5 and 6 request that anticipated incidents, incidents still in progress and completed incidents be reported. The Form is designed to gather information leading to the determination of the names of the organizations or groups involved, the leaders, the type of organization, the nature of the incident and the source of the information concerning the incident. Form 421 (Security Summary Report) requires information about the individuals who may be connected with potential civil disorders, including such basic personal data as date and place of birth, marital status, name of spouse, age, race, physical description, occupation and employer, motor vehicle record and the names and addresses of associates. In addition, the form requries a narrative which ideally would include, among other items, citizenship, habits or traits, places frequented, financial status, past activities, and observations on the subject by the source of the information.

25. *See* Donner, section II for examples of the proliferation of state and local intelligence units.

26. *Id.*

An example of intelligence activity at the local level parallel to the state and federal activities is provided in *Holmes v. Church*[27] in which plaintiff, upon application for a pistol permit, was subjected to investigation and surveillance by the Department of Police of the City of New Rochelle, New York. The decision to place plaintiff under surveillance was made despite the finding that he was not engaged in criminal activity, suspected of criminal activity or known to have a criminal record.[28] Defendant had "maintained on file information of and reports on the conduct and association and activities of the plaintiff. . . ."[29] Upon a showing that the application for a pistol permit was proper in all respects and not related to criminal or political activity in any way, plaintiff was granted a permanent injunction enjoining the Police Department of the City of New Rochelle from all further acts of surveillance or investigation of plaintiff and providing for the destruction of the entire file developed through prior investigation and surveillance.[30]

The increase of intelligence units at all levels of government is not a result of unilateral decisions in each locale. Rather, the decision to establish intelligence units has been prompted by the findings and suggestions of high level federal and state commissions created to analyze and report on the causes of civil disorders.[31]. For example, the *Report of the National Advisory Commission on Civil Disorders* specifically directed its attention to the role of police intelligence in preventing civil disorders and made the following suggestions:

> Intelligence—the absence of accurate information both before and during a disorder—has created special control problems for the police. Police departments must develop means to obtain adequate intelligence for planning purposes, as well as on-the-scene information for use in police operations during a disorder.
>
> An intelligence unit staffed with full-time personnel should be established to gather, evaluate, analyze, and disseminate information on potential as well as actual civil disorders. It should provide police administrators and commanders with reliable information essential for assessments and decision-making. It should use undercover police personnel and informants but it should also draw on community leaders, agencies, and organizations in the ghetto.[32]

---

27. 70 Civ. 5691 (S.D.N.Y., June 10, 1971).
28. *Id.* at 3, para. 6.
29. *Id.* at 2.
30. *Id.* at 3-5.
31. *See* note 20 *supra.*
32. *Rights in Conflict, The Official Report To The National Commission on the Causes and Prevention of Violence, Signet Books* at 78.

Another indication that both the frequency and the depth of surveillance has increased is the number of suits being brought against various levels of government for the infringement of constitutional rights through present police investigatory practices. At this time, there are approximately twenty ACLU sponsored suits against the FBI, the Army and state and municipal police departments in which the plaintiff is seeking relief from obtrusive acts of surveillance.[33] Perhaps the most important of these is *Kenyatta v. Hoover*[34] which is a class action for declaratory and injunctive relief against the FBI based on the surveillance of lawful political activities revealed in the *Media* FBI documents.[35] In this action, the ACLU is attempting to block future FBI intelligence operations in the area of lawful political activity and to force the destruction of existing dossiers compiled on the plaintiffs. Plaintiff asserts that the FBI conducted surveillance which "exceeds the lawful needs and statutory authority" of the agency and which is "beyond the constitutional authority of the executive branch";[36] that the FBI gathered information about the founders (including plaintiff Kenyatta), organization structure and private meetings of the executive board of the plaintiff's Greater Philadelphia Black Economic Development Conference;[37] and that the FBI sought and gained knowledge of the unpublished telephone number of plaintiff Kenyatta and the bank statements of the checking accounts of plaintiff's National Black Economic Development Conference, Pennsylvania Office.[38] Documents of unquestioned authenticity support these primary allegations. It is therefore certain that the surveillance was conducted, which leaves at issue only the question of whether the FBI had the authority to conduct such surveillance. The ACLU believes that the practices challenged in *Kenyatta* are indicative of political surveillance undertaken by the

---

33. *See, e.g.,* Fifth Avenue Peace Parade Committee v. Hoover, 70 Civ. 2646 (S.D.N.Y. 1971); People against Racism v. Laird, 69 Civ.–(D.D.C., complaint filed Dec. 17, 1969); Tatum v. Laird, 44 F.2d 947 (D.C. Cir. 1971), *cert. granted,* No. 71-288 (1971); ACLU v. Westmoreland, 70 Civ. 3191 (N.D. Ill. 1970), *appeal docketed sub nom.,* ACLU v. Laird, 71 Civ. 1159 (cir. 1971); Cannon v. Davis, #978116 (Sup. Ct. of the St. of Calif., complaint filed June 6, 1970), not reported; Bach v. Mitchell, (D. Wis., 1971, not reported).

34. (E.D. Pa., complaint filed Oct. 27, 1971). *See also Tatum v. Laird,* 44 F.2d 947 (D.C. Cir. 1971), *cert. granted,* No. F1-288 (1971) which will be the first Supreme Court test of the First Amendment argument formulated by the ACLU which substantially extends the present scope of doctrine of the "chilling effect."

35. See notes 16 and 19 *supra.*

36. Complaint, *Kenyatta v. Hoover,* 71 Civ., not reported (E.D. Pa., Complaint filed Oct. 27, 1971) at 10, para. 16.

37. *Id.* at 6-7, para. 8.

38. *Id.*

FBI and other agencies of the Federal government, including the Army, which is beyond the authority of the executive branch.[39]

Members of both houses of Congress are beginning to show an increasing awareness of the problems of political surveillance. Senator Sam J. Ervin (D.—N. C.) has held hearings on the issue of privacy and record-keeping[40] which have documented the existence of widespread political surveillance.[41] Congressman Mikva (D.—Ill.), himself a target of such surveillance, has introduced a bill to protect the political rights and privacy of organizations and individuals and to define the authority of the armed forces to collect, distribute and store information about civilian political activity.[42] The primary reason behind these developments is the vigorous assertion of the right to dissent. A secondary reason is the increased capability of enforcement agencies to conduct widespread surveillance—a result of the present availability of the benefits of advanced technology.

The Law Enforcement Assistance Administration has made funds available to police departments at all levels to develop experimental means and methodology of law enforcement.[43] In Mt. Vernon, New York, for example, the LEAA has financed a remote camera surveillance system which provides continuous visual surveillance of approximately one mile of public streets.[44]

Advances in technology made outside the field of law enforcement have also been employed to aid police efforts. Perhaps the most important among these is the computer which enables the various agencies to collect, collate, store, retrieve and disseminate great quantities of information in fast and efficient manner.[45] Increasing surveillance has meant a dramatic increase in the amount of informa-

---

39. *See* note 33, *supra* for a partial listing of suits being brought on this ground. *Cf.* Note, *Wiretapping—Power of the U.S. Attorney-General to Authorize Wire Tapping Without Judicial Sanction*, 60 KY. L. REV. 245 (1971).

40. *See generally Senate Hearings*, note 2 *supra*.

41. *Id.* (Statement of Christopher Pyle, Feb. 24, 1971). *See also* DATAMATION 41 (April 25, 1971); N.Y. TIMES §1 (Mar. 5, 1972); col. 4 (Feb. 29, 1972); Kondracke, *Army has closed political computer, but Justice Dept. maintains bigger one,* CHICAGO SUN-TIMES 26, col. 1 (Mar. 9, 1970); Franklin, *Federal Computers Amass Files on Suspect Citizens,* N.Y. Times 1, (June 28, 1970).

42. H.R. 136, 92nd Cong., 1st Sess. (1971). *See also* S.995, 92nd Cong., 1st Sess. (1971) introduced by Senator Birch Bayh and H.R. 4375, 92nd Cong., Sess. (1971) introduced by Representative Edward Koch.

43. *See* Goulden, *The Cops Hit the Jackpot,* THE NATION 520 (Nov. 23, 1970). *See also* Barkan, *Big Brother Won't Wait Until 1984,* GUARDIAN 2 (Feb. 2, 1972).

44. *See* Belair and Bock, *Police Use of Remote Camera Systems for Surveillance of Public Streets,* 4 COLUM. HUMAN RIGHTS L. REV. 4 (HRLR 143, 1972).

45. The instruments of surveillance developed by our advanced technology are cataloged in Part Two, *New Tools for Invading Privacy,* WESTIN, PRIVACY AND FREEDOM 65-168 (1967). Westin's work has spawned many inquiries into the capability of the devices being developed by the new technology and the impact of the computer on privacy, chief among which are: MILLER, THE ASSAULT ON PRIVACY: COMPUTERS, DATA BANKS

tion which law enforcement agencies must handle and the computer has provided the optimum means.[46] The computer and the related science of cybernetics[47] permit the manipulation and management of vast quantities of disparate bits of information and afford government officials the ability to conduct "dataveillance" (review presently stored information on a particular subject) for the purpose of retriev-

---

AND DOSSIERS (1971) [hereinafter Miller]; FERKISS, TECHNOLOGICAL MAN (1969); LONG, THE INTRUDERS (1967). Although the computer has vastly increased our ability to manipulate large quantities of information, its direct impact has been overrated. Emphasis should be placed on the data being fed into the data bank—how is it collected, evaluated and recorded before being prepared for the computer? It is this pre-computer information gathering that concerns this paper since it is believed that safeguards against the invasions of privacy, particularly in a political context, must begin and be maintained in the initial stages of data gathering. But handling information by computer does involve secondary questions of privacy. The most extensive analysis of these problems can be found in Miller *supra. See also* Miller 261, *Selective Bibliography* 261-69.

46. Political surveillance has resulted in the creation of "dissident data banks," a term used to designate computer storage of intelligence gathered on known and potential dissidents.

47. For a view of the development of computers, see BERNSTEIN, THE ANALYTICAL ENGINE (paper ed. (1966)) and for an examination of the different generations of computer development, see Taylor, *Computer Systems,* COMPUTERS AND THE LAW 40 (American Bar Assn. Standing Comm. of Law and Technology, 2d ed. 1969). To obtain a perspective on the impact of the computer and the related science of cybernetics, see CLARKE, PROFILES OF THE FUTURE (1965); KAHN AND WEINER, THE YEAR 2000 (1967); BOGUSLAW, THE NEW UTOPIANS, A STUDY OF SYSTEM DESIGN AND SOCIAL CHANGE (1965); *Hearings on the Computer and Invasion of Privacy before Subcomm. of the House Comm. on Govt. Operations,* 89th Cong. 2d Sess. 7 (1966) (statement of Vance Packard); Miller, *Personal Privacy in the Computer Age: The Challenge of a New Technology in an Information-Oriented Society,* 67 MICH. L. REV. 1091, 1093-1106 (1969). For an example of the scientific community's views of the impact of the computer on our society [in an] excerpt from a speech by Dr. Glenn T. Seaborg, Chairman of the Atomic Energy Commission, reprinted in *Hearings on Computer Privacy Before the Subcomm. on Administrative Practice and Procedures of the Senate Comm. on the Judiciary,* 90th Cong., 1st Sess. 248 (1968):

> Springing from our Scientific Revolution of recent decades is what is being called our "Cybernetic Revolution." This revolution which, comparatively speaking, is only in its infancy today amplifies (and will to a large extent replace) man's nervous system. Actually, this is an understatement because computers amplify the collective intelligence of men—the intelligence of society—and while the effect of the sum of men's physical energies may be calculated, totally different and compounded effect results from combining facts and ideas. ... Add this effect to the productive capacity of a machine driven by an almost limitless energy source like the atom and the resulting system can perform feats almost staggering to the imagination. That is why I refer to cybernation as a quantum jump in our growth. (quoted in Miller at n.2).

See generally Main, *Computer Time-Sharing—Everyman at the Console,* FORTUNE, Aug. 1967 at 88; Burck, *The Computer Industry's Great Expectations,* FORTUNE, Aug. 1968 at 93; Diebold, *The New World Coming,* SAT. REV., July 23, 1966 at 17; Michael, *Speculations on the Relation of the Computer to Individual Freedom and the Right to Privacy,* 33 GEO. WASH. L. REV. 270 (1964); Ruggles, *On the Needs and Values of the Data Banks,* in *Symposium—Computers, Data Banks, and Individual Privacy,* 53 MINN. L. REV. 211 (1968).

ing, collating, or evaluating those bits of information relevant to the subject of the records check.[48]

B. Collection, Dissemination and Investigation as Harassment

The gathering of data is a rather strong implication that information collected will be used for a specific purpose. When information is gathered on political dissidents, in particular, it is critical to the preservation of the right to dissent that that purpose be both legitimate and within the statutory authority of the collecting agency. It is therefore proper to ask what justification the agency must have to collect and use the information about the dissident. In other words, to what standards must the agency adhere to stay within its legal parameters and what safeguards are available to the dissidents should the agencies transcend those standards and infringe upon his constitutionally protected rights?

A consideration of data collection and dissemination and investigation is the necessary precursor to defining legal standards to which an agency must constitutionally adhere.

The decision to place a subject under surveillance apparently may be made unilaterally by any agency at any level of government.[49] It does not seem to matter whether the subject is engaged in criminal or political activities; he is equally vulnerable.[50] Presently,

---

48. Information collected for use and storage may cast its subject in a "false light" if it is incomplete. Likewise, inaccurate data obviously imperils both the subject and the user, since neither is fairly represented. Data collected for specific reasons is only as complete and accurate as those collecting it take time to make it. Usually this is dictated by the purpose for which the information is collected. *See* Karst, *The Files: Legal Controls over the Accuracy and Accessibility of Stored Personal Data,* 31 LAW & CONTEMP. PROB. 342 (1966).

Where the purpose of data gathering is to monitor the subject, information need not be accurate beyond the whereabouts and associations of the individual. In addition, much of the agent or informer reporting is highly subjective and often reflects personal bias. *See* examples listed in Donner, section III and accompanying notes and note 69 *infra.* Information of this sort, when computer stored and retrieved, presents difficult problems of interpretation because it is retained in raw form and is political in nature. Who should have access? How does one safeguard stored information? The problem is particularly acute in time-shared storage banks. *See* Ware, *Security and Privacy in Computer Systems,* 30 AFIPS CONFERENCE PROCEEDINGS 279 (1967); Allen, *Danger Ahead! Safeguard Your Computer,* HARV. BUS. REV. Nov.-Dec. 1968, at 97, 99; and generally, Petersen and Turn, *System Implications of Information Privacy,* 30 AFIPS CONFERENCE PROCEEDINGS 291 (1967).

49. Interview with Mr. Frank Askin, Professor of Law, Rutgers University School of Law on February 16, 1972. Mr. Askin is also an attorney for the ACLU involved in suits against obtrusive government surveillance, *i.e.,* Tatum v. Laird, 444 F.2d 947 (D.C. Cir. 1971). *cert. granted,* No. F1-288 (1971). *See also* Donner, section IX.

50. See note 17, *supra.* The "national security" exception is used to circumvent the usual warrant requirements of the Fourth Amendment. The problem is of course who determines which acts jeopardize the national security. Where it is the law enforcement agency itself with the discretion to conduct surveillance at will, there is reason to suspect a bias in favor of surveillance on the grounds of safety and insurance.

therefore, the agency need not conform to any particular standards in order to subject an individual or a group to surveillance. However, the usual justifications which accompany the decision are the actuality or likelihood of acts either criminal in nature or detrimental to the national security.[51] Such justifications appear to be a bastard form of the "probable cause" standard, as that term is understood in criminal law, but is in reality little more than the agency's own policy of self-restraint. Indeed, former Attorney General Mitchell has made the claim that surveillance activities, including wire-taps, are within the sole discretion of the executive branch.[52]

Once the collection of information is under way, the agency may be required to adhere to a number of different standards depending upon the nature and scope of the surveillance to be conducted. For example, to search a man's home, inspect his papers or tap his phone, the agency must show that such a search is "reasonable" under the circumstances, and that they have "cause" to believe that the search will furnish information which bears upon the probable criminal conduct of the subject.[53] In these circumstances, the agency would be required to secure the approval of a neutral magistrate and to obtain a warrant specifying the purpose and scope of the search before going forward. However, the Fourth Amendment has essentially developed as a rule of criminal law and is largely ignored in the civil context.[54] Although there have been indications that the reach of the Amendment will be extended,[55] nothing has been done to suggest that it will embrace civil problems; such an extension is necessary to reach the problems engendered by political surveillance.

The First Amendment provides applicable standards which, however, are discretionary and too uncertain to be considered viable stan-

---

51. *See* United States v. Sinclair, Criminal No. 44375 (E.D. Mich., Jan. 25, 1971) and United States v. Smith, 321 F. Supp. 424 (C.D. Cal. 1971) in which the use of the national security justification is illustrated.

52. *See* Note, *Wiretapping—Power of the U.S. Attorney-General to Authorize Wiretapping Without Judicial Sanction,* 60 KY. L. REV. 245 (1971); Comment, *Warrantless Electronic Surveillance of Dissident Domestic Organizations under the National Security Exception,* 5 VALP. U. L. REV. 651 (1971). *See also* United States v. United States District Court for E.D. of Mich., 444 F.2d 651 (6th Cir.), *cert. granted,* 403 U.S. 932 (1971).

53. *See* U.S. Const. amend. IV:

The right of the people to be secure in their persons, houses, papers, and effects, against unreasonable searches and seizures, shall not be violated, and no warrants shall issue, but upon probable cause, supported by oath or affirmation, and particularly describing the place to be searched, and the persons or things to be seized.

54. Hufstedler, *The Directions and Misdirections of a Constitutional Right of Privacy,* THE RECORD 546, 555 (1971) [hereinafter Hufstedler]. See Part III, *infra.*

55. *See* Bivens v. Six Unknown Named Agents of Federal Bureau of Narcotics, 403 U.S. 388 (1971); Berch, *Money Damages for Fourth Amendment Violations by Federal Officials: An Explanation of Bivens v. Six Unknown Named Agents of Federal Bureau of Narcotics,* LAW & SOC. ORDER 43 (1971) [hereinafter Berch].

dards for the conduct of surveillance. For example, the "nexus" test would require an agency to demonstrate a direct interest in the information sought.[56] Presumably, this test could be met by showing the relevance of the surveillance to the national security, to the criminal conduct of the subject and perhaps to the need to maintain order within society. But what degree of relevance is required? What other interests are sufficiently compelling and direct?[57]

A second First Amendment standard based on the doctrine of the "chilling effect" is being developed and has become the principal weapon of the ACLU in this field.[58] But it too has its limitations as a guide to the conduct of surveillance. To invoke this standard, there must exist a viable and direct threat of infringement upon the rights of speech and association, and surveillance which does not so impinge evades its compass. In addition, it is extremely difficult to determine the point where the *chill* is sufficient to satisfy the doctrine which severely limits its utility as a guideline.

A final standard is the right to privacy. Privacy here is to be understood as the "claim of individuals, groups, or institutions to determine for themselves when, how and to what extent information about themselves is communicated to others."[59] This standard, although viable in theory, is weak in practice because of its broad embrace and lack of constitutional profile. It is safe to say that, at

---

56. *See* Gibson v. Florida Legislative Investigation Committee, 372 U.S. 539 (1963). *Contra,* Uphaus v. Wyman, 360 U.S. 72 (1959). *But see* Goldman v. Olson, 286 F. Supp. 35 (W.D. Wis. 1968); and Part II, *infra.*

57. See Part II, *infra.*

58. *See* Askin, *Police Dossiers and Emerging Principles of First Amendment Adjudication,* 22 STAN. L. REV. 196 (1970'. *See, e.g.,* Tatum v. Laird, 44 F. 2d 947 (D.C. Cir. 1971), *cert. granted,* No. F1-288 (1971).

59. WESTIN, PRIVACY AND FREEDOM 7 (1st ed. 1967). *See also* Fried, *Privacy,* 77 YALE L. J. 475 (1968). The struggle to define the right of privacy appears to have been a difficult exercise because it cuts across so many concerns of the individual. *See* Dixon, *The Griswold Penumbra: Constitutional Charter for an Expanded Law of Privacy?,* 64 MICH. L. REV. 197, 199 (1965); "Under this emotional term [the right to privacy] march a whole congeries of interests, some closely interrelated, some almost wholly unrelated and even inconsistent."

Perhaps one of the better definitional statements was written by Warren and Brandeis, *The Right to Privacy,* 4 HARV. L. REV. 193 (1890).

See also an attempt in *Office of Science and Technology of the Executive Office of the President, Privacy and Behavioral Research* 8-9 (1967):

> . . . what is private varies for each person and varies from day to day and setting to setting. Indeed, the very core of the concept is the right of each individual to determine for himself in particular setting or compartment of his life how much of his many-faceted beliefs, attitudes and behavior he chooses to disclose. Every person lives in different worlds and in each his mode of response [is] different. . . . The right to privacy includes the freedom to live in each of these different roles without having his performance and aspirations in one context placed in another without [his] permission.

present, the right to privacy alone constitutes neither a barrier to surveillance nor a usable guideline for its conduct; however, it can be, and often is, used to reinforce other standards.[60]

Any of these standards may easily be avoided and do little to safeguard the individual or group from unwarranted surveillance. And where the dissident is concerned, they offer only *ex post facto* relief—that is, the sanctions which may be used to enforce the guarantees of the First Amendment are available only after obtrusive acts of surveillance have been accomplished.[61] Therefore an agency which has determined its target has considerable latitude in determining how and to what extent surveillance is to be conducted. At this point and in this context data collection by means of surveillance can be used to harass the subject. Reliance upon agency restraint is an invitation to intentional or unintentional abuse of broad discretion,[62] which in either case, is real and harmful to the subject.[63]

Information is often gathered from secondary sources such as government records, associates and acquaintances, neighbors, business contacts and relatives. Much of the information obtained is often inaccurate or misleading and the absence of access to the file makes it impossible to challenge its accuracy or content.[64] Intelligence reports are notoriously subjective,[65] and files are seldom, if ever, *massaged* to separate accurate from partially or wholly biased information.

Once such information has been gathered and stored, a second opportunity for abuse and harassment arises. It may be disseminated to disparate enforcement agencies or other parties[66] (on the collector's own initiative or on request), providing the opportunity for continuing surveillance to augment a file and permitting secondary and even tertiary exercise of the discretion in the conduct of the surveillance.

---

60. *See, e.g.,* United States v. White, 401 U.S. 745, 751; *id.* at 781 (Harlan, J., dissenting); Katz v. United States, 389 U.S. 347, 359 (1967); Griswold v. Connecticut, 381 U.S. 479 (1965).

61. *See* Part II, *infra,* for a discussion of the scope of First Amendment protection against unwarranted acts of surveillance.

62. *See* N.Y. Times 1, col. 4 (Feb. 29, 1972).

63. *See, e.g.,* N.Y. Times 33, col. 3 (March 6, 1972). *See also* Mikva, *A Nation of Fear,* THE PROGRESSIVE 18, 19-20 (Feb. 1971) and for a case of unsupervised surveillance in which the government played on unsavory role, *see* United States v. Jones, 292 F. Supp. 1001, 1008-09 (D.D.C. 1968).

64. See note 48, *supra.*

65. Donner, section IV. For examples, see Complaint, Kenyatta v. Hoover, 71 Civ. _____ appendices E, F, H. and K (E.D. Pa., Complaint filed Oct. 27, 1971) and Brief for Appellants, Appendix at 12-17, Tatum v. Laird, 444 F.2d 947 (D.C. Cir. 1971).

66. *Id. See also* Donner, section II (excerpt from the Annual Report of the Massachusetts Division of Subversive Activities, 1969; Media document dated November 13, 1970).

Information in a police dossier is hardly benign, and when it is released under authority of the department to the employee, to acquaintances or the public generally, it carries a presumption of authenticity that may work severe hardship on the subject.[67] But such result need not be immediate. It may be that the subject's reckoning with the contents of the file will be deferred, and at some later date he will be confronted with the information.[68]

This renewed surveillance and dissemination may cause harassment in several ways. If the subject has knowledge of the surveillance and the existence of a dossier, it is logical to assume that his speech or normal association may be inhibited. If he has no such knowledge, it is more likely that he will be injured by the dissemination of the information because a lack of knowledge precludes explanation or defense.[69]

It must be reiterated at this point that the subject of surveillance may be engaged in lawful or unlawful activity.[70] Nonjudicially authorized surveillance may be conducted to obtain anything shy of the information for which a warrant is clearly required. The dissident is accorded the same status as those suspected of criminal or treasonable acts although he has committed no act requiring the forfeiture of constitutional safeguards. He is unable to ascertain the contents of the dossier of which he is the subject, and is therefore denied the opportunity to challenge its implications. Nor is this all. An intervening step or circumstance which invites the attention of the police may cause the subject to be investigated,[71] which entails

---

67. Some problems involved in the dissemination of information (together with the ability to disseminate) are outlined in Miller 38-53. That information in power is a premise well established. For a discussion, see Shils, *Privacy and Power,* reprinted in *Hearings on Computer Privacy before Subcommittee on Administrative Practice and Procedures of the Senate Committee on the Judiciary,* 90th Cong., 1st Sess. 231 (1968). See also note 2, *supra* for cases in which dissemination of political intelligence was thought to be harmful.

68. There is an obvious distinction between the authority of a government and private data-collector. The government has a superior—but not all-inclusive—right to require information subject to our legal protections. The private sector must have other reasons for compelling disclosure such as a reasonable benefit to the individual as in a favorable credit-rating. But a serious difficulty arises when either sector solicits information about a person and stores it without his knowledge. If such information is later disseminated, the individual is unaware of its import and is deprived of defense. The argument for disclosure by collecting agencies, in cases where national security or other such compelling reasons are not involved, is largely based on this premise.

For an example of the alleged harm that attends the improper use of dissemination, *see* Robertson v. Mitchell, C-71581 (N.D. Cal., complaint filed Mar. 24, 1971).

69. Comment, *Chilling Political Expression by Use of Police Intelligence Files,* 5 HARV. CIV. RIGHTS CIV. LIB. L. REV. 71, 74 (Jan., 1970).

70. See cases cited in note 2 *supra.*

71. Investigation of individuals engaged in lawful activity has been alleged to be harassment *per se. See* Brief for Appellants at 23-28, Tatum v. Laird, No. 24,203 (D.C. Cir. January, 1971); Brief for Plaintiffs—Respondents at 38, 40-41, Anderson v. Sills, No. A-150-69 (Super N.J. January 13, 1970).

an overt police effort to create as complete a file on the subject as possible and which involves the direct contact with the associates and acquaintances of the subject. Still, in the case of the political dissident, there may well have been no criminal act or intent or danger to the national security—surveillance resulted from the decision to make his beliefs known. Or, more specifically, the decision to exercise his First Amendment rights of speech and association have caused him to be labeled, recorded and placed under surveillance.

Judge Ferguson, in *United States v. Smith*, stated the problem succintly:

> [T]he government seems to approach these dissident domestic organizations in the same fashion as it deals with * unfriendly foreign powers. The government cannot act in this manner when only domestic political organizations are involved even if those organizations espouse views which are inconsistent with our present form of government. To do so is to ride roughshod over numerous political freedoms which have long received constitutional protection. The government can, of course, investigate and prosecute criminal violations whenever these organizations, or rather their individual members, step over the line of political theory and general advocacy and commit illegal acts.[73]

The difficulty of course is not with the agencies whose mission it is to keep order or the dissidents who seek to disseminate their political views; rather, it lies with the policies and sanctions presently drawn from the constitutional standards. It is submitted that increasing political surveillance, the relative lack of policy guidelines in the conduct of surveillance and the superior capability and resources of law enforcement agencies have created an imbalance between the need for order and the right to dissent in favor of the government and to the detriment of our constitutional liberties. Therefore, it is necessary to forge the means of reasserting those liberties by retailoring the policy, standards and sanctions which insure them.

PART II. THE AMBIT OF FIRST AMENDMENT PROTECTION

New interpretations of the scope of the First Amendment are emerging and appear to be coalescing into a doctrine which would

---

72. 321 F. Supp. 424 (C.D. Cal. 1971).
73. *Id.* at 429.

extend the protections afforded by the Amendment to political dissidents who organize for social and political change.[74] A significant, although minor, step in the development of this doctrine was taken in *Anderson v. Sills*[75] and *Holmes v. Church*.[76] The thrust of plaintiffs' argument, accepted by both courts, was that police surveillance may be enjoined as an unconstitutional violation of the rights of free expression and assembly secured by the First Amendment because of the *chilling effect* on the individual's right to speak and associate freely. More precisely, this theory requires that governmental surveillance that "inhibits the exercise of first amendment rights by persons not directly or immediately threatened with punishment or other direct sanction . . . is constitutionally vulnerable."[77] This doctrine was developed to counteract the arguments that individuals and organizations engaging in dissent from existing governmental policies cause the illegal civil disorders that the police seek to prevent, and that surveillance and the creation of dossiers on lawful protestors will aid in the prevention of illegal disorders.[78] The specific issue with which the doctrine deals is the annoyance, intimidation and harassment imposed by the implication of criminality or subversive intent so strongly suggested by police surveillance and record-keeping.

The doctrine, however, is new and in need of further judicial development. It is unclear, for example, whether the existence of a valid governmental purpose such as the maintenance of order is sufficient to justify surveillance activities which impede or inhibit lawful political conduct. Should an analysis of the problems generated by the friction between the right to dissent and the need for order utilize a "balancing" or "nexus" test? Is it the likelihood, the form, or the impact of governmental action which is to be examined in determining abridgements of the First Amendment? If this new doctrine is to prosper, these and the many related problems sure to arise must be given close consideration to determine the scope of protection afforded by the First Amendment.

---

74. *See generally* Askin, *Police Dossiers and Emerging Principles of First Amendment Adjudication*, 22 STAN. L. REV. 196 (1970) [hereinafter Askin]; Brennon, *The Supreme Court and the Meiklejohn Interpretation of the First Amendment*, 79 HARV. L. REV. 1 (1965). *Compare* American Communications Association v. Douds, 339 U.S. 382 (1950) and Dennis v. United States, 341 U.S. 494 (1951) *with* Dombrowski v. Pfister, 380 U.S. 479 (1965) and United States v. Robel, 389 U.S. 258 (1967) for a dramatic indication of the development of First Amendment law over the last two decades.

75. 106 N.J. Super. 545 (Ch. Div. 1969), *rev'd and remanded,* 56 N.J. 210, 265 A. 2d 678 (1970).

76. 70 Civ. 5691 (S.D. N.Y. June 10, 1971).

77. Askin, *supra* note 74, at 199.

78. *Id.* at 198.

A. The Doctrine of the Chilling Effect

The doctrine of the *chilling effect* as developed in recent years, has extended the reach of First Amendment protections,

> ... from a private right not to be prosecuted or otherwise sanctioned for speech ... to a public right to keep government from interfering with free trade in the marketplace of ideas.[79]

Perhaps the most significant factor in this development came in *Dombrowski v. Pfister* which recognized that the rights of free expression and association are "of transcendental value to all society, and not merely to those exercising their rights."[80] This acknowledged a First Amendment proscription of any act which constricts, or is likely to constrict, not only the exercise but the uninhibited existence of those rights. Or, in other words,

---

79. *Id.* at 202.

80. 380 U.S. 479, 486 (1965). *Dombrowski* was an action under the Civil Rights Act, Title 42 U.S.C. § 1983 (1964), for declaratory and injunctive relief restraining defendants from prosecuting or threatening to prosecute plaintiffs for alleged violations of a Louisiana antisubversive activities law. *Dombrowski* is responsible for the development of the Constitutional doctrines of *vagueness* and *chilling effect*. See note 81, *infra.* But, in addition, the case dealt with the federal abstention and anti-injunction doctrine. The Court addressed itself to the controversy over the interpretation of the Federal Anti-Injunction statute, 28 U.S.C. § 2283 (1964), which provides that:

> A court of the United States may not grant an injunction to stay proceedings in a state court except as expressly authorized by Act of Congress ... or where necessary in aid of its jurisdiction, or to protect or effectuate its judgements.

However, the Court evaded the issue of whether § 1983 is an exception and construed the word *proceedings* in a way which permitted an injunction against the prosecution at issue. The rationale was that no state *proceedings* were pending where the grand jury had not been convened and indictments had not been obtained until after the complaint seeking the injunction had been filed. On this basis, it was determined that an injunction could issue upon a finding that the Louisiana law violated due process because its language is vague, uncertain and overbroad. The irreparable injury, necessary to injunctive relief, was established by showing the likelihood of substantial impairment of expressional rights if plaintiffs were to await state disposition of the issues and the later review of any adverse determination by the Supreme Court. Landry v. Dailey, 288 F. supp. 183 (1968) reaffirmed *Dombrowski* on the question of federal injunctive power. *Landry* held that allegations that prosecutions for violations of state statutes and municipal ordinances which had been applied in an unconstitutional manner, for the purpose of discouraging plaintiffs' civil rights activities, *presented factual issues requiring a plenary hearing and precluding dismissal of an action seeking an injunction against state court prosecutions. See* Schlam, *Police Intimidation Through "Surveillance" May be Enjoined as an Unconstitutional Violation of Rights of Assembly and Free Expression—Part II,* 3 CLEARINGHOUSE REV. 157, 162 (November, 1969) [hereinafter Schlam]. And it was clearly established that such allegations were actionable under the Civil Rights Act.

the injury to be remedied is not only personal but also societal; it must be gauged by the impact on those who will not complain to the courts because of the very nature of the injury.[81]

The *Landry* Court was concerned over the *Dombrowski* evasion of the apparently irreconcilable interpretations of § 1983 and the Federal Anti-Injunction Statute by holding that no *proceedings* were pending:

> ... that the lawful exercise of constitutionally protected rights should depend on such a fortuitous distinction would indeed be anomalous (at 224).

A construction of the anti-injunction statute which precluded injunctive relief for all pending prosecutions would undercut the utility and scope of 42 U.S.C. § 1983. Relief would be dependent upon the "mere fortuity" of a "person affected by such harassment" instituting a "suit in the federal court before formal charges were brought against him in the state courts (*Landry* at 224). *Landry* recognized the inherent conflict between § 1983 and the anti-injunction statute, together with the circumlocution of the issue in *Dombrowski,* and concluded that:

> ... When the anti-injunction statute and the Civil Rights Act are viewed in their historical posture, their relationship becomes clearer. Section 1983, a product of a later Congress and an expression of an overwhelming Congressional concern for the protection of federal rights from deprivation by state action, would seem to have been to be an exception to the general limitation of section 2283 (at 223).

Taken together, *Dombrowski* and *Landry* seem to anticipate a federal injunctive power applicable to state prosecutions under laws, either vague or overboard, which impinge upon the expressional rights. Presumably, relief could be sought under § 1983 and the Fourteenth Amendment or under the First Amendment doctrine of the *chilling effect* as presented in Anderson v. Sills, 106 N.J. Super. 545 (Ch. Div. 1969), *rev'd. and remanded,* 56 N.J. 210, 265 A. 2d 678 (1970); Tatum v. Laird, 44 F. 2d 947 (D.C. Cir. 1971), *cert. granted,* No. 71-288 (1971). *See also* Note, *Limiting the section 1983 Action in the Wake of Monroe v. Pape,* 82 HARV. L. REV. 1486 (1969); Carter v. Carlson, 447 F.2d 358 (D.C. Cir. 1971).

81. Askin, note 74, *supra* at 202. *See* Note, *Chilling Political Expression by Use of Police Intelligence Files,* 5 HARV. CIV. RIGHTS CIV. LIB. L. REV. 71 (January 1970) and Note, *The Chilling Effect in Constitutional Law,* 69 COLUM. L. REV. 808 (1969) for recent analysis of the chilling effect. *See also* Schneider v. Smith, 390 U.S. 17 (1968); Keyishian v. Board of Regents of New York, 385 U.S. 589 (1967); Elfbrandt v. Russel, 384 U.S. 11 (1966); Lamont v. Postmaster General, 381 U.S. 301 (1965), *aff'g* Heilberg v. Fixa, 236 F. Supp. 405 (N. D. Cal. 1964) for cases employing the doctrine.

The *Dombrowski* (note 80, *supra*) line of cases support the theory that the *chilling effect* that possible prosecution works on the expressional rights secured by the First Amendment cannot be viewed with indifference—such prosecution should be enjoined where valid statutes are used in bad faith, or vague and overboard statutes restrain lawful activity.

Clear examples of the effects of threatened or potential prosecution are provided by cases involving freedom of association. *See, e.g.,* Brandenberg v. Ohio, 395 U.S. 444, 449 n. 4 (1969); Shuttlesworth v. City of Birmingham, 394 U.S. 147, 153 (1969); NAACP v. Alabama, 357 U.S. 449 (1958); Local 309 v. Gates, 75 F. Supp. 620 (D.C. N.D. Ind. 1948).

The chilling effect can be used to enjoin state action unless the state can demonstrate a *compelling interest* in such action and show a *substantial* connection between the interest and the information sought. Watkins v. United States, 354 U.S. 178, 198 (1957). These requirements have led to the development of a balancing test by which the superior interest (state or plaintiff) is determined. This, in turn, has led to considerable discussion of the viability of such a test when First Amendment rights are concerned. Compare American Communications

Two important procedural effects flow from the expansion of the doctrine. The requirements of both standing and justiciability are loosened, thereby decreasing the burden of proof for the plaintiff.[82] For example, plaintiff need no longer establish that he is directly "hit" by the action complained of, or that an injury has actually been sustained.[83] The courts lowered the procedural barriers so that they could proceed to the merits and determine the impact of the governmental action which elicited the complaint. Substantively, the doctrine protects pure speech, association and action which falls between *speech* and *speech-plus*, and gives the court permission to look to the detriment, or the probable detriment, to the aggregate rights of all those similarly situated in addition to the individual case before it.

The doctrine has been applied most effectively in *Lamont v. Postmaster General*,[84] in which a federal statute authorizing the Postmaster General to withhold delivery of foreign correspondence of *communist political propaganda*[85] was challenged. The statute also required the Post Office to notify the addressee that his mail was being held pending his written request for its delivery. If delivery were so requested, the addressee would be listed as one who authorized the receipt of communist propaganda. The petitioners, who were willing to acknowledge their willingness to receive mail classified as *communist propaganda*, were allowed to maintain the suit even though they were not personally aggrieved by the legislation.[86] Both the District and the Supreme Courts found that the statute had a probable injurious impact on society as a whole[87] and held the stat-

---

Association v. Douds, 339 U.S. 382, 399-400 (1950) with Konigsberg v. State Bar, 366 U.S. 36, 68-69 (Black, J., dissenting) and with United States v. Robel, 389 U.S. 258, 268 n. 20 (1967). The net effect, and the great appeal of the chilling effect doctrine is that

... it permits the court to look to the detriment to the aggregate [expressional] rights of all those in the group affected rather than on the individual before it. An allowable state inquiry must be directed at active participation in an organization [or activity] with illegal aims. ...

Schlam, note 80, *supra* at 163. *See generally* Note, *The Constitutional Right to Anonymity: Free Speech, Disclosure and the Devil*, 70 YALE L. J. 1084 (1961).

82. *See, e.g.,* Jenkins v. McKeithen, 395 U.S. 411 (1969); Zwickler v. Koota, 389 U.S. 241 (1967); Dombrowski v. Pfister, 380 U.S. 479 (1965).

83. *See, e.g.,* Lamont v. Postmaster General, 381 U.S. 301 (1965), *aff'g* Heilberg v. Fixa, 236 F.Supp. 405 (N.D. Cal. 1964).

84. *Id.*

85. 39 U.S.C. § 4008 (1964).

86. *See* Lamont v. Postmaster General, *supra* note 83; Bates v. City of Little Rock, 361 U.S. 516 (1960); NAACP v. Alabama, 357 U.S. 449 (1958). *See generally* Askin, *supra* note 74, at 197-98 n. 12. Note, *Parties Plaintiff in Civil Rights Litigation*, 68 COLUM. L. REV. 893 (1968).

87. *See* discussion of *Lamont* in Askin, *supra* note 74, at 203-04.

ute to be in violation of the addressee's First Amendment rights because of the likelihood that the "addressee [will] feel some inhibition in sending for literature which federal officials have condemned as 'communist political propaganda.' "[88]

The *Lamont* theory has not been uniformly applied. In *Vietnam Veterans Against the War* v. *Nassau County Police Department*,[89] a request for a preliminary injunction was denied for a want of showing irreparable harm to the First Amendment rights of the petitioners. In this case, police attended, by invitation, a march and a meeting of the veterans and gathered information, including photographs, to be filed in dossiers on the group and its leaders. The veterans objected to the data collection and brought suit relying on *NAACP* v. *Button*[90] and *Tatum* v. *Laird*.[91] *Button* had employed a First Amendment argument based on the right of association in which the court said:

> ... there is no longer any doubt that the First and Fourteenth Amendments protect certain forms of orderly group activity.... [W]e have affirmed the right "to engage in association for the advancement of beliefs and ideas." *NAACP* v. *Alabama ex rel. Patterson,* 357 U.S. 449, 460 (1958).

But the court in *Vietnam Veterans* employed a test balancing the state interest in the collection of data and the maintenance of dossiers against the First Amendment rights of the petitioners; the burden was placed on the petitioners to show that they were chilled, not on the police to show that the information gathered was necessary to a legitimate governmental purpose. The court relied primarily on the second *Sills* decision,[93] and presumed that the information gathered would be used in a lawful exercise of police discretion.[94]

The confusion evident in these contrasting decisions is grounded in the standard by which a court determines whether governmental action

---

88. Lamont v. Postmaster General, 381 U.S. 301, 307 (1965). *See* Heilberg v. Fixa, 236, 409 (1964) and Lamont v. Postmaster General, 229 F. Supp. 918, 919 (S.D.N.Y. 1964).

89. 10 CRIM. L. RPTR. 2152 (E.D.N.Y. December 1, 1971).

90. 371 U.S. 415 (1963).

91. 44 F. 2d 947 (D.C. Cir. 1971), *cert. granted,* No. 71-288 (1971).

92. 371 U.S. at 430.

93. Anderson v. Sills, 56 N.J. 210, 256 A. 2d 678 (1970).

94. The court successfully avoided the consideration of the merits by imposing the burden of showing irreparable harm upon plaintiffs. The logic of the court is questionable since it unearths the traditional motions of justiciability of Poe v. Ullman, 367 U.S. 497 (1961) in favor of Dombrowski v. Pfister, 380 U.S. 479 (1965). *See generally* Note, HUAC *and the "Chilling Effect": The Dombrowski Rationale Applied,* 21 RUTGERS L. REV. 679 (1967).

which inhibits the exercise of First Amendment rights is actionable. Since not all impediments to the free exercise of First Amendment rights are unconstitutional,[95] it is necessary to select a standard by which to distinguish the unconstitutional from the constitutional impediments. The courts have developed two such standards: the balancing and nexus tests.

The balancing test weighs,

> ... the probable effects of the statute upon the free exercise of the right of speech and assembly against the congressional determination ... of conduct [likely to] cause substantial harm. ...[96]

Various methodologies have been employed which have had the same practical effect as the balancing test but which have claimed theoretical distinctions.[97] It has been the results which have interested the Court, as Chief Justice Vinson has indicated:

> When particular conduct is regulated in the interest of public order, and the regulation results in an indirect, conditional, partial abridgement of speech, the duty of the court is to determine which of these two conflicting interests demands a greater protection under the particular circumstances presented.[98]

But this view has not been universally accepted. Justice Black consistently argued against its use, and in *Konigsberg v. State Bar*,[99] he articulated the view that, although there may be incidental abridgements of speech or association through government action, the government, despite the legitimacy of its purpose, may not take action which directly inhibits those rights secured by the First Amendment. The Warren Court, in *United States v. Robel*,[100] moved toward Black's view that,

---

95. *See* Brandenburg v. Ohio, 395 U.S. 444, 455 (1969) (Douglas, J., concurring); Shuttlesworth v. City of Birmingham, 394 U.S. 147, 155 (1969); and Gregory v. City of Chicago, 394 U.S. 111, 118 (1969) (Black, J., concurring).

96. American Communications Associations v. Bouds, 339 U.S. 382, 399 (1950).

97. *See* Corwin, *Bowing Out "Clear and Present Danger,"* 27 NOTRE DAME LAW 325, 349-56 (1952).

98. American Communications Associations v. Douds, 339 U.S. at 399.

99. 366 U.S. 36, 68-69 (1969) (Black, J., dissenting). Black's position is that speech and the ... speech portion of speech-plus activities [are] entitled to the full protection of pure speech, but the state has the power to act upon the non-speech aspects where it is necessary to protect legitimate state interests.

... government is restricted to acting upon unprotected expression and association; it cannot act upon the protected merely because it is rationally or reasonably related to the unprotected.[101]

Former Chief Justice Warren, speaking for the majority in *Robel*, took the following position:

> Faced with a clear conflict between a federal statute, enacted in the interest of national security and the individual's exercise of his First Amendment rights, we have confined our analysis as to whether Congress has adopted a constitutional means in achieving its concededly legitimate legislative goal. In making this determination we have found it necessary to measure the validity of the means adopted by Congress against both the goal it has sought to achieve and the specific prohibitions of the First Amendment. We have ruled only that the constitution required that the conflict between congressional power and individual rights be accommodated by legislation drawn more narrowly to avoid the conflict.[102]

The "nexus test," was also developed prior to *Robel*. The Court, in *Gibson* v. *Florida Legislative Investigation Committee*,[103] articulated the test as follows:

> [I]t is an essential prerequisite to the validity of an investigation which intrudes into the area of constitutionally protected rights of speech, press, association and petition that the state convincingly show a *substantial relation between the information sought and a subject of overriding and compelling state interest*[104] (emphasis added).

In *Gibson*, the Florida Legislative Investigation Committee sought an NAACP membership list to determine whether that organization had been infiltrated by communists. The Court held that the nexus test had not been met since there was no showing of a *substantial* relation between the information sought and a compelling state interest insofar

---

101. Askin, note 74, *supra*, at 209.
102. 389 U.S. at 268 n. 20.

103. 372 U.S. 539 (1963). For a discussion of the development of the nexus test, *see* Askin, *supra* note 74 at 212-216. *Compare* Gibson v. Florida Legislative Investigation Committee, *supra* note 100 with Uphaus v. Wyman, 360 U.S. 72 (1959). *See also* DeGregory v. Attorney General, 383 U.S. 825 (1966).
104. 372 U.S. at 546.

as the NAACP was concerned. This means that the state interest must be directly related to the conduct investigated, and that the nexus test will not be satisfied by subjective inferences or suspicions.[105] In this way, nexus requirements were often couched in language indicative of the balance doctrine which has undercut the efficacy of the nexus test.[106]

In applying these two tests to the dissident situation, one commentator has stated that:

> the *Robel* standard bars the state from attempting to justify such data gathering [investigation and dossier maintenance] by some imprecise balancing of a vague and undefined interest in public order against the constitutional rights involved. The nexus standard demands that the state at a minimum demonstrate a direct relationship between protest and unlawful activity.[107]

If it is unable to do this, the state may be said to have chilled the exercise or existence of First Amendment rights. At this juncture, the *Dombrowski* and *Lamont* line of cases can provide access to the courts for the adjudication of the constitutionality of the means and purpose of the government action alleged to infringe upon those rights permitting dissent. Accordingly, government surveillance activities undertaken in a speculative and arbitrary fashion, as described in Part I, would not survive a constitutional challenge. This doctrine, however, has not yet received the approval of the Supreme Court, nor has it been widely accepted in the district or state courts.[108] Moreover, it has had only limited success in the proscription of political surveillance.[109]

The standards themselves present certain questions for which the doctrine presents no answers; for example, who will decide the

---

105. *See* Askin, *supra* note 74 at 217. *See* Goldman v. Olson, 286 F. Supp. 35 (W.D. Wis. 1968).

106. *Id.* at 213. *See, e.g.,* Uphaus v. Wyman, 360 U.S. 72 (1959).

107. *Id.* at 217. *See also id,* at 217 notes 105, 106 and 107.

108. *See, e.g.* Tatum v. Laird, 44 F. 2d, 947 (D.C. Cir. 1971) *with* Vietnam Veterans Against the War v. Nassau County Police Dept. *supra* note 89. *See also* Fifth Avenue Peace Parade Committee v. Hoover, 70 Civ. 2646 (S.D.N.Y. 1971); Anderson v. Sills, 106 N.J. Super 545 (Ch. Div. 1961), *rev'd and remanded,* 56 N.J. 210, 265 A.2d 678 (1970); Aronson v. Gearusso, 436 F. 2d 955 (1971); Handschu v. Murphy, 71 Civ. 2203 (S.D.N.Y. 1971).

109. Compare Holmes v. Church, 70 Civ. 5691 (S.D.N.Y. June 10, 1971) with Vietnam Veterans Against the War v. Nassau County Police Dept., note 89, *supra. See also* Fifth Avenue Peace Parade Committee v. Hoover, 70 Civ. 2646 (S.D.N.Y. 1971); Anderson v. Sills, 106 N.J. Super. 545 (Ch. Div. 1961), *rev'd. and remanded,* 56 N.J. 210, 265 A 2d 678 (1970); Aronson v. Gearusso, 436 F. 2d 955 (1971); Handschu v. Murphy, 71 Civ. 2203 (S.D.N.Y. 1971).

legitimacy of the stated governmental interest, and the constitutional permissibility of the means of implementation.[110] At present, such decisions are made on a unilateral basis by the agencies which decide to conduct surveillance and how, when and against whom it is to be conducted.

It is submitted that the problems of political surveillance go beyond the cognizable reach of the First Amendment, even that of the scope of the protections afforded by the expanded chill doctrine, and involve the invasion of individual privacy.[111] In order to invoke the doctrine to enjoin the surveillance a petitioner must have knowledge of it—without such knowledge, there can be no chill and no relief.[112] Requiring the existence of the evil, or at least the machinery for its implementation,[113] before relief for probable or actual injury may be sought, may be too little too late. The privacy of a dissident may well be invaded long before he has knowledge of an intent or an act of surveillance. Moreover, if we assume that the procedural requirements of standing and justiciability can be met and the standards properly employed, the only relief available is an injunction against future harm—there is no remedy for injury suffered except in extraordinary circumstances. Finally, prohibitions of the First Amendment voiced in the emerging doctrine are subject to avoidance as long as agencies continue to make unilateral interpretations of the ambit of the First Amendment protections. In effect, these factors reduce the doctrine to an after-the-fact remedy.[114] For these reasons, the chilling effect doctrine alone, even if developed as indicated, is insufficient to safeguard the right of lawful dissent.

---

110. *See* Part Iv, *infra. See also,* Askin *supra* note 74 at 213 and following for a discussion of the questtions which the use of the chilling effect will engender.

111. *See* Part III, *infra See* CLARK, CRIME IN AMERICA 287 (1970). *See also* United States v. White, 401 U.S. 745, 756 (1971) (Douglas, J., dissenting).

112. Even if petitioner has knowledge of the surveillance, and can demonstrate a chilling effect he must meet the additional requirements of presenting a justiciable issue and showing irreparable harm. *See, e.g.*, Tatum v. Laird, 44 F. 2d 947 (D.C. Cir. 1971), *cert. granted,* No. 71-288 (1971) which is going to the Supreme Court on the issue of justiciability and Vietnam Veterans Against the War v. Nassau County Police Department, 10 CRIM. LAW. RPTR. 2152 (E.D.N.Y. December 1, 1971) in which a claim for injunctive relief was denied for failure to show irreparable harm.

113. To obtain standing, it would seem that at least the instrumentality to accomplish the injury complained of must be in existence before the controversy would be ripe enough for adjudication. *See, e.g.*, Anderson v. Sills, 106 N.J. Super. 545 (Ch. Div. 1969), *rev'd. and remanded,* 56 N.J. 210, 265 A. 2d 678 (1970) in which the plan for police data gathering was in existence and in the process of implementation (distribution of the memorandum had occurred) before suit was brought.

114. The term after-the-fact refers not to the necessity of an injury being sustained prior to suit but to the likelihood of its occurring before the surveillance can be enjoined if present practice is continued.

PART III: FOURTH AMENDMENT INTERESTS
IN POLITICAL FREEDOM

The Fourth Amendment, like the First Amendment, safeguards the individual from governmental abridgement of substantive rights. While the First Amendment establishes the expressional rights which insure the opportunity for political dissent, the Fourth Amendment sustains "the right of people to be secure in their persons, houses, papers, and effects, against unreasonable searches and seizures. . . ."[115] Unlike the First Amendment, the Fourth Amendment creates procedural requirements for governmental action.[116] In the context of political surveillance, the Fourth Amendment shields the dissident from *unreasonable searches and seizures*, of not only his personal property but also his actions[117] and statements.[118] More precisely, the Amendment affords the individual protection against the disclosure of information which he seeks to preserve as private.[119]

That which is regarded as private may also be divulged. The individual may elect to communicate information; it may be demanded of him by warrant; or, it may be surreptitiously "stolen" from him through unwarranted government surveillance. It is the latter case which engenders the Fourth Amendment interest in privacy and political freedom.

A. The Nature of the Fourth Amendment Interest

The Court, in *Katz* v. *United States*[120] took a significant step toward delineating the emergent Fourth Amendment interest in privacy. The *Katz* decision culminated a series of cases which together establish general principles for the applicability of the Fourth Amendment: that verbal communication is within the sweep of Fourth Amendment protection; that the presence or absence of a trespass no longer bears upon the reasonableness of a search; and that the principal concerns of the Fourth Amendment are not property rights but rather

---

115. U.S. CONST. amend. IV.

116. *Id.*

117. *See* Criminal Law: *Unreasonable Visual Observation Held to Violate Fourth Amendment,* 55 MINN. L. REV, 1255 (1971). This comment is based on State v. Bryant, 787 Minn. 205, 177 N.W. 2d 800 (1970).

118. Katz v. United States, 389 U.S. 347 (1967); Wong Sun v. United States, 371 U.S. 471 (1963).

119. *See* Warden v. Hayden, 387 U.S. 294, 304 (1967) in which the Court declared that "the principal object of the Fourth Amendment is the protection of privacy rather than property." *See also* United States v. White, 401 U.S. 745, 778 (1971) (Harlan, J., dissenting).

120. 389 U.S. 347 (1967).

the interests of privacy.[121] The privacy to which the Amendment addresses itself is not merely "the right to be let alone" for which Brandeis argued in *Olmstead v. United States*,[122] but the right to control the extent to which information about ourselves is communicated to others.[123]

Although the definition proposed by Brandeis is ambiguous, his objective was clearly defined:

> To protect that right every unjustifiable intrusion by the government upon the privacy of the individual . . . must be deemed a violation of the Fourth Amendment.[124]

The more recent definition, which focuses on the individual's control over the dissemination of information about himself is more amenable to this interpretation. The plain object of any governmental "search" is the collection of information about its subject. Information, therefore, is basic to both individual privacy and Fourth Amendment protection, and the Fourth Amendment interest in privacy implies individual control over such information.[125]

It may, however, be necessary from time to time to subordinate such individual control to a superior public interest, e.g., the maintenance of order, the prevention of crime and the security of the nation. The Fourth Amendment anticipates this need and protects the individual in this circumstance by requiring a showing of probable cause and reasonableness before a warrant will issue authorizing and proscribing the "search." Mr. Justice Harlan, dissenting in *United States v. White*, has concluded that any "official investigatory action that impinges on privacy must typically, in order to be constitutionally permissible, be subjected to the warrant requirements."[126] If this thesis is accepted, it follows that the warrant is a prerequisite to *any* surveillance activity of the government. Mr. Justice Jackson, in his opinion for the Court in *Johnson v. United States*,[127] clearly described the purpose and the importance of the warrant requirement:

---

121. *See* United States v. White, 401 U.S. 745, 768 (1971) (Harlan, J., dissenting). Harlan's dissent traces the development of Fourth Amendment law and considers the values which the Amendment seeks to protect.

122. 277 U.S. 438, 471 (1928) (Brandeis, J., dissenting).

123. *See* WESTIN, PRIVACY AND FREEDOM 7 (1st ed. 1967). *See also* Fried, *Privacy*, 77 YALE L.J. 475, 482 (1968). See note 59 *supra*.

124. Olmstead v. United States, 277 U.S. 438, 478-79 (1928).

125. *See* Hufstedler, note 54 *supra* at 550-54; Comment, *Privacy and Political Freedom: Application of the Fourth Amendment to "National Security" Investigations*, 17 U.C.L.A. L. REV. 1205, 1208-10 (1970); Bergstrom, *The Applicability of the "New" Fourth Amendment to Investigations by Secret Agents: A Proposed Delineation of the Emerging Fourth Amendment Rights to Privacy*, 45 WASH. L. REV. 785, 791 (1970) [hereinafter Bergstrom].

126. 401 U.S. 745, 781 (1971) (Harlan, J., dissenting).

127. 333 U.S. 10 (1948).

The point of the Fourth Amendment, which often is not grasped by zealous officers, is not that it denies law enforcement the support of the usual inferences which reasonable men draw from evidence. Its protection consists in requiring that those inferences be drawn by a neutral and detached magistrate instead of being judged by the officer engaged in the often competitive enterprise of ferreting out crime. . . . The right of the officers to thrust themselves into a home is . . . a grave concern, not only to the individual but to a society which chooses to dwell in reasonable security and freedom from surveillance. When the right of privacy must reasonably yield to the right of search is, as a rule, to be decided by a judicial officer, not by policeman or government enforcement agent.[128]

Recently, in *Camara v. Municipal Court,*[129] the Court brought administrative searches within the scope of the Fourth Amendment, emphasizing,

. . . the desirability of establishing in advance those circumstances that justified the intrusion into a home and submitting them for review to an independent assessor. . . .[130]

The primary concern of the Court was that administrative searches involved a governmental invasion of privacy, and that it was "against the possible arbitrariness of invasion that the Fourth Amendment with its warrant machinery was meant to guard."[131]

The procedural prerequisites specified in the Fourth Amendment[132] have been further clarified in recent holdings such as *Chimel v. California,*[133] in which the Court emphasized the importance of an independent predetermination of the need for the desired information by a neutral magistrate to fulfill the "reasonableness" requirement of the Fourth Amendment.[134] This requirement has been extended further in *Terry v. Ohio*[135] and *Davis v. Mississippi*[136] which proscribe the "incident-to-arrest" exception to the warrant requirement. In

---

128. *Id.* at 13-14.
129. 387 U.S. 523 (1967).
130. United States v. White, 401 U.S. 745, 781 (1971) (Harlan J., dissenting). *See* Camara v. Municipal Court, 387 U.S. 523, 528-29, 532-37 (1967).
131. 401 U.S. at 782 (Harlan, J., dissenting). *See* Camara v. Municipal Court, 387 U.S. at 539.
132. See note 53 *supra. See also* Katz v. United States, 389 U.S. 347, 356-57 (1967).
133. 395 U.S. 752 (1969).
134. 395 U.S. at 7.
135. 392 U.S. at 1 (1968).
136. 394 U.S. 721 (1969).

Terry, the Court held that "any restraint of the person, however brief and however labeled, was subject to a reasonableness examination,"[137] and announced that,

> ... the Fourth Amendment governs all intrusions by agents of the public upon personal security and makes the scope of the particular intrusion, in the light of all the exigencies of the case, a central element in the analysis of reasonableness.[138]

The foregoing discussion indicates that governmental surveillance of political dissidents may well be within the scope of the Fourth Amendment. Certainly, searches conducted without a warrant which do not fall within a clearly defined exception are invasions of privacy. They are also violations of the Fourth Amendment because they destroy the individual's ability to control the dissemination of information about himself. Surveillance, like a "search," seeks and obtains information at the expense of the individual's control over the dissemination of such information. If the information sought by surveillance were of the same kind sought by the typical search, the surveillance would clearly be within the reach of the Fourth Amendment and warrantless surveillance would therefore be prohibited.

Information acquired by police surveillance of political dissidents, however, often differs from that sought by the typical government search[139] because it may be partially or wholly public, *i.e.*, it may have been communicated by the individual to a non-specific audience. The

---

137. 392 U.S. at 19.

138. *Id.* at 18 n. 15. *See also* Davis v. Mississippi, 394 U.S. 721, 727 (1969).

139. Much of the information gathered by police intelligence units is of a quasi-public nature which in large part has become known via the news media. *See* Franklin, *Federal Computers Amass Files on Suspect Citizens*, N.Y. Times 1, Col. 1 (June 27, 1970); L.A. Times 16, Sec. A, Col. 1 (April 19, 1970). Such information, to the extent that it is gathered by newsmen, is governed by Time, Inc. v. Hill, 385 U.S. 374 (1967). *See* Comment, *Privacy, Defamation, and the First Amendment: The Implications of Time, Inc. v. Hill*, 67 COLUM. L. REV. 926 (1967). Gathering of information by government employees for the purpose of creating a dossier to monitor individuals poses the threshold problem of whether such information can lawfully be gathered, and if so, to what uses it may be put. If the individual intended its dissemination, the information may be used for any purpose which does not impinge upon First Amendment rights (*i.e.* create a chilling effect). Where the individual has not intended the information to become public his privacy is immediately at stake, and although the newsman can make public newsworthy information with virtual impunity, it is questionable whether the government can further capitalize upon it. *See* Katz v. United States, 389 U.S. 347, 351-52 (1967) in which a plurality stated:

> What a person knowingly exposes to the public, even in his own house or office, is not a subject of the fourth amendment protection. . . . But what he seeks to preserve as private, even in an area accessible to the public, may be constitutionally protected.

private or public quality of information should be a factor in determining the applicability of the Fourth Amendment to government surveillance-searches. Other factors should also be considered: the reason, mode and extent of the surveillance; the use(s) to which the information obtained is to be put; and the effect of the surveillance on the subject.[140]

Fourth Amendment warrant procedure would mean prior judicial inquiry into the "probable cause" which prompted the decision to conduct surveillance and would limit the practice of unilateral decision-making. It would screen all requests to conduct surveillance by balancing the need for the surveillance against the invasion of privacy the surveillance entails and would drastically reduce the instances of indiscriminate and unnecessary surveillance and surveillance used as harassment. As judicial monitoring of surveillance was extended, the individual would gradually be afforded the opportunity to exercise lawfully his First Amendment rights with relative impunity unless the application for a warrant became a perfunctory affair. This latter circumstance is admittedly a possibility, but in *Stanford* v. *Texas*, the Court held that the,

> ... constitutional requirement that warrants must particularly describe the things to be seized is to be accorded the most *scrupulous exactitude* when the things are books and the basis of their seizure is the ideas which they contain[141] (emphasis added).

This standard of "scrupulous exactitude" could arguably apply equally to warrants authorizing the surveillance-search or seizure of any expression, written or otherwise produced and permitted by the First

---

Justice Harlan, concurring (at 361), stated that there must be an "actual (subjective) expectation of privacy and ... be one that society is prepared to recognize as reasonable." Harlan elaborated upon this view in his dissent in United States v. White, 401 U.S. 745, 786 (1971):

> The critical question, therefore, is whether under our system of government, as reflected in the Constitution, we should impose on our citizens the risks of the [government] listener or observer without at least the protection of a warrant requirement.

The information that individuals seek "to preserve as private" seems clearly beyond reach of the government without a warrant. *See* Katz v. United States, 389 U.S. 347, 351-52 (1967); Bergstrom, note 125 *supra* at 790.

140. *See* Appendix to Petitioner's Brief for Certiorari, Tatum v. Laird, 444 F. 2d 947 (D.C. Cir. 1971), *cert. granted,* No. F1-288 (1971), reprinted in 4 COLUM. HUMAN RIGHTS L. REV. (Winter, 1972). The appendix documents socio-psychological effects of surveillance.

141. 379 U.S. 476 (1965).

Amendment, such as political dissent. The warrant would then prescribe the constitutional limits of the search and would necessarily have been drawn to prevent infringements upon the rights and values secured by the First and Fifth Amendments.

B. Political Surveillance and Informational Privacy

If gathering information[142] from or about a subject is the proper objective of a surveillance-search and seizure, it follows that the warrant requirements of "reasonableness" and "probable cause" would apply in every instance of surveillance of political dissidents.[143] These procedural requirements would, in turn, eliminate unilateral decisions to conduct surveillance and would require each decision to be made according to the standard of reasonableness.

To apply the Fourth Amendment to the surveillance of political dissidents is to force a consideration of the need asserted by the government by a neutral magistrate. The standards by which the sufficiency of the showings of the government are measured are critical—they must be flexible enough to permit the warrant to issue only when necessary and yet afford protection in all other circumstances. Standards developed in *Camara*, *Terry*, *Chimel* and *Davis* utilize a balancing test which weighs the need to search against the seriousness of the resulting invasion of privacy, emphasizing reasonableness of the search (means as well as objective) over the probable cause requirement.[144] The test is extremely flexible. The relative balance between privacy and the need to search or conduct surveillance may be determined after considering such factors as the intimacy of the information sought, the gravity of the suspected criminal behavior or the likelihood of infringement upon First Amendment rights.[145]

The privacy against which a need to search is balanced is that which permits the individual to control the dissemination of information about himself. Court construction of a test which determines whether or not the government can intrude upon individual lives

---

142. *See* note 139, *supra*

143. The primary exceptions to the Fourth Amendment warrant requirement are searches and seizures incident to a lawful arrest, Chimel v. California, 395 U.S. 752 (1969); by knowing consent, Bumper v. North Carolina, 391 U.S. 543 (1968); in hot pursuit, Warden v. Hayden, 387 U.S. 294 (1967); upon abandonment, Massachusetts v. Painter, 389 U.S. 560 (1968); with custodial perogative, Harris v. United States, 390 U.S. 234 (1968) and Chambers v. Maroney, 399 U.S. 42 (1970); and by necessity with probable cause, Carroll v. United States, 267 U.S. 132 (1925).

144. *See* United States v. White, 401 U.S. 745, 784 (1971) (Harlan, J., dissenting). *See also* Hufstedler, note 54 *supra* at 562.

145. Balance as used here does not imply weighing the government's need to search against First Amendment rights but against the individual privacy involved.

implicitly recognizes the viability of this right to control information about oneself and makes possible the application of the Fourth Amendment to *any* government action which seeks information from or about an individual.[146]

This rationale in no way forecloses surveillance of any kind to the government. It merely assures that the government can justify its action. In the context of political dissent where First Amendment rights are involved, it is of paramount importance that the government make all efforts to refrain from infringing upon the rights of speech and association. The Fourth Amendment requirement that the government demonstrate its need to search provides an opportunity for the government to meet the "nexus" requirements of the First Amendment chill doctrine and for the prior determination of the constitutionality of the statute's application or its mode of implementation. Such prior determination could arguably be instrumental in maintaining the balance between the right to dissent and the need for order by defining the legal parameters of government action before the fact. In addition, the prior determination to the grounds for the issuance or denial of a warrant would be subject to attack in a claim for relief from the warrant.

There are of course many kinds of surveillance and any argument that the warrant requirement should attach to some forms and not to others is to argue the "shape of the table" and to ignore the substantive rights which the requirement is designed to protect. Title III of the *Omnibus Crime Control and Safe Streets Act* of 1968,[147] for example, expressly excludes secret agents equipped with mechanical recording or transmitting devices from the probable cause and prior judicial authorization requirements for electronic surveillance. This exception seems unwarranted in view of the fact that the object of the "search" is information regardless of the methodology employed. It is counterproductive to permit the government to escape the warrant requirement of a showing of reasonableness by its means of surveillance when the object of its actions is the same. The means as well as the objective must be reasonable, and the various modes of surveillance must not be permitted to obfuscate the substantive values which the Fourth Amendment seeks to secure.[148]

---

146. It is the identity of interests which links privacy and the Fourth Amendment: if privacy can be said to be the right to control information about oneself and the Fourth Amendment protects people against unreasonable government intrusions, then, as against the government, the Fourth Amendment secures control over information about himself to the individual.

147. 18 U.S.C. § 2510 *et. seq.* (1964).

148. *See* Hufstedler, *supra* note 54, at 562.

The validity of the Title III exception has been questioned on the ground that *Katz* could be construed to impose the warrant requirement on the use of participant monitors.

> In *Katz* the court reasoned that the defendant has a right to rely upon the security of the phone booth against the "uninvited ear" of the recording device which was placed on top of the phone booth. The situation in *On Lee* v. *United States*, 343 U.S. 747 (1952), where the microphone hidden on a secret agent transmitted the conversation directly to a federal official outside the laundry, would seem to be a perfect example of the "uninvited ear" referred to in *Katz*. Since the enclosed phone booth excluded the public from hearing, only the bookmaker to whom Katz was talking was expected to receive Katz' communication. In *On Lee* the enclosed laundry excluded the public from hearing and confined the conversation to the defendant and Chin Poy.
> The only real difference between the cases is that in *On Lee* the electronic device was brought in by one of the parties while in *Katz* it was not. Yet this is irrelevant. In both cases an uninvited and unknown second object received information that was intended only for one person and was not "knowingly expose[d] to the public."
> The test of privacy as "control . . . over information about ourselves" is very similar to *Katz* in this regard. The participant monitor cannot waive the other's right to privacy by secretly changing the [expectations] of his privacy.[149]

Although this argument is severely limited in view of the recent decision in *United States v. White*[150] in which the use of a participant monitor was approved, it has considerable merit. The Court has held that notice after the fact in electronic surveillance is sufficient to meet reasonableness requirements,[151] thereby detracting from the argument that such surveillance should be immune from the warrant requirement. Moreover, because the surveillance activities of the government, including electronic surveillance by participant monitors, do not usually present exigencies which render prior judicial authorization unfeasible, the requirements should be insisted upon.[152] Where the government has validly determined its need to conduct surveillance or a search, it usually already has sufficient information to satisfy the warrant

---

149. *See* Bergstrom, *supra* note 125, at 808-09.
150. 401 U.S. 745 (1971).
151. *See* Katz v. United States, 389 U.S. 347, 355n.16 (1967).
152. *See* Bergstrom, *supra* note 125, at 813-14.

requirements, including the name or identity of the suspect, the suspected criminal conduct, the place where the search will occur, the duration, the nature of the information sought, and the kind of surveillance to be authorized.[153] Indeed, if such information were not available, the surveillance-search would be exploratory, unreasonable *per se* and an unnecessary invasion of privacy. Moreover, "[e]ven a more specific search should be rejected if there is a very low probability of recovering much relevant information."[154]

The implementation of this analysis could be effected if

the short, but significant, step [of identifying] the right of privacy as the right to preserve the autonomy of one's personality against unreasonable government intrusions [were taken].[155]

Following this course, any governmental surveillance designed to discover and collect information about a person would be a "search" and the reasonableness thereof would depend on the balance established between the need to search (the public interest) and the invasion of privacy the search would entail. In referring to this balancing process, Judge Shirley M. Hufstedler wrote:

[T]he weight is on the side of the private right unless there is *strong justification* if favor of the government action, and the government has chosen a *reasonable means* for vindicating its overriding interest. When governmental action consists of protecting the constitutional rights of one group of private citizens against the competing interest of privacy to others of its citizens, the societal interests of each are similarly weighed against the other, except that the scale is not initially tipped as it is when the interests that are opposed are fundamental private rights and the general public interest.[156] (emphasis added).

Mr. Justice Brandeis, dissenting in *Olmstead v. United States,*[157] articulated this view and urged its implementation:

---

153. *See* Omnibus Crime Control and Safe Streets Act of 1968 § 802, 18 U.S.C. § 2510 *et. seq.*

154. *See* Bergstrom, *supra* note 125.

155. *See* Hufstedler, *supra* note 54, at 559. The Court in *Katz* missed the opportunity to establish this right, see Katz v. United States, 389 U.S. 347, 350 (1967).

156. Hufstedler *supra* note 54, at 562.

157. 277 U.S. 438 (1928).

> The makers of our constitution recognized the significance of man's spiritual nature, of his feelings and of his intellect. They knew that only a part of the pain, pleasure and satisfactions of life are to be found in material things. They sought to protect Americans in their . . . sensations. They conferred, as against the Government, the right to be let alone—the most comprehensive of rights and the right most valued by civilized men. To protect that right, every unjustifiable intrusion by the government upon the privacy of the individual, whatever the means employed, must be deemed a violation of the Fourth Amendment. And the use, as evidence in a criminal proceeding, of facts ascertained by such intrusion must be deemed a violation of the Fifth.[158]

Neither the Brandeis view nor the instant analysis has been given full recognition in the courts. Judge Hufstedler argues that one of the more significant reasons for this failure is the tendency of the Court to employ the Fourth Amendment strictly as a rule of criminal law.[159] The effect of this approach is to deprive the Fourth Amendment of the full and pervasive reach of Constitutional authority and severely undercut the use of the privacy analysis, because it is seldom, if ever, employed in the criminal context. The time to give full recognition to the scope of the Fourth Amendment is well overdue.

C. A "New" Constitutional Profile of Privacy

Privacy has long been a vague and imprecise concept. It has been inferred from individual amendments,[160] from grouped amendments,[161] and even from the entire Bill of Rights,[162] but it has never been accorded the status of a specifically defined constitutional right. It is submitted that this has resulted directly from the Court's reluctance to read the Fourth Amendment in a civil rather than a criminal context.

The most visable use of the Amendment has been in criminal cases in which the exclusionary rule has been invoked to suppress illegally obtained evidence and to deter police from impinging upon the substantive rights afforded by the Amendment. But the exclusionary rule is

---

158. *Id.* at 478-79.

159. *See* Hufstedler, *supra* note 54, at 555.

160. *See, e.g.,* Stanley v. Georgia, 394 U.S. 557 (1970) and Watkins v. United States, 354 U.S. 178 (1957) (First Amendment).

161. *See, e.g.,* Boyd v. United States, 116 U.S. 616 (1886) (First and Fourth Amendments).

162. *See, e.g.,* Griswold v. Connecticut, 381 U.S. 479 (1965).

"not a defining part of the Amendment; rather, it is only one of the many possible ways to enforce its more generally applicable guarantees."[163] Nevertheless, the rule's effect has become synonomous with that of the Amendment, and the "message most widely received is that the Amendment is a shield for the guilty."[164] The prevalence of this view is understandable since the "visible beneficiaries" of the rule are those who have submitted to searches and seizures which have "yielded evidence of crime."[165] "People subjected to illegal searches that turn up nothing incriminating do not appear in the criminal process,"[166] and illegal searches do not "surface in . . . civil proceeding[s] because legislatures and courts have not created effective legal remedies."[167] This view is articulated by Judge Hufstedler as follows:

> A vivid illustration of the product of hostility to the exclusionary rules is the plurality opinion in *United States* v. *White*, 401 U.S. 745 (1971). . . . In reaching [its] conclusion [that there is no constitutional distinction between an informant's verbally reporting a conversation that he has had with a person suspected of a crime and his secretly recording and simultaneously transmitting every word of the conversation to third persons] the opinion emphasized that "one contemplating illegal activities must realize and risk that his companions may be reporting to the police" (at 752) and that a wrongdoer must be held to realize and to assume the risk that his companion may choose electronic means for his police reporting.[168]

The risk contemplated by the Court ignores the difference between human and non-human mediums of information transfer. No cognizance is taken of the fact that the speaker has completely lost control over the communication of information concerning himself because he has no knowledge of the identity or number of his auditors. Judge Hufstedler has drawn the following conclusions:

> Had the police officer in *White* physically secreted himself in White's house to eavesdrop upon his converstion with the

---

163. Hufstedler, *supra* note 54, at 555.
164. *Id.*
165. *Id.*
166. *Id.*
167. *Id.*
168. *Id.* at 555-56.

informer, the evidence thus acquired would have been in stark violation of the Fourth Amendment, even if the informant had expressly chosen that method of "reporting." To say that there is no violation of the Amendment because the intrusion was electronic is to resurrect Taft's *Olmstead* and to bury *Katz*. . . .

The implications of the plurality opinion are far more devastating than its apparent holding. The opinion raises the critical question: Must one who is not contemplating illegal activities likewise realize and likewise risk that his companions are informers, monitoring and transmitting his conversation to the army, to the welfare office, or to some other governmental agency bent on dossier collection?[169]

In the context of lawful political dissent, the question raised by Judge Hufstedler becomes very meaningful, particularly when one considers the present police practice of initiating surveillance unilaterally. Where unnecessary illegal violations of privacy occur, there is no remedy. The exclusionary rule merely prevents the submission of evidence illegally obtained; it does nothing for the individual engaged in lawful conduct who has had his privacy invaded on spurious grounds. One can only suppose that such would not be the case if the Court had earlier developed the Fourth Amendment in a civil as well as a criminal context.

The exclusionary rule has been subjected to severe criticism of late, and is in danger of being limited or overruled. In *Bivens* v. *Six Unknown Named Agents of Federal Bureau of Narcotics*,[170] the court held that one who has been subjected to an unreasonable search and seizure by federal officers can assert a claim for money damages upon

---

169. *Id.* at 556.

170. 403 U.S. 388 (1971). The exclusionary rule was developed to suppress evidence seized in violation of the Fourth Amendment by federal officers to be used in federal prosecutions. Weeks v. United States, 232 U.S. 383 (1914). In Wolf v. Colorado, 338 U.S. 25 (1949), the Court made the Fourth Amendment requirements applicable to state evidence-gathering processes, but refused to compel the use of the exclusionary rule. This refusal was based on the assumption that alternative methods of meeting the Fourth Amendment requirements would be developed by the states themselves. 338 U.S. at 31. By 1961, the assumption of the Court had proven unfounded because the states had not developed satisfactory alternatives to the exclusionary rule. The result was Mapp v. Ohio; 367 U.S. 643 (1961) which enforced the use of the rule by the states. *See* Linkletter v. Walker, 381 U.S. 618, 637 (1965).

The rule has come under heavy criticism for its failure to accomplish its deisgnated purpose of preventing police lawlessness. *See* Oaks, *Studying the Exclusionary Rule in Search and Seizure*, 37 U. CHI. L. REV. 665, 672-736 (1970); Allen, *The Wolf Case: Search and Seizure, Federalism, and the Civil Liberties*, 45 ILL. L. REV. 1 (1950). *Cf.* Note, *Police Liability for Invasion of Privacy*, 16 CLEV.-MAR. L. REV. 428 (1967).

which relief may be granted.[171] The money damages sought and obtained in *Bivens* seem an appropriate remedy, especially in cases where innocent parties have suffered violations of their Fourth Amendment rights.[172] It is logical to assume, moreover, that if the warrant requirements of the Fourth Amendment were rigorously applied the incidence of such claims would be minimal.

If the approval of the right to claim money damages for Fourth Amendment violations stands, it will virtually assure the development of a recognizable federal right to privacy. Together with the exclusionary rule, this right will impel the application of the procedural requirements of the Fourth Amendment in order to reduce the incidence of suit and will necessitate the application for a warrant before any surveillance-search or seizure is undertaken by the government save in those instances of clearly defined exceptions.[173] Finally, the courts will be compelled to develop the reasonableness test and the federal concept of privacy, securely grounded in the Fourth Amendment.

PART IV: IMPLEMENTATION AND USE OF THE CONSTITUTIONAL SAFEGUARDS

The result of blending the emerging First Amendment doctrine and the Fourth Amendment privacy analysis is the security of the right to dissent. The warrant requirements would screen all decisions to conduct surveillance of dissidents, attach immediately upon such decisions, and require particularly strong showings of the need to search before authorizing surveillance in any context in which First Amendment rights are involved. The use of First Amendment chilling effect doctrine would serve to enjoin activities which, regardless of their authorization, impinged upon the rights of speech and association. Although the need which the government must show in applying for warrants to conduct political surveillance is higher where the First Amendment is involved, it is not impossible to secure a warrant; the government must give a full and detailed description of the precise

---

171. *See* Berch, *supra* note 55; N.Y. Times 19 col. 1 (Mar. 13, 1971).

172. *See* Berch, *supra* note 55, at n. 1; Hill, *Constitutional Remedies*, 69 COLUM. L. REV. 1109, 1149 (1969); McDiarmid, *Fourth Amendment Remedies: Money Damages to Right Prior Wrongs*, 2 COLUM. SURVEY OF HUMAN RIGHTS L. 1 (1969-70). *See generally* Katz, *The Jurisprudence of Remedies: Constitutional Legality and the Law of Torts in Bell v. Hood*, 117 U. PA. L. REV. 1 (1968); Developments in the Law—*Remedies Against the United States and Its Officials*, 70 HARV. L. REV. 827 (1957); N.Y. Times 19, col. 1 (Mar. 13, 1972).

173. See notes 164 and 143 *supra* for discussion of the exclusionary rule and the exceptions to the warrant requirement.

activities to be undertaken. In addition, these procedures offer the opportunity of legal remedy for abuses; under the Fourth Amendment, information gathered by unwarranted surveillance is subject to the exclusionary rule, if prosecution is to follow, or if none, then a claim for money damages.[174] With warranted surveillance, the sufficiency of the grounds for the improperly issued warrant may be challenged, and if successfully attacked, the exclusionary rule or the claim for money damages may be invoked.

Once government acts of surveillance infringe upon First Amendment rights, or the instrumentality for such infringement exists, the plaintiff can seek injunctive relief under the chilling effect doctrine. Such relief may be particular in that it applies to the plaintiff alone or it may be expanded to enjoin governmental acts affecting those similarly situated. The privacy grounded and made specific in the Fourth Amendment is supported and definitionally strengthened by the First Amendment and its "penumbra,"[175] and together the two amendments provide safeguards and relief before and after the fact of surveillance.

The primary obligation of the judiciary in implementing these doctrines is the development of the tests for their applicability. In First Amendment situations, the *nexus test* must be developed and refined. Under the Fourth Amendment, the *reasonableness* requirement, interpreted in terms of the need to conduct surveillance being weighed against the invasion of privacy entailed, should be developed by judicial decision. The judiciary should determine particularly what exceptions to the warrant requirement should continue to be permitted, under what circumstances a warrant will issue, and whether and when injunctive relief or money damages will be granted.

Although affirmative judicial action can revitalize constitutional recognition of the right to dissent, it remains for Congress to insure the necessary authority and to announce the appropriate policy. Chief Justice Burger, dissenting in *Bivens* v. *Six Unknown Named Agents of Federal Bureau of Narcotics*,[176] strongly argues for such legislative guidance in creating a claim for money damages for Fourth Amendment violations. He objects, not to the fact that the remedy be available, but to the Court fashioning it. Similarly, Mr. Justice Harlan,

---

174. *See generally* Berch, note 55, *supra*. Punitive damages are available under 42 U.S.C. § 1983 (1970) whether or not they are available under the state law. *See* Adickes v. S.H. Kress & Co., 398 U.S. 144 (1970); Basista v. Weir, 340 F.2d 74 (3d Cir. 1965).

175. *See* Stanley v. Georgia, 394 U.S. 557 (1969) and Griswold v. Connecticut, 381 U.S. 479 (1965).

176. 403 U.S. 388, 411 (1971).

dissenting in *White*, points to the clear need for the delineation of a Congressional policy toward government surveillance.[177]

Despite the fact that these requests for Congressional action arise from different situations and from different sides of the question, it indicates that a national policy on surveillance and privacy must be established. Issues of particular importance are: the immunity to suit of federal officers in violation of Fourth Amendment safeguards; access to court for those whose privacy is transgressed; the evaluation of Fourth Amendment rights for the purposes of awarding money damages; the imposition of punitive damages in instances of grossly negligent or willful intrusions upon privacy; and the creation of the due process rights for those about whom information has been gathered, stored and disseminated. The last point goes beyond the simple act of dissemination of information gained in surveillance to other law enforcement agencies. It bears on such questions as notice that information is on file or has been disseminated, access to such information to verify its accuracy, and the right to challenge the retention, use and further dissemination of such information.[178] And it is of particular importance to the individual subjected to surveillance but against whom no action is brought,[179] and to those falsely arrested or otherwise harmed by the data collection or dissemination.[180] Any action taken by Congress should address itself not only to present problems, but to those being spawned by new advances in law enforcement.[181] Most importantly, it should clearly invoke the warrant system in the civil context in order to restrict any unilateral decision to conduct surveillance to those areas specifically deemed exceptions.

---

177. 401 U.S. 745, 790-92 (1971). *See also* N.Y. Times 19 col. 1 (March 13, 1972).

178. *See Freedom of Information Act,* 5 U.S.C. § 552 (1967) for an example of the first hesitant steps toward giving citizens access to information gathered and held by the government.

179. *See generally* Morrow v. District of Columbia, 417 F. 2d 728 (D.C. Cir. 1969). *See also* Longton, *Maintenance and Dissemination of Records of Arrest Versus the Right to Privacy,* 17 WAYNE L. REV. 995 (1971).

180. *See, e.g.,* Menard v. Mitchell, 430 F. 2d 486 (D.C. Cir. 1970), *rev'd and remanded,* 328 F. Supp. 718 (1971).

181. *See, e.g.,* Goulden, *The Cops Hit the Jackpot,* THE NATION 520 (Nov. 23, 1970); The Institute for Defense Analysis, TASK FORCE REPORT: SCIENCE AND TECHNOLOGY 72 (1967).

POLICE USE OF
REMOTE CAMERA SYSTEMS
FOR SURVEILLANCE
OF PUBLIC STREETS

7

ROBERT R. BELAIR
and CHARLES D. BOCK*

In the late 1960's, a few urban police departments began experimenting with low light level, all weather, television cameras to conduct 24 hour surveillance of public streets.[1] What follows is an overview of the nature and extent of such camera surveillance, and an analysis of its Constitutional implications.

PART I: THE MT. VERNON EXPERIMENT[2]

Police in Mt. Vernon, New York own what is probably the most advanced and certainly the best publicized of the handful of operational camera surveillance systems.[3] The Law Enforcement Assistance Administration (LEAA), a division of the Department of Justice created by the Omnibus Crime Control and Safe Streets Act of

---

*Staff members, *Columbia Human Rights Law Review*.

1. Olean, N.Y. has the first operational remote controlled camera surveillance system in the U.S. The other sites are Mt. Vernon, N.Y., Hoboken, N.J., Saginaw, Mich. and San Jose, Calif, all of which have camera systems in various stages of operation or development. Police in Toronto, Canada may have been the first urban law enforcement agency to deploy closed circuit televison cameras in public places. Toronto Star 1 (July 25, 1968). For the purposes of this paper "public street" takes its obvious meaning. It is a public place and "traditionally public places refers to any regions in a community freely accessible to members of that community.,. . ." Goffman, BEHAVIOR IN PUBLIC PLACES 9 (1963).

2. Mt. Vernon, N.Y. is a Westchester County suburb of New York City with a population of approximately 80,000. It covers an area of four square miles and has a business district of five blocks.

3. For perhaps the best popular description of the Mt. Vernon system, *see* T.V. Guide (August 13, 1971). *See also* Time Magazine 46 (May 10, 1971); The Cleveland Press (April 20, 1971); Chicago Tribune (April 14, 1971); Buffalo Courier Express (March 28, 1971).

1968[4] has funded the Mt. Vernon project[5] and views the program as a prototype for future television surveillance systems.[6]

A description of Mt. Vernon's experiment borrows inevitably from the vocabulary of George Orwell's *1984*.[7] Mt. Vernon's two low light level television cameras[8] were installed in April of 1971 and are positioned one block apart on the city's major business street.[9] The camera system's light amplification ability enables the police to maintain 24 hour surveillance of even a poorly lit street.[10] Mounted conspicuously on utility poles, the cameras peer down on the street from their remotely controlled, motorized perches. The policeman operating the system at department headquarters a few blocks away uses a

---

4. 42 U.S.C. § § 3701, 3711-3795 LEAA's purpose is to improve America's criminal justice system by dispersing funds primarily in the form of block grants to state criminal justice planning agencies. The state planning agencies, in turn, distribute the money to local law enforcement agencies.

5. Under Contract No. C41670, the Office of Crime Control Planning (New York State's planning agency) has received $47,000 to fund the Mt. Vernon system for a one year period beginning in April of 1971.

6. Dr. Irving Guller, Professor of Psychology at John Jay School of Criminal Justice (part of the New York City's University System) is evaluating the effectiveness of the Mt. Vernon System for the Office of Crime Control Planning and LEAA. Designs for future television surveillance systems await Dr. Guller's report to be published in the spring of 1972. Telephone interviews with Dr. Guller (Feb. 20, 22, 1972).

7. GEORGE ORWELL, *1984* (1949). For a description of *Oceania's* television surveillance system, *see id.* at 6.

8. Low light level TV (LLLTV) camera systems have been used by the military since the early 1960's. LLLTV cameras are passive devices. They do not radiate or emit a beam such as in infra-red systems. As a result it is impossible to detect the fact that you are being observed by one of them. These cameras operate on a light amplification principle. Donald T. Heckel (Sylvania Electronic Systems) and Captain Michael T. Court (Mt. Vernon Police Dept.) *The Mt. Vernon Story: The World's First Police Operated LLLTV System* undated mimeo) at 1.

9. The cameras are on Fourth Street at the intersection of First and Second Street respectively. The street contains about 100 stores and small businesses. During the day the pedestrian and vehicular traffic is heavy. The police department describes the street as a "high business crime area." Interview with Lt. Nicholas Beianco, Director of the Bureau of Administration and Records. Mt. Vernon Police Dept., in Mt. Vernon, New York, Dec. 10, 1971, and Feb. 24, 1972.

10. The heart of the entire system is the day/night type camera. It is completely automatic after installation and adjusts its own gain so that the picture output looks the same in bright sunlight as it does at night. It can operate over a scene illumination range of 0.0001 (starlight) to 10,000 foot candles (bright sunlight). Heckel, *supra* note 8, at 5.

This night vision capability is the technological breakthrough chiefly responsible for moving the cameras from banks, apartment lobbies, industrial cities, etc., where they have long been a fixture and putting them on the streets. *See* WESTIN, PRIVACY AND FREEDOM 70-73 (1967) for a description of the early uses of closed circuit television.

Probably the largest public facility targeted system was recently installed by the Paramus, N.J. Police Dept. on the roof of Bamberger's Dept. Store in the Garden State Plaza shopping center. The camera scans the parking lot for 1500 feet in all directions transmitting pictures to two monitoring screens in an outdoor security room. The developer of the system, Michael B. Arnold of Televig. 1 Systems (Olean, N.Y.) said that the Paramus project was the first in the nation. The demonstration project was underwritten partially by the New Jersey State Law Enforcement Planning Agency. (The LEAA State Planning Agency for N.J.). Bergen Evening Record A-10 (Feb. 27, 1970).

12-button control panel and three monitors (the third monitor has a split screen and an instant replay capability) to rotate the cameras 355° in a horizontal plane and 120° in a vertical plane.[11] With this maneuverability the cameras have a combined effective surveillance range of more than one mile.[12] The police operator can manipulate the camera's telescopic lens to read a car license plate one-half mile away from the camera's location, or from the same distance, provide a close-up of a pedestrian's face.[13] With almost equal ease, the cameras can apparently photograph through a store or apartment window.[14] Each camera is encased in a steel housing and comes complete with windshield wipers, windshield sprayers, a ventilating fan and heaters.

Sylvania Electronic Systems engineers, developers of the Mt. Vernon system, are currently installing a video tape machine that will record for instant or delayed playback everything that transpires on camera. On replay, 24 surveillance hours can be monitored in 48 minutes. The tape can also be shown in slow motion.[15] The expense of the magnetic tapes— roughly $60.00 per 24 hour recording period —will preclude their permanent retention. After from 15 to 30 days of storage, Mt. Vernon police expect to erase and reuse a tape on which no criminal activity is recorded.[16]

For at least four reasons, Mt. Vernon's video tape cameras widen the scope of such surveillance: Activities that initially go unnoticed by human monitors can later be reviewed; events that are of no ostensible police interest when they occur may become important days or weeks later; the opportunity for instant replay may improve police decision making; and finally, a video tape of a criminal act is normally admissible in court.[17]

---

11. The cameras are connected to the police station by coaxial cable and telephone wires strung through the city's sewer system. Heckel, *supra* note 8, at 2.

12. T.V. GUIDE, *supra* note 3. Lt. Beianco, *supra* note 9, suggests that one mile translates to about six Mt. Vernon city blocks.

13. Interview with Dr. Irving Guller, *supra* note 6.

14. In an upcoming network documentary on the Mt. Vernon surveillance system entitled *The Fear Killers*, and narrated by ex-astronaut John Glenn, the police described their distinguished guest's surprise when, during a demonstration, the camera strayed inside a street front restaurant and provided the viewers a crystal clear close-up of an unknown patron's sandwich. Interview with Lt. Beianco *supra* note 9. Bernard Cohen, a writer for the New York office of the Associated Press reported that during a demonstration of the system the camera's ability to look inside apartment windows was left in doubt. Interview with Bernard Cohen, in New York City (Feb. 8, 1972).

Dr. Irving Guller maintains that the angulation of the cameras makes it impossible to peep in the street front windows of apartments on the second story or higher. Guller *supra* note 6.

15. Interview with Lt. Beianco *supra* note 9.

16. *Id.*

17. *See* note 275, *infra.*

The Impact of Camera Surveillance on Crime. According to Mt. Vernon and LEAA officials crime deterrence is the primary purpose of remote controlled camera surveillance of public streets.[18] Detection and apprehension of criminal suspects is a secondary goal. LEAA and its think tank, the National Institute of Law Enforcement advocate both the deterrence and the apprehension models of camera surveillance systems. Covert mobile camera systems that temporarily saturate suspected crime areas and are particularly geared to criminal detection and apprehension have been designed and funded.[19] However, conspicuously placed, permanently positioned, remote controlled, 24 hour cameras surveillance units may have an impact that both poses a new element in the law enforcement equation and provides the subject matter of this article.

Initial analysis of the crime pattern in Mount Vernon suggests that the camera system has been effective in combating street crimes. During the non-surveillance period, April through November of 1970, 99 incidents of street crime were reported in the camera surveillance area. From April to November 1971 with the cameras in place, only 49 incidents were reported.[20] An evaluation of the Mt. Vernon system commissioned by LEAA and the New York State office of Crime Control Planning and authored by Dr. Irving Guller, Professor at John Jay School of Criminal Justice, will conclude that during the experiment's one year period crime in the camera surveillance area was reduced by slightly better than 50%.[21]

Interestingly, despite the decrease in the number of crimes reported during 1971, the number of arrests in the surveillance area remained constant. This statistic suggests that the prospect of official surveillance contributed as much to the cop's on the beat enthusiasm as it did to the criminal's reticence.

Only one other surveillance system comparable to Mt. Vernon's has been tested. In Olean, N.Y., five conventional closed circuit tele-

---

18. Interview with Dr. Guller, *supra* note 6. *See also* statement by Douglas Lipton then Deputy Director of the Westchester Regional Crime Control Planning Board, Mt. Vernon Daily Argus 1 (April 9, 1971). An executive of Sylvania, which installed the system, and Mt. Vernon Police agreed: "The primary purpose of this system is to act as a crime deterrent." Sunday News 1 § 2 (Apr. 11, 1971). While it is quite true that no attempt is made to hide the cameras an impromptu survey taken by the authors suggests that a sizable minority of the street's population is somehow unaware that two 29 pound sets of electronic eyes clearly visible 22 feet above their heads are watching them.

19. *See* note 43, 44 *infra*.

20. Interview with Lt. Beianco, *supra* note 9.

21. Interview with Dr. Guller, *supra* note 6. [For convenience, reference to the LEAA evaluation will hereinafter be cited as the Guller Report.] During the first 10 weeks after the system was operational, crime prevention appetites were whetted by a crime decrease in the camera surveillance area of 71%. T.V. GUIDE *supra* note 3.

vision cameras patroled that city's three block business district. After one year of operation (1968-1969) the project was discontinued in part because officials felt that the small upstate community had too little street crime to justify the costs of intensive surveillance.[22]

Evidence provided by the Mt. Vernon surveillance system has not as yet contributed to a conviction at trial. In nearly a year of operation the police have witnessed only three attempted robberies via the monitors. In all of these cases the individual was apprehended and upon learning of his *television appearance* promptly pleaded guilty.[23] One Mt. Vernon police official explained that when a suspect learns that his activity was observed by the camera, "it's like catching the guy red-handed."[24]

The Increasing Use of Camera Surveillance Systems. The impending success of the Mt. Vernon surveillance project may dispose of three issues previously thought fatal to the operation of large scale visual surveillance systems--underdeveloped technology, excessive cost and unfavorable public opinion. Officials expect to conclude that the Mt. Vernon system has proven technologically capable of providing daytime and nighttime, all weather, close-up and wide angle street surveillance with remarkably clear picture resolution.[25] Sylvania Electronic System's engineers are also confident that the system is now sufficiently *debugged* to operate reliably.[26]

The second lesson Mt. Vernon teaches is that the cost of establishing and maintaining a 24-hour remote-controlled visual surveil-

---

22. N.Y. Times 58, col. 4 (April 11, 1971) *See also Report by the Committee on Telecommunications of the National Academy of Engineering to the Department of Housing and Urban Development Communication Technology for Urban Development* 127 (June 1971). Olean police officials felt that the camera system was not entirely effective. Because the cameras did not have a low light level capacity, the quality of the monitor's picture declined markedly at night. The system's zoom lens ability was also limited.

During the one year experiment no illegal activities were photographed by the cameras. Indeed one of the more exciting uses of the surveillance system occurred when two youths were spotted entering the local bank after business hours. An investigating officer dispatched by a worried camera observer found a bank officer chatting with his son and a companion. Telephone interview with Michael Luty, Chief of the Olean Police Dept., Mar. 15, 1972.

23. Interview with Lt. Beianco *supra* note 9.

24. *Id.* In Santa Barbara, California, the police used cameras to record interrogations of drunken drivers. After seeing the film the next morning the drivers invariably pleaded guilty.

25. Interview with Dr. Guller, *supra* note 6. As late as spring of 1971 the National Academy of Engineering expressed concern that a camera could not be developed that "at night when the illumination is provided by discrete light sources, namely street lamps, and where moving vehicles, street signs, traffic lights, etc. introduce highly concentrated bright light spots in the picture, the camera (will) maintain full resolution and visibility in the surrounding dark areas." *Report of the National Academy of Engineering, supra* note 22 at 120. Indications are that Sylvania's LLLTV cameras meet this requirement.

26. Mt. Vernon officials suggest that system reliability was and to some extent continues to be an issue. At times unbeknownst to Mt. Vernon citizens' both cameras were "down." Repair is described as a "big deal" and "the major obstacle to expansion of the system." Interview with Dr. Guller, *supra* note 6, interview with Lt. Beianco, *supra* note 9.

lance system is probably not a deterrent for medium and large sized cities.[27] Mt. Vernon Police Captain Michael Court has stated publically that the City will break even on the $47,000 yearly cost of its system. "It would take three men to patrol that area over a 24 hour period. That's $30,000 a year so in about 19 months we break even."[28]

An important pilot study by the National Academy of Engineering[29] estimates that it would cost 1.5 million dollars a year for 140 cameras to provide 24 hour surveillance of the 58.5 miles of streets in New York City's 71st Precinct (Brooklyn). The same expenditure for foot patrolmen would provide visual surveillance for only 2% of the precinct's streets per minute. A comparable expenditure for squad cars would cover just over 10% of the precinct per minute.[30] Although expenditures of 1.5 million dollars or even $47,000 exceed the capacities of many police budgets, LEAA grants have proven to be an easily obtainable and prolific source of funds.[31]

Garlan Morse, President of the Sylvania Electric Products Division of General Telephone and Electronics Corporation, predicted to the New York Times in April of 1970 that law enforcement agencies will be spending 500 million a year on electronic gear by 1975. Morse credits LEAA pilot projects with starting the boom.[32]

If Mt. Vernon illustrates that the technology and the financing for 24-hour visual surveillance systems is available, it also suggests that public support for such systems, at least when confined to busi-

---

27. Olean, N.Y., with a population of 20,000 and little street crime, falls outside this category. The cost of the Olean system was fully underwritten for one year by a local cable T.V. concern. However, it must be noted that the Olean experiment preceded the lush days of the LEAA pork barrel. *See* Goulden, *Tooling up for Repression: The Cops Hit the Jackpot,* THE NATION 520 (Nov. 23, 1970).

28. TIME MAGAZINE 46 (May 10, 1971). Because the monitors and controls for the cameras are located in the Police Department's communications room, monitoring duties were shared by communications personnel. The Guller Report, *supra* note 6, will criticize Mt. Vernon's failure to provide full time operators. Consequently, the Department plans to use police cadets or the handicapped as operators in the near future. The *Report by the National Academy of Engineering, supra* note 22, at 126, recommends one operator per every four viewing screens.

29. *See supra* note 22.

30. *Report of the National Academy of Engineering, supra* note 22, at 127.

31. To date, every remote camer_ surveillance system proposal except the Olean, N.Y. system has had substantial LEAA funding. In Mt. Vernon the entire tab is picked up by LEAA and doubtless the Mt. Vernon venture will be characterized by some as the advent of 'Big Brother.' But to be objective about it, there is nothing the cameras will see—and perhaps see

One source estimates that LEAA spent 50 million dollars in 1970 on electronic crime fighting gear. *See* Goulden, *supra* note 27, at 527. A review by the authors of LEAA 1970 blocks grants indicates that at least 40 states have substantial electronic surveillance projects underway. Most are "criminal justice information systems" - computers.

32. *See* Goulden, *supra* note 27 at 527.

ness districts, is equally available.[33] One persuasive conclusion about Mt. Vernon is that businessmen and the local media combined to *sell* the camera system.[34] The Guller Report will recommend that future LEAA camera system appropriations contain a "public relations package." As well, Dr. Guller urges, that "every possible news medium should be solicited for its cooperation."[35] The Westchester Civil Liberties Union was the lone formal critic of the surveillance systems.[36]

Predictably, the response within the law enforcement community has been extremely enthusiastic.[37] Sylvania and Mt. Vernon representatives have received hundreds of requests for information from police forces around the country.[38]

The National Academy of Engineering has recommended to the Justice Department "that an experimental television surveillance system be designed, installed and tested, and that the demonstration project (involving an annual budget of 1.5 million dollars and 140 cameras) cover approximately two square miles within a typical urban area.[39]

---

33. The Guller Report, *supra* note 6, will conclude that Mt. Vernon's citizens raised very few civil liberties or privacy objections. Olean Police Chief Michael Luty also reported that local residents did not object to the surveillance system.

34. A poll of business men operating in the camera surveillance area found overwhelming enthusiasm for the cameras. Guller Report, *supra* note 6.

Sal Quaranta, Executive Director of the Mt. Vernon Chamber of Commerce expressed public enthusiasm for the experiment. "When breakins occur now the person will be seen either getting in or out of the store. I would also like to see a camera installed on Gramatan avenue." MT. VERNON DAILY ARGUS 1 (Apr. 9, 1971). The Mt. Vernon Daily Argus has editorially endorsed the system. *See* MT. VERNON DAILY ARGUS 1 (Apr. 9, 1971).

Another local paper concluded, "Surveillance is nearly always a controversial subject, and doubtless the Mt. Vernon venture will be characterized by some as the advent of 'Big Brother.' But to be objective about it, there is nothing the cameras will see—and perhaps see more sharply from a distance at night—that dozens of policemen would not also see if they were deployed in the area in saturated strength. Far from having anything to fear, the innocent person should feel a greater sense of security because of the added dimensions of invisible but very real protection." Mamaroneck Times, Mamaroneck, New York (Jan. 18, 1971).

35. Guller Report, *supra* note 6.

36. Jerry Gutman, Director of the Westchester CLU and a well respected civil liberties activist has publically characterized the system as an "outrageous invasion of privacy." T.V. GUIDE *supra* note 3

(Court action to enjoin the continued operation of the cameras has stalled for lack of suitable plaintiffs.)

37. "Closed Circuit television, now a crime-fighting, traffic decongestant reality in Mt. Vernon, may be pressed into service as 'electronic eyes' in parks, penitentiaries, business sections and other parts of Westchester if county and community officials have their way." Sunday News 1, § 2 (Apr. 11, 1971).

Many law enforcement officials regard the device, called low light level television, or LLLTV, as a potentially powerful tool in patrolling dark areas by remote control. Buffalo N.Y. Courier Express (Mar. 22, 1971). Dr. Guller predicts that after his report is made public "there'll be a clamor for the camera systems. The inhibitions that surround the camera's use will be dispelled." Guller, *supra* note 6.

38. Interview with Lt. Beianco, *supra* note 9.

39. *See Report of the National Academy of Engineering, supra* note 22 at 122.

In the wake of Mt. Vernon's experiment, police in several cities are implementing remote-controlled camera surveillance systems of various types or have at least received LEAA funding for future systems. For example, police in Hoboken, New Jersey are installing three closed circuit remote-controlled television cameras to observe a fourteen block downtown area.[40] San Jose, California[41] and Saginaw, Michigan[42] are working to implement Mt. Vernon style surveillance systems. A number of states and local communities are developing covert or mobile camera surveillance systems. Some communities have received LEAA funds for purchase of LLLTV equipment without detailing the kind of visual surveillance system they intend to establish.

For example, in 1970 a $150,000 LEAA award to the Delaware Agency to Prevent Crime created a 25 man unit to make surreptitious nighttime movies and video tapes. Some of the money will provide the police with decoy trucks and costumes,

> [the rental trucks] are to be used as the basis on which patrol is to be conducted under covert conditions: *e.g.*, uniforms of dry cleaners, salesmen, public utilities etc. make it possible to be in the neighborhood without being obvious.[43]

LEAA gave the Florida Inter-Agency Law Enforcement Planning Council a discretionary grant of $150,000 in June of 1970 to create a similar unit in Tampa, Florida.[44] Washington, D.C. will receive $50,000 from LEAA to implement the Mayor's Command Center Television System.[45] Indiana is buying four LLLTV cameras and fifteen video tape machines for use in that state's ten largest cites at

---

40. LEAA Grant #71-DF-528. $46,161 is budgeted for 1971.

41. Barkan, *Big Brother Won't Wait Until 1984*, GUARDIAN 2 (Feb. 2, 1972) (Robert Barkan was a senior engineer at Sylvania's Electronic Defense Laboratories. He is currently a member of the Pacific Studies Center).

42. LEAA grant #70-DF-416. $3,352 was appropriated for a one year pilot study.

43. *See* Goulden, *supra* note 27 at 529.

44. LEAA grant #70-DF-170. STAVS (Sensortized Transmitted Alarm Video System) envisions a selective enforcement unit of ten video tape equipped vehicles.

45. *District of Columbia Comprehensive Plan for 1971* (Annual criminal justice planning and appropriations documents are submitted by the State Planning Agency in each state. The title of the document and the SPA varies from state to state but for the sake of clarity all of the plans will be generically referred to as comprehensive plans.)

Apocalyptically, the proposal concludes: "Technological development, however, is rapidly creating both the capability and many detailed uses for the mass telecommunications media subsumed under the heading of a 'wired city'." (Part II, at 427).

a cost approaching $100,000.[46] Kansas,[47] Georgia,[48] Iowa,[49] Hawaii,[50] Texas,[51] New Hampshire,[52] Minnesota,[53] New Jersey,[54] and even Alaska[55] all expect to have video surveillance systems of varying degrees in the near future.

A related kind of observational surveillance, police helicopter patrols, have also experienced dramatic growth. Normally, helicopter surveillance systems rely on human eyesight, video tape and camera units and occasionally roof-top strobe light alarm systems or some combination of the above.[56]

---

46. *1971 Indiana Comprehensive Plan* at 122.

47. *1971 Kansas Comprehensive Plan* at 393. The state is spending $316,667 on video surveillance equipment.

48. *1971 Georgia Comprehensive Plan.* In part II-B at 7, the plan makes the following predictions:

> Modern Technology will be looked toward for other crime deterrent devices. Improved street lighting systems and electronic surveillance through closed circuit television cameras conspicuously positioned are two more ways that science has and will work with law enforcement.

49. *1971 Iowa Comprehensive Plan,* part I at 221. The state expects to buy six LLLTV cameras and monitors.

50. *1971 Hawaii Comprehensive Plan* at 226, 339. Hawaii will spend $75,000 for the purchase and installation of a closed circuit television building perimeter for their central police facility.

51. *Texas Comprehensive Plan,* part III at 39.

52. *1971 New Hampshire Comprehensive Plan,* part I at 257. Program Number 7-D-5: "$100,000 is to be spent on closed circuit television and sound control systems."

53. *1971 Minnesota Comprehensive Plan,* part I at 214.

54. *1971 New Jersey Comprehensive Plan,* at C40. Over the next five years New Jersey will spend almost 3 million dollars on electronic gear to make crime targets less inviting and vulnerable. "The project may include surveillance devices, such as closed-circuit television or portable television units . . . . "

55. *1971 Alaska Comprehensive Plan* at 320, 433. By 1975 the ten largest cities in the state will have "video surveillance systems of an automated nature to provide filmed coverage of high crime areas."

56. *1971 Alabama Comprehensive Plan* at C-129. A $280,000 program for helicopter observation patrols.

California has been the most energetic is pursuing funds for airborne observation—*1971 California Comprehensive Plan:*

> $181,934 for San Francisco's "Operation Skywatch," $98,286 for Kern County helicopter patrol, $96,766 for Ventura County's computer assisted helicopter patrol, Grant # 71-DF-491 will provide Riverside, Calif., with helicopters, Grant # 71-DF-611—a total of $465,000 appropriated for helicopters with "airborne portable video tape equipment and stabilized binoculars,"Grant # 70-DF-094 to fund a study by the California Council on Criminal Justice for demonstration and evaluation of closed circuit airborne television capabilities which has proven to be a great asset in recording and analyzing ground activities.

Atlanta, Georgia,is establishing a helicopter patrol. *1971 Georgia Comprehensive Plan,* part II at J-1. Chicago, Illinois, is also beginning helicopter ground observation. *1971 Illinois Comprehensive Plan,* part II at 59. Maryland plans a helicopter patrol. *1971 Maryland Com-*

Little prescience is required to observe that television surveillance systems may soon become a vital and accepted part of police hardware.[57] Given a warm public climate, and state-of-the-art technological improvements, the use of 24-hour camera surveillance systems could exceed even the ambitious proposal of the National Academy of Engineering.[58] The assertion has been made that remote camera systems of the Mt. Vernon type would be extremely effective in residential areas.[59] Officials at the National Institute of Law Enforcement posit that the technology is available to create a computerized video tape system that would search for and mark all places in a tape where programmed characteristics occurred.[60]

At the 1969 Carnahan Conference, one government official concluded:

There is a great unrestricted area of electronic surveillance and electronic counter-crime measures in which there needs to be expansion and further innovation.

Generally, no legal limitations on electronic surveillance of large public areas exist. The challenge is wide open.[61]

Any empirical analysis of existant and planned visual surveillance systems marches ineluctably toward one conclusion: police use of technology to conduct visual surveillance of public areas is rapidly coming of age.[62]

---

prehensive Plan at 826. Grant # 71-DF-969 will provide Seattle, Washington with helicopters for ground surveillance.

See Jelkens, *Some Legal Aspects of Aircraft Usage as an Aid to Law Enforcement, 3 Journal of California Law Enforcement* 128-142 (Jan., 1969).

57. *See* Barkan, note 41, *supra* at 3: "The current sensor and T.V. surveillance projects are smallscale but the combined interests of engineers, industry and government are pushing for rapid escalation, unimpeded by legal regulation."

58. *See generally Report of The National Academy of Engineering,* note 22, *supra.*

59. Dr. Guller suggests that if the public continues to fully accept camera surveillance there are no practical obstacles to their use in residential areas, particularly if a strobe light alarm were installed on each residence thereby obviating landscaping obstacles and the greater distances between houses. Interview with Dr. Guller, *supra* note 6.

60. Telephone interviews with officials at the National Institute of Law Enforcement (Unfortunately none of the officials spoke for personal attribution.)

61. *See* Barkan, note 41, *supra* at 3.

62. Surveillance technology of all varieties has undergone rapid advancement over the last decade. Warnings about this growth have been sounded from many sources. *See* Lopez v. United States, 373 U.S. 427 (1963) (Brennan, J., dissenting); Osborn v. United States, 385 U.S. 323 (1966) (Douglas, J., dissenting); PACKARD, THE NAKED SOCIETY (1964); M. BRENTON, THE PRIVACY INVADERS (1964); ROSENBERG, THE DEATH OF PRIVACY (1969); WESTIN, PRIVACY AND FREEDOM (1967); MILLER, THE ASSAULT ON PRIVACY (1971); *Hearings Before the Subcomm. on Constitutional Rights of the Senate Comm. on the Judiciary,* 92d Cong., 1st Sess. (1971); *Hearings on the Computer and Invasion of Privacy Before a Subcomm. of the House Comm. on Government Operations,* 89th Cong., 2d Sess. (1966). *See* Westin, note 10, *supra,* at 365-66, for a summary of this development:

The body of this note evaluates this kind of electronic visual surveillance in terms of its potential conflict with First and Fourth Amendment freedoms. Other constitutional provisions less forthright than the First Amendment and the Fourth Amendment in safeguarding the central freedoms of speech, behavior, association and personal security from government encroachment by surveillance will not be substantively discussed. This note concludes with a brief consideration of remote camera surveillance and the public policy alternatives it impels.

PART II. REMOTE CAMERA SURVEILLANCE AND THE FIRST AMENDMENT

On its face, the proposition that one feels inhibited by the spectre of being videotaped by the police is not to be contradicted. The behavorial consequences of police monitoring of public streets are, however, not readily ascertainable. The First Amendment protects many forms of communication and association, on public streets and other places, from both direct and indirect limitation by the state. It also shelters expression from government-induced inhibitions, which unnecessarily curtail free speech and association. If 24-hour remote camera surveillance of public streets creates cognizable inhibitions, a potential constitutional conflict is presented.

Governmental action which indirectly restrains speech is constitutionally less suspect, however, than regulation of the content of speech. Compelling state interests may constitutionally support government disclosure of information which deters expression, as long as such inquisition does not unnecessarily sweep away First Amendment guarantees.[63] In establishing these criteria (all to be discussed

---

A technological breakthrough in techniques of physical surveillance now makes it possible for government agents and private persons to penetrate the privacy of homes, offices, and vehicles; to survey individuals moving about in public places; and to monitor the basic channels of communication by telephone, telegraph, radio television and data line . . . . As of the 1960's the new surveillance technology is being used widely by government agencies of all types and at every level of government, as well as by private agents for a rapidly growing number of businesses, unions, private organizations, and individuals in every section of the United States. Increasingly permanent surveillance devices have been installed in facilities used by employees or the public . . . . Finally the scientific prospects for the next decade indicate a continuing increase in the range and versatility of the listening and watching devices, as well as the possibility of computer's processing of recordings to identify automatically the speakers on topics under surveillance. These advances will come just at the time when personal contacts, business affairs, and government operations are being channeled more and more into electronic systems such as data phone lines and computer communication.

63. *See* American Communications Association v. Douds, 319 U.S. 382 (1950).

below), courts have traditionally balanced the nature of the speech, the state interest served by its curtailment and the method used by the state to effectuate its purpose. When disclosure or compilation of information arguably conflicts with First Amendment rights, the relationship between its content and the government's objective in obtaining is crucial. The central problem for constitutional litigation, then, it is the technique the state chooses to serve its ends. It is in this light that our discussion of remote camera surveillance and the First Amendment begins.

A. Coercive Government Activity And Free Expression

As Circuit Judge Wilkey suggested in *Tatum v. Laird*,[64] First Amendment cases relevant to our inquiry involving the freedom of expression and association may fall into one of three categories:[65] (1) cases where some legal or criminal sanction was imposed or threatened to be imposed on persons who exercised their First Amendment rights;[66] (2) cases involving some element of government compulsion, either to testify regarding one's political ideas or beliefs, or to identify oneself in order to exercise First Amendment rights;[67] and (3) situations where the government threatens to publicize the names of alleged politically controversial persons for the purpose of inhibiting the exercise of their First Amendment rights.[68] Cases not falling clearly into one of the three categories, but also holding concrete and identifiable[69] government sanctions or directives unconstitutional because of their infringement upon First Amendment rights,

---

64. 444 F.2d 947 (D.C. Cir. 1971).

65. *Id.* at 953. Judge Wilkey's categories result from an analysis of the cases cited by plaintiff in that case. The categories are helpful for our purposes although their rigid contours need not be adhered to in an analysis of cases not cited in *Tatum.*

66. The court cited United States v. Robel, 389 U.S. 258 (1967) (criminal prosecution or loss of employment); Dombrowski v. Pfister, 380 U.S. 479 (1965) (threat of criminal prosecution); NAACP v. Button, 371 U.S. 415 (1963) (criminal prosecution and disbarment); National Student Association v. Hershey, 412 F.2d 1103 (D.C. Cir. 1969) (draft reclassification). *Id.* at 953 n.13.

67. Here the court cited Lamont v. Postmaster General, 381 U.S. 301 (1965) (Post Office compelled the affirmative act of requesting delivery of mail thought to be communist propaganda); Talley v. California, 362 U.S. 60 (1960) (requiring identification of the "speaker" on political handbills); NAACP v. Alabama, 357 U.S. 449 (1958) (requiring filing of membership lists by organization unpopular in its locale); Sweezy v. New Hampshire, 354 U.S. 234 (1957) and Watkins v. United States, 354 U.S. 178 (1957) (compelling testimony regarding beliefs and associational ties).

68. Hentoff v. Ichord, 318 F. Supp. 1175 (D.D.C. 1970). This is decidedly a less broad category than the two forementioned.

69. This does not imply that "indirect" government encroachment on First Amendment rights are not included. *See* United Mine Workers v. Illinois State Bar, 389 U.S. 217, 222(1967):

are legion.[70] The right to freely associate lies at the foundation of many of these decisions.[71] The injury in cases involving disclosure and loyalty oaths, for example, included harassment of unpopular groups,[72] loss of employment[73] and "a public stamp of disloyalty,"[74] penalties which clearly deter membership in controversial organizations.[75] In addition, loyalty oath requirements brought with them the threat of perjury[76] and discouragement of the free spirit that, for instance, "teaching requires."[77]

The First Amendment would, however, be a hollow promise if it left government free to destroy or erode its guarantees by indirect restraints so long as no law is passed that prohibits free speech . . . as such. We have therefore repeatedly held that laws which actually affect the exercise of these vital rights cannot be sustained merely because they were erected for the purpose of dealing with some evil within the state legislature's competence, or even because the laws do in fact provide a helpful means of dealing with such an evil.

Cf. Schneider v. State, 308 U.S. 147 (1939); Cantwell v. Connecticut, 310 U.S. 296 (1940); and Keyishian v. Board of Regents, 385 U.S. 589 (1967).

70. *See, e.g.,* cases only as far back as 1939. In that year, in *Schneider, note 69, supra,* a municipal ordinance enforcing the legitimate state purpose of keeping streets clean by forbidding distribution of printed matter was struck down.

A registration requirement imposed on a labor union organizer before making a speech was held unconstitutional in Thomas v. Collins, 323 U.S. 516 (1945). A tax ordinance requiring the furnishing of a list of organizational contributors was invalidated in Bates v. City of Little Rock, 361 U.S. 516 (1960). In Shelton v. Tucker, 364 U.S. 479 (1960), public employment for teachers was constitutionally protected from the precondition of disclosure of organizational ties by the applicant. In similar holdings, broad loyalty oath requirements as a condition of public employ have been resoundingly turned back. Cramp v. Board of Public Instruction, 368 U.S. 278 (1967), for example, involved a Florida statute requiring every employee of the state to swear in writing that he had never lent his "aid, support, advice, or counsel" to the Communist Party. Failure to take the oath would result in loss of employment. The Court found that the statute's vagueness was intolerable in view of the inhibiting effect it had on free speech (at 287). *In accord* Baggett v. Bullitt, 377 U.S. 360 (1964).

71. *See, e.g.,* Liveright v. Joint Committee of the General Assembly, 279 F. Supp. 205 (M.D. Tenn. 1968) (legislative committee's subpoena of civil rights organization's records).

72. Dombrowski v. Pfister, 380 U.S. 479 (1965). The Supreme Court voted that because of established bad faith harassment by the police which threatened immediate and irreparable injury, the Federal District Court was justified in enjoining threatened prosecution under a state criminal statute. Essential was the fact that plaintiff would not have an opportunity to raise his constitutional defense in time to avoid injury. *Cf.* Cameron v. Johnson, 390 U.S. 611 (1968) and Younger v. Harris, 401 U.S. 37, 48-49 (1971).

73. Shelton v. Tucker, 364 U.S. 479 (1960).

74. Sweezy v. New Hampshire, 354 U.S. 234 (1957).

75. The Supreme Court has recognized that "the threat of sanctions may deter . . . almost as potently as the actual application of sanctions." NAACP v. Button, 371 U.S. 415, 433 (1963). The "threat" of sanctions was held to discourage membership in Shelton v. Tucker, 364 U.S. 479 (1960); NAACP v. Alabama, 357 U.S. 449 (1958); and Gibson v. Florida Legislative Investigation Committee, 372 U.S. 539, 555-556 (1963).

76. *See* Elfbrandt v. Russell, 384 U.S. 11 (1966) and Keyishian v. Board of Regents, 385 U.S. 589 (1967).

77. *See* Keyishian v. Board of Regents, 385 U.S. 589 (1967) and Shelton v. Tucker, 364 U.S. 479 (1960).

In other cases, speech without organized association has been the basis for relief from overzealous state action,[78] *e.g., Talley v. California*,[79] where the court struck down an ordinance that made it a criminal offense to distribute handbills that did not identify the preparer, distributor or sponsor.

All of these cases involved to some degree, a "chilling effect"[80] resulting from sanctions on the exercise of First Amendment rights, while almost all involved vague or overbroad state regulation, investigation or other form of restraint.[81] An examination of these decisions reveals that the Supreme Court has been more sensitive to overbroad and vague state statutes[82] when First Amendment issues are raised. Statutes which carry the threat of prosecution, and are *vague* as to their prohibitions, have been found to place upon individuals the burden of restricting their conduct to that which is unquestionably safe. "Free speech may not be so inhibited."[83] Similarly, *overbroad* regulations which sweep away, unnecessarily, First Amendment rights which are fundamental in the constitutional system, are suspect before the scrutiny of the court.[84]

However, the mere establishment of threatened harm producing *chilled* expression or association does not appear automatically to

---

78. *See* Coates v. Cincinnati, 402 U.S. 611 (1971) in which a Cincinnati ordinance made it illegal for three or more persons to assemble on sidewalks and there conduct themselves in a manner annoying to persons passing by. Justice Stewart's majority opinion found the ordinance both unconstitutionally vague because it subjects the exercise of the right of assembly to an unascertainable standard and overbroad because it authorizes the punishment of constitutionally protected conduct. *Cf.* Gregory v. Chicago, 394 U.S. 111 (1969); Edwards v. South Carolina, 372 U.S. 229 (1963). *Compare* Cox v. Louisiana, 379 U.S. 536 (1965) *with* Adderley v. Florida, 385 U.S. 39 (1966).

79. 362 U.S. 60 (1960).

80. *See* Dombrowski v. Pfister, 380 U.S. 479 (1965).

81. *See* Keyishian v. Board of Regents, 385 U.S. 589 (1967) (lóyalty oath); Dombrowski v. Pfister, 380 U.S. 479 (1965) (statute defining subversive organization); NAACP v. Button, 357 U.S. 449 (1958) (overbroad "bar" statute).

82. In Dombrowski v. Pfister, 380 U.S. at 486, the Court commented that

Because of the sensitive nature of constitutionally protected expression, we have not required that all those subject to overbroad regulations risk prosecution to test their rights. For free expression—of transcendental value to all society and not merely to those exercising their rights—might be the loser.

83. Baggett v. Bullitt, 377 U.S. 360, 372 (1964).

84. *See* United States v. Robel, 389 U.S. 258 (1967). The court invalidated § 5 (a)(1)(D) of the Subversive Activities Control Act which presumptively excluded all Communist Party members from government employ regardless of the nature of the individual's purpose in being a member, or knowledge of the organization's specific goals. The Court cited NAACP v. Button, 357 U.S. at 438, Shelton v. Tucker, 364 U.S. at 488, and Aptheker v. Secretary of State, 378 U.S. 500, 512-13 (1964) for the proposition that "it has become axiomatic that precision of regulation must be the touchstone in areas so closely touching our most precious freedoms."

invalidate the state action.[85] Rather, the Supreme Court has almost always[86] spoken of the need for balancing[87] First Amendment rights and state interests.[88] The test applied to instances of *chilled* First Amendment rights thrusts upon the government the burden of establishing a compelling interest,[89] and a substantial connection between that interest and the burden imposed on the individual.[90]

B. Anderson v. Sills and Non-Coercive Police Information Gathering

Unfortunately, *chill* upon First Amendment rights resulting from disclosure of information has only been recognized by the Supreme

---

85. This seems valid despite recent flirtations with a doctrine of "absolutism," United States v. Robel, 389 U.S. 258, 268n.20 (1967). *See* discussion in Askin, *Police Dossiers and Emerging Principles of the First Amendment*, 22 STAN. L. REV. 196, 207-211 (1970); *Chilling Political Expression By Use of Police Intelligence Files: Anderson v. Sills*, 5 HARV. CIV. RIGHTS – CIV. LIB. L. REV. 79-80 (1970); Gunther, *Reflections on Robel*, 20 STAN. L. REV. 1140 (1968) for recent views on the vitality of the balancing doctrine.

86. United States v. Robel, 389 U.S. 258 (1967), at least on its face, would have to be counted as an exception.

87. *See* Barenblatt v. United States, 360 U.S. 109 (1959). *See also* Younger v. Harris, 401 U.S. 37 (1971) at 51:

> [T]he existence of a chilling effect, even in the area of First Amendment rights, has never been considered a sufficient basis, in and of itself, for prohibiting state action. Where a statute does not directly abridge free speech, but—while regulating a subject within the states' power—tends to have the incidental effect of inhibiting First Amendment rights, it is well settled that the statute can be upheld if the effect on speech is minor in relation to the need for control of the conduct and the lack of alternative means for doing so.

88. The debate over whether or not *Robel* marked a turning point towards the Justice Black "absolute" position, Konigsberg v. State Bar of California, 366 U.S. 36, 68-69 (1971) (Black, J., dissenting) and away from the balance test of Justices Frankfurter, Harlan, Vinson, American Communications Association v. Douds, 319 U.S. 382 (1950), if not made superfluous by Younger v. Harris, 401 U.S. 37 (1951), seems to be an academic one at best. Under the "absolute" theory a perfectly valid government interest which directly abridged speech would be invalidated in the face of the First Amendment's protection. It strains the imagination to conceive of a "perfectly valid" governmental interest which would require the direct abridgement of protected First Amendment activity. For example, if a valid governmental exercise is the direct squelching of crime, there is no protected right of expression; whereas, the right to send letters of protest to one's congressman is unqualified, and no direct government abridgement of that right is "valid." The long history of constitutional jurisprudence indicates that simultaneous findings of absolute validity of conflicting state and individual interests are mutually exclusive.

89. The doctrine that the state action is subject to "strict scrutiny" and that the state must demonstrate more than a "rational basis", *i.e.*, a "compelling interest", to justify its action when fundamental freedoms are curtailed is clearly explicated by the Supreme Court in Shapiro v. Thompson, 394 U.S. 618 (1969) (equal protection test for state infringement on the right to travel). First Amendment cases requiring the "compelling interest" test are reasonably clear and very numerous. *See* Justice Harlan's concurring opinion in Talley v. California, 362 U.S. 60, 66 (1960). *Compare* Schneider v. State, 308 U.S. 147, 161 (1939) *with* NAACP v. Alabama, 357 U.S. 449, 463-64 (1958), *and* Sweezy v. New Hampshire, 354 U.S. 234, 265 (1957), (concurring opinion).

90. *See* Watkins v. United States, 354 U.S. 178, 197-98 (1957).

Court in cases in or near Judge Wilkey's categories set out above. In the cases which raise issues closest to those presented by the use of remote cameras, the First Amendment has provided a legally cognizable right outweighing government interests only where concrete, identifiable sanctions have been used or threatened for the purpose of coercing action resulting in disclosure of information about individuals or groups.[91]

Lower courts, in *Anderson v. Sills* and *Tatum v. Laird*, on the other hand, have considered issues concerning the inhibition of free expression by governmental information gathering that does not coerce, threaten or restrict activity directly.[92] Unlike cases dealt with to date by the Supreme Court they present the question of whether or not mere knowledge of government surveillance (without coercion to testify, reveal membership lists, take a loyalty oath, refrain from protest activities in certain places[93] or identify oneself in order to "speak" or hold a job) curtails First Amendment freedoms. Moreover, they frame the issue of whether or not a government activity which *chills* without coercion, can be upheld as legitimate despite the

---

91. Talley v. California, 362 U.S. 60 (1960), is a prime example. The invalidated ordinance required the disclosure of a handbill author's identity in order to distribute the handbills. Although the Court leaned heavily on the importance of anonymity in the exercise of free speech, it did not say that if anonymity were lost to the individual through state action other than coercion or direct threat of sanction, such action would be invalidated. Remote cameras provide the latter fact situation.

92. *See* 106 N.J. Super. 545 (1969), *rev'd and remanded*, 56 N.J. 210, 265 A.2d 678 (1970) and 444 F.2d 947 (D.C. Cir. 1971) respectively. In *Tatum*, plaintiffs sought a declaratory judgment that the Army's surveillance of lawful civilian political activity was unconstitutional, for an injunction restraining similar future activities and a destruction of data already obtained. In Federal District Court defendant was granted a motion to dismiss on the grounds that plaintiff had failed to state a claim upon which relief could be granted. Circuit Judge Wilkey ruled that plaintiffs did indeed present a justiciable controversy, but remanded for further findings as to harm to the plaintiffs, the nature of the Army's surveillance and its relationship to the military's proper function. The Army has asked the Supreme Court to hear an appeal to the assumption of jurisdiction by the Circuit Court.

Judge Wilkey's decision does not deal with the merits (and therefore will not be treated outside of this footnote). It is interesting, however, that the court granted plaintiffs' standing for reason of their having sufficient adversary interest, but remanded for an ascertainment of the plaintiffs' injuries. This was deemed necessary although the plaintiffs alleged more than an inhibition of their right to "speak" controversially. Admittedly, the record before the court was not complete, but the remand remains indicative of the difficulties in such a case, even before a judge receptive to the plaintiffs' claims. Of further note was the emphasis by the court on the fact that the Army, by tradition nearly immune from judicial scrutiny, was the source of plaintiffs' *chill* rather than a "civilian investigative agency." *Cf.* Davis v. Ichord, 442 F.2d 1207 (D.C. Cir. 1970) and Holmes v. Church, 70 Civ. 5691 (S.D.N.Y. June 10, 1971).

93. *See* Edwards v. South Carolina, 372 U.S. 229 (1963); Cantwell v. Connecticut, 310 U.S. 296 (1940); Cox v. Louisiana, 379 U.S. 536 (1965).*See also* Adderly v. Florida, 385 U.S. 39 (1966).

psychological[94] inhibition or expression it creates.[95] In other words, these cases question whether the threshold of legitimacy for non-coercive government activity which inhibits expression will be as low as it has been for coercive state action, which the courts have been ready to label overbroad or vague when the First Amendment "squeeze" has been demonstrated.[96] Herein would appear to be the legal dilemma posed by extensive remote camera surveillance.

In *Anderson*, the Superior Court of New Jersey, in granting the plaintiff a summary judgment, held unconstitutional a directive (or memorandum) of the Attorney General to local officials requesting the compilation of extensive information concerning participants in rallies, protests and other protected events, the alleged purpose of which was the avoidance of potential civil disorder problems. In granting standing to the plaintiff civil rights organization, Judge Matthew noted a "marked relaxation of standards of justiciability where governmental action inhibits the exercise of First Amendment rights."[97] Although the standing question,[98] *per se*, is outside the scope of this paper, the court's position regarding standing is indicative of the approach it took toward the merits of the case.

The court moved from inhibition of expression by directly threatened sanctions,[99] or coerced identification as a condition of

---

94. *See* Askin, appendix to Tatum v. Laird, 444 F.2d 947 (D.C. Cir. 1971), *cert. granted*, No. 71-288 (1971) reprinted in 4 COLUM. HUMAN RIGHTS L. REV. (1972); GOFFMANN, BEHAVIOR IN PUBLIC PLACES; THE FREE PRESS OF GLANCE (1963); Miller, *Personal Privacy in the Computer Age: the Challenge of a New Technology in an Information−oriented Society*, 67 MICH. L. REV. 1089 (1969).

95. Government activities which presented a coerced threat to the exercise of First Amendment rights have been held illegitimate or not sufficiently compelling in their over-breadth or their vagueness, despite the general legitimacy of their underlying purpose. *See* United States v. Robel, 389 U.S. 258 (1967).

96. Not all coercive government action curtailing what might otherwise be included as First Amendment rights is unconstitutional. *See* O'Brien v. United States, 391 U.S. 367 (1968) (government prohibition of draft card burning); Kovacs v. Cooper, 336 U.S. 77 (1949) (prohibition of the use of soundtrucks on residential streets at night); Cox v. Louisiana, 379 U.S. 536 (1965) (license requirement for a parade on a public highway); Konigsberg v. State Bar of California, 366 U.S. 36 (1961) (Bar committee questions regarding prospective lawyer's membership in the Communist Party). *Cf.* Law Students Research Council v. Wadmond, 401 U.S. 154 (1971).

97. 106 N.J. Super. 545, 550 (1969). In reaching its decision, the court relied on Lamont v. Postmaster General, 381 U.S. 301 (1965); Dombrowski v. Pfister, 380 U.S. 479 (1965); and Straut v. Colissi, 293 F. Supp. 1339 (1968).

98. *See* Comment, *Chilling Political Expression By Use of Police Intelligence Files: Anderson v. Sills*, 5 HARV. CIV. RIGHTS CIV. LIB. L. REV. 72-78 (1970).

99. Such as the existence of an overbroad criminal statute used by police to harass a civil rights organization. *See, e.g.*, Dombrowski v. Pfister, 380 U.S. 479 (1965).

the exercise of free thought[100] to *chill* resulting from the mere knowledge of an intelligence gathering scheme, with relative ease:

> ... the constitutional doctrine requires that we consider any burden placed upon First Amendment rights that might reasonably be expected to interfere or to prevent their exercise as constituting an impermissible infringment on those rights.[101]

Relying heavily on *United States v. Robel*,[102] Judge Matthews sounds the death knell of the balancing test[103] on the one hand, but bases his decision on "overbreadth" on the other, implicitly recognizing the need to balance.[104] The court's position on the need to balance, however, can be regarded as the least significant part of the holding. Crucial to the opinion is the court's recognition that the plaintiffs were significantly *chilled* in the exercise of their First Amendment rights by the mere knowledge that the police were keeping files on them *and* its finding that the threshold of legitimacy for government action, in this instance, is no higher than it has been for instances of more concrete and immediate coercion, sanction or threat thereof.

The Supreme Court of New Jersey felt differently and reversed the decision.[105] Chief Judge Weintraub held that, "[t]he constitutional issue was presented in a hypothetical way within an aura of surmise and speculation,"[106] and found it, "important to note what is and is not before us."[107] The case neither presented a statute imposing criminal liability for its violation[108] nor one affecting the

---

100. Lamont v. Postmaster General, 381 U.S. 301 (1965) (governmental scheme requiring addressees of foreign Communist propaganda to return a reply card if they wanted material delivered by the Post Office).

101. 106 N.J. Super. 545, 554 (1969).

102. 389 U.S. 258 (1967).

103. 106 N.J. Super. 545, 555-56.

104. *Id.* at 557. The Judge ordered a destruction of the information gathering apparatus, "except where such information will be used to charge persons with specifically defined criminal conduct." Anderson v. Sills, 106 N.J. Super. 545 (1969). Therefore, it seems clear that when criminal conduct is scrutinized the government has a legitimate interest outweighing the possible First Amendment right of a criminal "suspect." Where persons other than criminal suspects are involved, First Amendment rights outweigh genuine government interests in protecting against future civil disorders.

105. 56 N.J. 210, 265 A.2d 678 (Sup. Ct. 1970). The court held that plaintiffs should not have been granted a summary judgment and that therefore a full hearing below was necessary. Not intending to deal with the merits, the court nevertheless discusses them rather freely.

106. *Id.* at 215.

107. *Id.* at 220.

108. *Id.* Cited were United States v. Robel, 389 U.S. 258 (1967); Dombrowski v. Pfister, 380 U.S. 479 (1965); Gibson v. Florida Legislative Investigation Committee, 372 U.S. 539 (1963); NAACP v. Button, 371 U.S. 415 (1963); Watkins v. United States, 354 U.S. 172 (1957).

right to public employment.[109] Nor did the Sills Memorandum pose the threat of statutory inhibition of the right to pursue a profession. In those instances, a statute on its face raises the question of whether, because of vagueness or overbreadth, it unnecessarily deters an individual from speech or activity protected by the First Amendment:[110] The Sills Memorandum, however, *"imposes no liability or obligation or restriction whatever upon the citizens,"*[111] and therefore, the catalogue of potential harms resulting from police intelligence gathering, that was so influential in the lower court, did not impress Judge Weintraub.[112] Moreover, he found it unnecessary to require of police activity, serving the legitimate purposes of crime prevention, the kind of precision which the constitution demands of legislative actions.[113]

The court did not deny the existence of a *chill* in the police surveillance situation, but found the "legality" of the government's curtailment of First Amendment rights, when weighed against "the competing interests of the citizens," to be "pivotal":[114]

The First Amendment itself would be meaningless if there were no constitutional authority to protect the individual from suppression by others who disapprove of him or the company he keeps.[115]

The gravamen of the court's stance appears to be that the executive branch may gather whatever information it reasonably believes to be necessary to enable it to perform the traditional police roles of crime detection and prevention, and that, "a court should not interfere in the absence of proof of bad faith or arbitrariness."[116] Furthermore, the judiciary must refrain from interference where a decision would be based on "nothing more" than a fear that police officers "will be unfaithful to their oaths or unequal to their responsibility."[117]

---

109. *Id.* The court relied on Keyishian v. Board of Regents of New York, 385 U.S. 589 (1967).

110. *Id.*

111. *Id.* (emphasis added).

112. 56 N.J. 210, 222 (1970).

113. 56 N.J. 210, 225 (1970). The court explains that it is a serious matter for the judiciary to interfere with the preventive measures devised by the executive branch of government in response to its constitutional obligation to protect all citizens. "Surely such interference may not rest upon a hypothetical exposition of what could happen under a set of forms in the hands of an officer indifferent to the restraints upon his office . . . the forms are necessarily comprehensive, leaving it to the local authorities to decide in their judgment what incidents are worthy of note and what information should be obtained as to the individuals concerned or involved" (at 225).

114. 56 N.J. 210, 226 (1970).

115. *Id.*

116. *Id.* at 229. *Compare* Dombrowski v. Pfister, 380 U.S. 479 (1965) *with* Younger v. Harris, 401 U.S. 415 (1963).

117. *Id.* at 229.

In sum, the court found that inhibition of First Amendment rights resulting from nothing more than police surveillance is legally cognizable *and* that the threshold of legitimacy for police activities inducing such a *chill* is *lower* than that which the Supreme Court has ruled necessary for government action which applies or threatens sanctions curtailing the exercise of free speech or association.[118] The threshold applicable to police surveillance, instructs Chief Justice Weintraub, depends upon intent, *i.e.*, bad faith or deliberate arbitrary treatment of citizens by the police.[119]

It seems, however, that in upholding the broad investigative power of the police,[120] the New Jersey court misread the nature of the plaintiff's complaint. It was not simply fear of bad faith action by the police[121] which the plaintiff's contended deterred the exercise of their First Amendment rights. Rather, the complaint alleged that the *chill* resulted from the knowledge that mere participation in a protected political demonstration might result in the compilation of a "police record." The record would include information about the individual and his affiliations, associates, employment and family.[122] This knowledge, the plaintiff alleged, would deter future political activity, particularly dissident political activity.[123] The existence of the record might mean public harassment, a stamp of disloyalty, discouragement of membership in certain organizations, difficulty in finding employment and possibly police harassment. These results were precisely those which concerned the Supreme Court in cases

118. *See* Dombrowski v. Pfister, 380 U.S. 479 (1965); Talley v. California, 362 U.S. 60 (1960); Lamont v. Postmaster General, 381 U.S. 301 (1965).

119. 56 N.J. 210, 229 (1970). Unfortunately, the Supreme Court has made it clear that its decision in *Dombrowski* did not depend so much on the mere existence of a threatening (overbroad) statute but its bad faith use by the police. *See* Younger v. Harris, 401 U.S. 415 (1963).

120. 56 N.J. 210, 230 (1970). In its generality, this statement is not to be denied. *See* Terry v. Ohio, 392 U.S. 1 (1968); Lewis v. United States, 385 U.S. 206 (1966); Hoffa v. United States, 385 U.S. 323 (1966); Osborn v. United States, 385 U.S. 323 (1966).

121. This was the test which the court set up. Fear alone was not enough, bad faith must have been proven.

122. *See* 56 N.J. 210, 217 (1970) for court's account of "Form 421." Included in the information to be gathered was:

> Spouse's Full Name. Type full name of spouse. If wife, include maiden name or names by any other marriages. Associates. Names and addresses of associates, include aliases and nicknames. Citizenship/naturalization date - parental background/occupation - armed forces service/digit status—membership, affiliation and/or status with organizations or groups - educational background - habits or traits - places frequented - parole/probation data on immediate family - financial/credit status - other records of past activities, findings and/or observations.

123. Dissident speech has always been carefully protected by the Supreme Court. *Compare* NAACP v. Alabama, 357 U.S. 449 (1958), *with* United States v. Robel, 389 U.S. 258 (1967), *and* United States v. O'Brien, 391 U.S. 367 (1968).

invalidating coercive State action.[124] On the basis of these Supreme Court's decisions, the New Jersey court could have invalidated the Sills Memorandum on the ground of overbreadth. The police activity in *Sills* could have been limited to surveillance of groups known to be bent on violent action as demonstrated by past activity.[125] Absent the element of coercion the court refused to circumscribe the surveillance activities.

C. The Remote Camera Plaintiff's Constitutional Attack

The use of "remote camera" surveillance impels a consideration of the relevant constitutional implications of these possibilities. Do the cameras present the same kind of threatened harms to the exercise of First Amendment rights as were alleged by the *Sills* and *NAACP v. Alabama* plaintiffs? If so, will courts treat them in the same way the Supreme Court treated them when they were afflicted by the threat of legal or criminal sanction or other governmental coercion? If not, will courts treat them and the police activity that inhibits association or expression, as did the New Jersey Supreme Court in *Anderson v. Sills*? Finally, how will the courts respond if "remote camera" plaintiffs can demonstrate only "uneasy feelings of inhibition"[126] rather than deterrents to First Amendment protected activities recognized by the Supreme Court?

The last question is the central one in determining the constitutionality of remote camera surveillance by police of public streets under the First Amendment. Under present law, it is also the most difficult question.[127] Ironically, it poses the ominous threat of a "watched society" critically dangerous to the vitality of life in the modern world.[128]

---

124. *See* NAACP v. Alabama, 357 U.S. 449 (1958); Sweezy v. New Hampshire, 354 U.S. 234 (1957); Watkins v. United States, 354 U.S. 178 (1957); Shelton v. Tucker, 364 U.S. 479 (1960); and Dombrowski v. Pfister, 380 U.S. 479 (1965). *See also* Askin, *Police Dossiers and Emerging Principles of First Amendment Adjudication*, 22 STAN. L. REV. 196, 211 (1970).

125. *See* Note, *Chilling Political Expression By Use of Police Intelligence Files: Anderson v. Sills*, 5 HARV. CIV. RIGHTS CIV. LIB. L. REV. 72-78 (1970).

126. *See* Olmstead v. United States, 277 U.S. 438, 478-479 (1928) (Brandeis, J., dissenting); Osborn v. United States, 385 U.S. 323, 354 (1960) (Douglas, J., dissenting); Freid, *Privacy*, 77 YALE L. J. 475 (1968); Note, *Chilling Effect in Constitutional Law*, 69 COLUM. L. REV. 808 (1969).

127. *Cf.* Tatum v. Laird, 444 F.2d 947 (1971), *cert. granted*, No. 71-288 (1971).

128. *See* Justice Douglas' dissent in Osborn v. United States, 385 U.S. 323 (1966):

We are rapidly entering the age of no privacy, where there are no secrets from government. The aggressive breaches of privacy by the government increase by geometric proportions. Wiretapping and "bugging" run rampant, without effective

The Camera's Potential for "Legal" Harm. First, it is important to distinguish the camera situation from the circumstance in *Sills*. The danger in *Sills* from plaintiff's perspective was police maintenance of files as part of a program of preventing civil disorder, the knowledge of which could easily deter further dissident activity for fear of repercussions by police. Furthermore, if it were to become public knowledge in a small community that a person was filed with the police as part of an investigation concerning civil disorders, he might be "stamped disloyal," suffer employment discrimination, be unable to join certain groups or be fearful of joining others, and be shunned by friends who might fear being included in the file.

In the case of police cameras, on the other hand, the only "file" is a videotape of all the people in the street. Public knowledge of being videotaped on a public street and nothing more could not result in being stamped disloyal, turned down for a job, scorned by associates, or inhibit membership—the harms that the Supreme Court has recognized as requiring the invalidation of state procedures. There is one potential danger in camera surveillance, however, which has been recognized in the context of First Amendment challenges to the state regulation: bad faith or abuse of function by the police.[129] The apprehension of misuse of the ready, replayable information[130] unlike that available from a policeman on the beat, may deter an individual from being seen with certain people, dressing as he chooses, or even standing around peaceably.[131] A law abiding citizen might fear further surveillance or a decision by the police that his appearance makes him a suspect of any crime in the area.[132]

---

judicial or legislative control . . . . The time may come when no one can be sure whether his words are being recorded for use at some future time; when everyone will fear that his most secret thoughts are no longer his own, but belong to the government; when the most confidential and intimate conversations are always open to eager prying ears. When that time comes, privacy, and with it liberty, will be gone. If a man's privacy can be invaded at will, who can say he is free? If his every association is known and recorded, if the conversations with his associates are purloined who can say he enjoys freedom of association? When such conditions obtain, our citizens will be afraid to utter any but the safest and most orthodox thoughts; afraid to associate with any but the most acceptable people. Freedom as the Constitution envisages will have vanished.

129. It is the very same harm which Judge Weintraub was willing to accept as controlling in *Sills*, but only if proven.

130. *See* Part I.

131. These are activities protected by the Fourteenth Amendment which, when restrained, curtail expression or association protected by the First Amendment, or at least it may be so argued. *See* Coates v. Cincinnati, 402 U.S. 611 (1971).

132. Perhaps this fear is as justifiable as the NAACP's fear of public harassment of its members as a result of disclosure of membership. NAACP v. Alabama, 357 U.S. 449 (1958) at 462:

The Cameras as a Coercive Force. In *NAACP v. Alabama*,[133] and the other Supreme Court cases discussed, the plaintiffs had to choose between exercising their First Amendment rights and risking criminal or legal sanction,[134] and acting within the challenged laws which infringed upon their right.[135] In the "camera" situation, plaintiffs are under no immediate governmental threat or compulsion if they choose to exercise their First Amendment rights. However, avoidance of the streets on which the cameras are placed may be the price of acting without fear of police abuse of the videotapes. Effectively, the government has conditioned the uninhibited exercise of First Amendment freedoms upon avoiding streets ostensibly free for public use. It is unlikely that this form of government "compulsion" to avoid certain public streets could be categorized with threats of legal criminal sanction. In *Lamont*, the Supreme Court struck down an "affirmative obligation" placed on addressees of foreign Communist propaganda to send a reply card in order to get delivery as an unconstitutional limitation on the exercise of First Amendment rights.[136] The Court found that the requirement conflicted with "uninhibited, robust and wideopen" debate and discussion contemplated by the First Amendment. This was the case only because the affirmative obligation was

> almost certain to have a deterrent effect, especially as respects those who have sensitive positions. Their livelihood may be dependent on a security clearance. Public officials, like schoolteachers who have no tenure, might think they would invite disaster if they read what the Federal Government says contains the seeds of treason.[137]

It is hardly a novel perception that compelled disclosure of affiliation with groups engaged in advocacy may constitute a[n] effective . . . restraint on freedom of association [directly abridged]. This court has recognized the vital relationship between freedom to associate and privacy in one's association.

It is less apparent that police abuse resulting in like damages, will take place, than it was that the membership lists would "get around" in *NAACP*. This is the problem. The contingency of police abuse adds one more hypothetical to the legitimate underpinning of a citizen's fears than the NAACP had to establish to prove deterrence. Dombrowski v. Pfister, 380 U.S. 479 (1965) leaves little room for judicial recognition of bad faith police action in the absence of substantiation.

133. 357 U.S. 449 (1958).
134. Dombrowski v. Pfister, 380 U.S. 479 (1965).
135. *See* Lamont v. Postmaster General, 381 U.S. 301 (1965).
136. *See* Murdock v. Pennsylvania, 319 U.S. 105 (1943) (Supreme Court held unconstitutional a flat license tax on the exercise of First Amendment rights) and Lovell v. Griffin, 303 U.S. 444 (1938) (a municipal licensing system for those distributing literature was held invalid).
137. Lamont v. Postmaster General, 381 U.S. 301 (1965).

The fears of persons exposed to the cameras are comparable to those which concerned the Court in *Lamont*. Is it possible to say that they impose the same dreadful obligation as did the Post Office reply card scheme in *Lamont* which the Court referred to as almost certain to have a deterrent effect? Would the obligation result from having to avoid the filmed street or refrain from free activity on the street?[138] The ultimate determination is whether fear of abusive police action is too conjectural to be counted as a sufficient limitation on the exercise on his First Amendment rights.

The Cameras and "Speech Plus." It is clear that the First Amendment covers non-political and non-controversial speech as well as the "robust debate" mentioned in *Lamont*.[139] Perhaps activity on a public street is "speech-plus" and therefore not protected in the same way under the First Amendment. Specifically,

First and Fourteenth Amendments do not afford the same kind of freedom to those who communicate ideas by conduct such as patrolling, marching, and picketing on streets and highways, as these amendments offered to those who communicate ideas by pure speech.[140]

This need not be overstated, in light of the fact that the "speech plus doctrine" pays particular attention to activity which incites lawlessness.[141] However, the doctrine is important to keep in mind in the camera situation, essentially because it is conduct which is being

---

138. *See* Schneider v. State, 308 U.S. 147, 163 (1939):

streets are natural and proper places for the dissemination of information and opinion; and one is not to have the exercise of his liberty of expression in appropriate places abridged on the plea that it may be exercised in some other places. *See also* Jameson v. Texas, 318 U.S. 413 (1943); Hague v. CIO, 307 U.S. 496, 514-516 (1939); Schneider v. Irvington, 308 U.S. 147, 162 (1940).

139. The first Amendment protects abstract discussion as well as vigorous advocacy. *See* NAACP v. Button, 371 U.S. 415, 42 (1963). *Cf.* Herdon v. Lowry, 301 U.S. 242, 259-264, (1937). The right of peaceable assembly in any numbers, whether for political purpose or not is equally well guarded by the First Amendment. *Cf.* De Jorge v. Oregon, 299 U.S. 353 (1937); Bond v. Floyd, 385 U.S. 116 (1966); United States v. Cruikshank, 92 U.S. 542 (1875).

140. Cox v. Louisiana, 379 U.S. 536, 555 (1965).

141. Picketing is "free speech-plus." *See* Justice Douglas's concurring opinion in Brandenburg v. Ohio, 395 U.S. 444, 455 (1969); Bakery Drivers Local v. Wohl, 315 U.S. 769, 775 (1942); Giboney v. Empire Storage Co., 336 U.S. 490, 501 (1949); Hughes v. Superior Court, 339 U.S. 460, 465 (1950); Labor Board v. Fruit & Vegetable Packers, 377 U.S. 58, 77 (1964) (Black, J., concurring) and *id.* at 93 (Harlan, J., dissenting); and Food Employees v. Logan Plaza, 391 U.S. 308, 326 (Douglas, J., concurring). Under the doctrine of these cases picketing can be regulated when it comes to the "plus" or "action" side of the protest. At that point the "clear and present danger" test had traditionally been applied. *Compare* Bridges v. California, 314 U.S. 252, 261-263 (1941) *with* Dennis v. United States, 341 U.S. 494 (1951).

watched.[142] Is the camera plaintiff to be afforded the same protection provided the political speaker or theorist,[143] and hence have the benefit of the same constitutional test? The "speech plus" doctrine sanctions governmental prohibition, generally speaking, when a "clear and present danger" results from *conduct*.[144] While it is possible that "pure speech," such as authorship of a book, creates a "clear and present danger," it is unlikely. So, the actor who speaks is subject to stricter scrutiny than is the writing theorist in the sense that his chance of directly inciting violent action is greater. When conduct is combined with speech the governmental power to regulate it is enhanced. But, persons subject to camera surveillance on public streets are not necessarily exercising First Amendment rights. When they do, it is combined with conduct and is subject to greater regulation. Of course (assuming that no "speech" on the street itself is contemplated), the "speech plus" doctrine does not affect the protection the Fourteenth Amendment provides to dress and behave peaceably as one chooses without arbitrary interference from the state.[145] If the cameras deter peaceable behavior protected by the Fourteenth Amendment in such a way as to *chill* the inclination to associate as one chooses on public streets, the constitutional claim is preserved despite the First Amendment "speech plus" doctrine.

The State's Interest in the Cameras. May it be alleged that the state's interest in maintaining remote camera surveillance is no more compelling than was the government's in curtailing the flow of communist literature in *Lamont*? Compare the police interest in preventing crime to that of having "loyal" teachers in *Shelton*, or in barring all communist party members from government employ as in *Robel*. Is the state's interest in enforcing the technical

---

142. *See* McKay, *The Preference For Freedom*, 34 N.Y.U. L. REV. 1182, 1203-1212 (1959). *See also* Brandenburg v. Ohio, 395 U.S. 444 (1969). The court overturned a Ku Klux Klan leader's conviction under the Ohio Criminal Syndicalism statute which forbade the advocation of violence to achieve political reform. The freedoms of speech and press were held not to permit a state to forbid advocacy of the use of force or of law violation except where such advocacy is directed to inciting or producing imminent lawless action and is likely to produce or incite such action. The distinction which the per curiam opinion drew between "speech plus" and "speech" is exemplified by the Court's citation to Noto v. United States, 367 U.S. 290, 297-8 (1961), "the mere abstract teaching . . . of the word, propriety or even moral necessity for a resort to force and violence, is not the same as preparing a group for violent action and steeling it to such action." It is this distinction, rather than one between activist expression and merely quiet speech or association which the Court has been careful to maintain. *Cf.* Yates v. United States, 354 U.S. 298 (1957); De Jonge v. Oregon, 289 U.S. 353 (1937) and Stromberg v. California, 283 U.S. 359 (1931).

Note, however, that conduct which does not incite to lawlessness, may still be regulated extensively despite First Amendment guarantees, under the notion that there is greater state interest in its control. *Cf.* O'Brien v. United States.

143. Hentoff v. Ichord, 318 F. Supp. 1175 (D.D.C. 1970).

144. *See* Amalgamated Food Employees Union v. Logan Valley Plaza, 391 U.S. 308 (1968)

145. *See* Tinker v. Des Moines School District, 393 U.S. 503 (1969).

requirements of a corporation statute (*NAACP v. Albama*) to be equated with the police interest in preventing crime? Crime prevention when stacked up against these sample state interests appears to be "compelling."[146] In addition, it can hardly be denied that the same citizens potentially chilled by the cameras harbor the "competing interest"[147] of having crime-free streets. Unquestionably, this is the kind of "competing interest" Judge Weintraub spoke of in the final *Anderson* decision, and this interest in bound to weigh heavily in the "balance." It is also a "balance" in which the governmental activity does not appear to be readily susceptible to narrowing to the particular evil sought to be corrected.[148] That the cameras achieve the desired preventive effect by virtue of the all-encompassing nature of their surveillance, can hardly be disputed. These factors do not portend well for remote camera plaintiffs under the standard Justice Black enunciated in the *Younger* case:

> Where a statute does not directly abridge free speech, but— while regulating a subject within the State's power—tends to have the incidental effect of inhibiting First Amendment rights, it is well settled that the statute can be upheld if the effect on speech is minor in relation to the need for control of the conduct and the lack of alternative means for doing so.[149]

In the last analysis, the problem is how the courts will handle the complaint that mere knowledge that the cameras exist, coupled with the knowledge of their great capacity for potential evil, inhibits the inclination to speak and associate freely. *Younger*,[150] may be further instructive. The Federal District Court permitted three individuals to intervene as plaintiffs in Harris' suit. Two were members of the Progressive Labor Party who claimed that the prosecution of Harris would inhibit them from peaceful advocacy of the Party's program. The third was a college history professor who felt uncertain as to his freedom under the act to teach the philosophy of Karl Marx. The District Court found the statute unconstitutional and enjoined the state court prosecution.[151] Justice Black's majority opinion reversing the lower court decision, disposed quickly of the

---

146. *See* Terry v. Ohio, 392 U.S. 1 (1968).
147. *See* Anderson v. Sills, 56 N.J. 210 (1970).
148. *See* United States v. Robel, 389 U.S. 258 (1969).
149. 402 U.S. 37, 51 (1971).
150. The Act had been held constitutional in Whitney v. California, 274 U.S. 357 (1927) which was overruled by Brandenburg v. Ohio, 395 U.S. 444 (1969).
151. *See* Justice Black's majority opinion. Younger v. Harris, 401 U.S. 37 (1971).

three intervenors: They had no "acute, live controversy" with the State; no one had been indicted, arrested or even threatened by the prosecutor.[152] Even if plaintiffs' allegations were true, they were not sufficient to

> bring the equitable jurisdiction of the federal courts into play to enjoin a pending state prosecution . . . . [P]ersons having no fears of state persecution except those that are imaginary or speculative are not to be accepted as appropriate plaintiffs in such cases.[153]

Would such plaintiffs have standing and a meritorious claim, if rather than seeking to enjoin a state court prosecution of another, they were directly attacking the constitutionality of the statute itself? As the court pointed out "a federal lawsuit to stop a prosecution in a state court is a serious matter.[154] In fact, Harris, who had standing was unable to get an injuction for lack of the kind of irreparable injury that was present in *Dombromski (i.e.,* "great and immediate," resulting from bad faith activities by the police.)[155]

Admittedly, as *Younger v. Harris* pointed out, a Federal Court injunction of a state court action is extraordinary and the damages shown must be great. Therefore, it is possible to look at the Court's disposition of the intervenor's "fears" as nothing more than a function of the extremity of their claim. However, there is nothing in the present case law to indicate that such a narrow view need be taken. On the other hand may it be hypothesized that fears of police abuse of remote camera videotapes are more substantial than those of criminal prosecution alleged by the unsuccessful intervenors in *Younger*? In the light of growing police surveillance and coextensively mounting sociological data of its potential ill effects, should courts even be concerned with the issue as defined by contexts like *Younger*?

In short, it appears that if remote camera subjects can establish clearly discernible limitations on the exercise of First Amendment rights, like public harrassment resulting from police use of the cameras, their case is measurably enhanced. Similarly, a demonstration of police abuse of the information would heighten the chance of success. But the fact that the cameras cannot easily be said to coerce, and the greater likelihood that plaintiffs would only be able to estab-

---

152. Younger v. Harris, 401 U.S. 37 (1971). This was the Court's disposition of the intervenors standing to sue. However, its implications for our discussion of the merits of the "remote camera case" is obvious.

153. *Id.* at 42.

154. *Id.*

155. Dombrowski v. Pfister, 380 U.S. 479 (1965).

lish an uneasy feeling when in the camera's range, is detrimental. These factors combine to provide a regrettably weak frontal attack on the remote camera surveillance technique based on its infringement of First Amendment rights.

PART III: OBSERVATION AS A SEARCH

We come now to the question of whether or not a camera system of the Mt. Vernon variety observes its targets in a manner protected by the Fourth Amendment's prohibition of unreasonable searches and seizures.[156] Phrased more analytically, the question to be asked is whether 24-hour visual observation and magnification of people in public places, indiscriminately and without probable cause, falls within the ambit of Fourth Amendment protections.

The Fourth Amendment protects people from warrantless and otherwise unreasonable searches where the individual has an expectation of privacy and that expectation is a reasonable one.[157] Thus the Fourth Amendment encompasses entirely non-trespassory intrusions[158] as well as the seizure of both tangible and intangible items.[159] Similarly, standing to raise Fourth Amendment issues is

---

15o. U.S. CONST. AMEND. IV:

The right of the people to be secure in their persons, houses, papers and effects against unreasonable searches and seizures shall not be violated and no warrants shall issue but upon probable cause, supported by oath or affirmation, and particularly describing the place to be searched, and the persons or things to be seized.

An excellent behaviorally oriented definition is found in FED. R. CIV. P. 62 (c):

Search necessarily implies prying into or uncovering of that which one has a right to and intends to and effectively does conceal from view or scrutiny of another.

157. The breakwater case of Katz v. United States, 389 U.S. 347, 353 (1967) swept away the requirement that the government engage in a trespass or physical intrusion before the protections of the Fourth Amendment become applicable. In now famous words, the Court declared that "the Fourth Amendment protects people and not simply areas," and therefore, where a person "justifiably relies" on privacy, it is an unreasonable search for the government to intrude either physically or in any other manner without a warrant. (In Katz, the government intercepted the defendant's conversations by placing a wall mike on the ceiling of a telephone booth he frequented). See note 217 infra.

158. The Katz decision thus overturned the Fourth Amendment's trespass requirement enunciated in Olmstead v. United States, 277 U.S. 438 (1928) and Goldman v. United States, 316 U.S. 129, 134-136 (1942).

159. Originally, the Fourth Amendment was thought to apply only to the search and seizure of tangible items. Katz at 364 (Black, J., dissenting). "[T]he framers' purpose [in the Fourth Amendment] was to limit its protection to tangible things." Id. at 365. See also Olmstead v. United States, 277 U.S. 438, 464-465 (1928) which implies that the Fourth Amendment is not concerned with hearing or sight. See note 174 infra.

not dependent on an individual's property rights.[160]

Where the police do not obtain a warrant[161] or where their search cannot be justified by exigent circumstances,[162] the search is unreasonable and the fruits of that search, both inculpatory and

---

In McDonald v. United States, 335 U.S. 451 (1948) and more explicitly in Silverman v. United States, 365 U.S. 505 (1961) and Wong Sun v. United States, 37 U.S. 471 (1963), the Court made it clear that the Fourth Amendment's overarching concern to prevent the invasion of an individual's "indefeasible right of personal security and personal liberty," Boyd v. United States, 116 U.S. 616, 630 (1886), mandated that invasions of privacy cognizable in intangible searches and seizures be protected by the Fourth Amendment:

> The exclusionary rule has traditionally banned from trial physical tangible materials observed either during or as a result of an unlawful invasion. It follows from our holding in Silverman v. United States, 365 U.S. 505 (1961) that the Fourth Amendment may protect against the overhearing of verbal statements as well as against the more traditional seizure of papers and effects. Similarly, testimony as to matters observed during an unlawful invasion has been excluded in order to enforce the basic constitutional policies . . . Thus verbal [or visual] evidence which derives so immediately from an unlawful entry and an unauthorized arrest as the officers' action in the present case is no less the fruit of official illegality than the more tangible fruits of an unwarranted intrusion.

Wong Sun v. United States, 371 U.S. 471, 484-485 (1963). *See also* Warden v. Hayden, 387 U.S. 294 (1967).

160. Jones v. United States, 362 U.S. 257 (1958).

161. The warrant requirement is at the foundation of the Fourth Amendment. Consistently, the Supreme Court has emphasized that:

> The informed and deliberate determinations of magistrates empowered to issue warrants . . . are to be preferred over the hurried action of officers . . . who may happen to make arrests.

United States v. Lefkowitz, 285 U.S. 452, 464 (1932). The Supreme Court in Chimel v. California, 395 U.S. 752 (1969) and Coolidge v. New Hampshire, 403 U.S. 443 (1971), has strengthened the importance of the warrant. The warrant will issue only upon probable cause presented before an impartial magistrate, 403 U.S. at 449, and must specifically describe the objects of the search and seizure, Marron v. United States, 275 U.S. 192 (1929).

Once a Court determines that a search has in fact been conducted without a warrant or without meeting the exigent circumstance standard, the search is *per se* unreasonable. In Katz v. United States at 357, the Court said:

> Over and again this Court has emphasized that the mandate of the [Fourth] Amendment requires adherence to judicial processes . . . and that searches conducted outside the judicial process, without prior approval by judge or magistrate, are *per se* unreasonable under the Fourth Amendment—subject only to a few specifically established and well delineated exceptions.

162. The Supreme Court has recognized a number of circumstances that by their very nature make procurement of a warrant impracticable or unnecessary. Chimel v. California, 395 U.S. 752 (1969) (incident to a lawful arrest); Bumper v. North Carolina, 391 U.S. 543 (1968) (by knowing consent); Warden v. Hayden, 387 U.S. 294 (1967) (hot pursuit); Massachusetts v. Painten, 389 U.S. 560 (1968) (abandonment); Harris v. United States, 390 U.S. 234 (1968) (custodial prerogative); and Carroll v. United States, 267 U.S. 132 (1925) (by necessity and with probable cause).

exculpatory, will be excluded in a federal[163] or state[164] criminal proceeding. Remedies more applicable than exclusion may also flow from a Fourth Amendment violation.[165]

Observation: In and Out of Plain Sight. When attempting to predict under what circumstances visual surveillance by the police ceases to be an inspection or investigation and becomes a search, it is helpful to speak in terms of two relatively distinct doctrines. The

---

163. Weeks v. United States, 232 U.S. 383 (1914). The "Week's exclusionary rule" provides that where agents of the federal government conduct a search and that search is not blessed by a warrant or exigent circumstance, any evidence (fruits) of the search will be excluded in a federal criminal prosecution.

164. In Mapp v. Ohio, 367 U.S. 643 (1961), the exclusionary rule was extended to the states.

165. The remedy that American Courts generally use to redress violations of Fourth Amendment rights is to exclude the fruits of the illegal search in a subsequent criminal prosecution. *See* Weeks v. United States, *supra* note 163. In regard to camera systems of the Mt. Vernon type, where the object is surveillance and not primarily apprehension and prosecution of criminal offenders, the exclusionary rule is a virtually empty remedy. Nevertheless, a determination of the applicability of Fourth Amendment protections to camera surveillance systems is important for two reasons.

First, exclusion of evidence in a criminal proceeding is not necessarily the only remedy for Fourth Amendment violations. Fourth Amendment protections may attach to government searches that threaten non-criminal sanctions. *See* Camera v. Municipal Court of San Francisco, 387 U.S. 523 (1967). *Cf.* Wyman v. James, 400 U.S. 309 (1971). Furthermore, the history of the Fourth Amendment makes clear that, where appropriate, remedies other than exclusion can be provided. *See* Boyd v. United States, 116 U.S.616 (1885) and particularly Wolf v. Colorado 338 U.S. 25 (1948) at 31:

> Granting that in practice the exclusion of evidence may be an effective way of deterring unreasonable searches, it is not for this Court to condemn as falling below the minimal standards assured by the Due Process Clause, a state's reliance upon other methods which, if consistently enforced, would be equally effective.

For a listing of state search and seizure remedies, other than exclusion, *see* Wolf v. Colorado, 338 U.S. at 30n.1. Recently, the courts and legal writers have expressed disenchantment with sole reliance on an exclusionary remedy and have instead sought more flexible responses to Fourth Amendment intrusions. *See* Lankford v. Gelston, 364 F.2d 197 (1966) providing injunctive relief from the Baltimore Police Department's pattern of unreasonable searches, and Bivens v. Six Unknown Named Agents of the Federal Bureau of Narcotics, 403 U.S. 388 (1971) holding that damages are recoverable from federal agents who violate the Fourth Amendment. For an unusual critique of the exclusionary rule, *see id.* at 411 (Burger, J., dissenting). *See also* Berch, *Money Damages for Fourth Amendment Violations by Federal Officials:* An *Explanation of Bivens v. Six Unknown Named Agents of the Federal Bureau of Narcotics,* 1971 LAW AND SOCIAL ORDER 43 (1971); Hufstedler, *Directions and Misdirections of Constitutional Right of Privacy,* 26 RECORD 546 (1971); Horowitz, *Excluding the Exclusionary Rule— Can There Be an Effective Alternative?* 47 L.A. BAR BULL. 91 January, 1972; Wingo, *Growing Disillusionment with the Exclusionary Rule,* 25 SW. L.J. 573 (1971).

Secondly, leaving aside the question of remedies, it is vitally important, for public policy reasons if no others, to assess the degree to which television surveillance systems threaten those freedoms protected by the Fourth Amendment. As the Supreme Court in the *Wolf* opinion observed:

> The security of one's privacy against arbitrary intrusion by the police—which is at the core of the Fourth Amendment—is basic to a free society. 338 U.S. at 27.

first and fundamental concept of visual observation is the plain sight rule.[166] Where a police officer is in a location that he has a legal right to be in, the plain sight rule holds that it is no search for him to observe any activities or objects coming within his clear view.[167] Conversely, where a police officer is illegally in a location anything he sees from that vantage point will be suppressed as the fruit of an illegal search.[168] The plain sight rule is thus, in essence, a doctrine of physical presence. Under this rule, the characterization of a visual observation as a search is ultimately dependent upon the physical location of the police officer.

A second and newer theory of visual surveillance has been impelled by the *Katz* decision.[169] This theory holds that where an individual has a reasonable expectation of freedom from visual surveillance it is a search for a police officer to make a visual intrusion.[170] However, courts have disagreed on the criteria to be used in determining when such an expectation is reasonable. Some courts have held that an individual cannot have a reasonable expectation of privacy if his activities are visible to a police officer who is in a position he has a legal right to be in.[171] Under this test the *Katz* doctrine is merely a restatement of the plain sight rule. Furthermore, this test does not protect an individual from situations in which the police are in a legal vantage point that normally would not allow them to observe the individual but by the employment of various deceptive or extra-sensory devices (two way mirrors, disguised peep holes, search lights, telescopes, *etc.*) the police are able to conduct visual surveillance. In reaction to this intrusive result, a few recent decisions have asserted that the reasonableness of an individual's expectation of freedom from visual surveillance is not determined simply by what the police can see from a legal location, but also considers the reasonableness of the method used by the police to obtain this view together with the seriousness of the resulting intrusion.[172] Arguably, the logic of these recent decisions extends Fourth Amendment protec-

---

166. The Supreme Court has often construed the plain sight rule and has done so in a number of contexts. *See, e.g.,* Chimel v. California, 395 U.S. 752, 763 (1969); Harris v. United States, 390 U.S. 234, 236 (1968) (objects falling within the plain view of an officer who has a right to be in the position to have the view are subject to seizure and may be introduced in evidence). The most recent treatment of the plain view doctrine in the context of an ongoing search is to be found in Coolidge v. New Hampshire, 403 U.S 443 (1971).

167. Harris v. United States, 390 U.S.234 (1968).

168. *See* notes 174-182 *infra* and accompanying text.

169. Katz v. United States, 389 U.S. 347, 353 (1967). *See* notes 239-252, *infra* and accompanying text.

170. *See* notes 240-253 *infra* and accompanying text.

171. *See* notes 181-182 *infra* and accompanying text.

172. *See* notes 240-253 *infra* and accompanying text.

tions to certain 24-hour remote camera surveillance situations.[173] To undertake the examination of this development it is necessary to review the case law of visual surveillance.

A. *Physical Presence and the Exclusion of Visual Fruits*

Under the physical presence theory of visual surveillance (a corollary of the plain view doctrine), once the police intrude on a constitutionally protected area and that intrusion is not accompanied by a warrant or exigent circumstance, the courts will exclude the visual fruits of the search. Thus, in *McDonald v. United States*,[174] the Supreme Court excluded an officer's testimony on gambling paraphernalia spotted when police broke into a rooming house and peeped over the top of a transom into the defendant's room. The court emphasized that the observations were made possible by an unauthorized physical intrusion in an area in which the defendant had, at least, an interest in excluding intruders.

Similarly, in *Brock v. United States*,[175] the Court of Appeals reversed a conviction for possession of moonshine liquor in part because the trial court admitted testimony as to what was seen by trespassing federal agents:

> Whatever quibbles there may be as to where the curtilage begins and ends, it is clear that standing on a man's premises and looking in his bedroom window is a violation of his right to be let alone.[176]

A police trespass of a porch,[177] a roof,[178] or the curtilage of a garage[179] in order to peer inside the building have also been characterized as intrusion necessitating the exclusion of visual fruits.[180]

A few post *Katz* cases continue to rely on the physical presence rationale to exclude the visual fruits of a search of the defendant's

---

173. *See* notes 255-266 *infra* and accompanying text.

174. McDonald v. United States, 335 U.S. 451 (1948). This holding implicitly overruled so much of *Olmstead* that implied that whatever was seen or heard was not a matter of Fourth Amendment concern. Olmstead v. United States, 277 U.S. 438, 465 (1928). *See* note 159 *supra*. *See also* McGinnis v. United States, 227 F.2d 598, 603 (1st Cir. 1955).

175. Brock v. United States, 223 F.2d 681 (5th Cir. 1955).

176. *Id.* at 685.

177. Whitley v. United States, 237 F.2d 787 (D.C. Cir. 1956).

178. United States v. Calabro, 276 F. Supp. 284 (S.D.N.Y. 1967).

179. Taylor v. United States, 286 U.S. 1 (1932). A unanimous Court excluded testimony of prohibition agents who used a flashlight to look through a small opening in the defendant's garage. Justice McReynolds characterized the warrantless presence of a six man squad of prohibition agents upon defendant's property as inexcusable.

180. *See* Mascolo, *The Role of Functional Observation in the Law of Search and Seizure: A Study in Misconception,* 71 DICK. L. REV. 379, 420 n.187-188 (1967). This article is one of the very few thoughtful analyses of visual surveillance and the Fourth Amendment. Mascolo cites the following cases as excluding fruits of an observation made possible by a

house.[181] For example, a Fifth Circuit Court of Appeals panel noted that:

> The main consideration in applying the test is to determine whether the observing officer had a right to be in the position to have that view. Many of the cases involving the plain view doctrine concern evidence recovered from autos located in public places. The rule lends itself to application in these situations because the observing officer is not required to trespass on private property in order to have a clear view of articles inside an automobile. However where the police officers trespass in order to secure the view we have not hesitated to find a search.[182]

Physical Presence: Plain View from a Legal Area. The plain sight rule continues to have particular vitality in those cases where a valid Fourth Amendment search is already underway and the police merely seize those suspect items that inadvertently come within their clear view.[183] Thus, once a determination is made that the police presence inside an individual's house is legal whether the police have a warrant[184] or probable cause,[185] are searching incident to an arrest[186]

---

physical intrusion of an area protected by the Fourth Amendment, McGinnis v. United States, 227 F.2d 598,603 (1st Cir. 1955); Williams v. United States, 263 F.2d 487, 489 (D.C. Cir. 1959); Simpson v. United States, 346 F.2d 291, 294 (10th Cir. 1965); Presley v. Pepersack, 228 F. Supp. 95, 104 (Md. 1964); Duncan v. State, 278 Ala. 145, 176 So.2d 840, 855 (Sup. Ct. 1965); State v. Hunt, 2 Ariz. App. 6, 406 P.2d 208, 214 (Ct. App. 1965); State v. Evans, 45 Hawaii 622, 372 P.2d 365, 369 (Sup. Ct. 1962); People v. O'Neill, 11 N.Y.2d 148, 227 N.Y.S.2d 416, 420 (1962); People v. Kramer, 38 Misc.2d 889, 239 N.Y.S.2d 303, 307 (Sup. Ct. App. Div. 1963); Barnes v. State, 25 Wis.2d 116, 130 N.W.2d 264, 269 (Sup. Ct. 1969). *See also* note 264 *infra*.

181. Root v. Gauper, 438 F.2d 361 (8th Cir. 1971), an unlawful police intrusion into a home will defeat the state's plain view contention. Squeella v. Avendana, 447 F.2d 575, 583 (5th Cir. 1971) (dicta) notes that illegal presence of law enforcement agent on curtilage makes observation through a window an illegal search. In United States v. Capps, 435 F.2d 637, 640 (9th Cir. 1970) the court upheld a search of defendant's car parked in his driveway using the following rationale:

> The Fourth Amendment's protections do not extend to the open field area surrounding a dwelling and immediately adjacent curtilage and therefore information gained as a result of a civil trespass on an open field area is not constitutionally tainted. . . .

182. United States v. Davis, 423 F.2d 974, 977 (5th Cir. 1970).

183. Harris v. United States, 390 U.S. 234 (1968); Coolidge v. New Hampshire, 403 U.S. 443 (1971).

184. United States v. Hamilton, 328 F. Supp. 1219 (Del. 1971); United States v. Patterson, 447 F.2d 424 (10th Cir. 1971); United States v. Thweatt, 433 F.2d 1226 (D.C.Cir. 1970); ker v. State of California, 347 U.S. 23 (1963).

185. Of course to legally search an individual's house without a warrant and instead with probable cause there must be a showing that in those circumstances it would have been impossible to seek a warrant. *See generally* Carroll v. United States, 267 U.S. 132, 153-154 (1925).

186. Chimel v. California, 395 U.S. 752 (1969); United States v. Titus, 445 F.2d 577 (2nd Cir. 1971).

or are responding to a call for assistance,[187] are invited guests[188] or pursuant to another judicially recognized reason,[189] any objects in the plain view of the officers can be searched.

Of course the plain sight rule cannot be used to justify the transformation of an officer's legal and specifically limited search of a residence into an exploratory search.[190] The Supreme Court noted:

> If the envelope were come upon in the course of a search for the suspect, the answer might be different from that where it is come upon, even though in plain view, in the course of a general indiscriminate search of closets, dressers, etc., after is is known that the occupant is absent.[191]

The plain view rationale also encompasses police observation of activities that are publicly visible (occurring in a public place or are in fact plainly visible from a public place).[192] Courts which have subscribed to this theory conclude that anything an officer can observe in such a location is not a subject of Fourth Amendment concern.[193]

Thus a series of decisions have held that where the police are standing on public walkways (including motel and apartment house walks) it is not a search if they peer through a residence's open

---

187. United States v. Barone, 330 F.2d 543 (2nd Cir. 1964) *cert. denied*, 377 U.S. 1004 (1964); Knisch v. Maryland, 271 A.2d 770, 10 Md. App. 565 (Ct. Spec. App. 1970); State v. Puryear, 94 N.J. Super. 125, 227 A.2d 139, 144 (Sup. Ct. 1967).

188. Bretti v. Wainwright, 439 F.2d 1042 (5th Cir. 1971); United States v. Welsch, F.2d 220 (10th Cir. 1971).

189. Vickory v. Superior Court, 10 Cal. App. 3d 110, 88 Cal. Rpts. 834 (Ct. App. 1970) (approaching house to ask a question). *See also* Giacona v. United States, 257 F.2d 450, 456 (5th Cir. 1958), *cert. denied*, 358 U.S. 873 (1958) (non-trespassory investigation) *and* Ellison v. United States, 206 F.2d 476, 478 (D.C. Cir. 1953).

190. Gilbert v. California, 388 U.S. 263 (1967).

191. *Id.* at 274-275.

192. In Coolidge v. New Hampshire, 403 U.S. at 465-466, the Supreme Court noted:

> ... the plain view doctrine would normally justify as well the seizure of other evidence that came to light during such an appropriately limited search. The court in *Chimel* went on to hold that "there is no comparable justification, however, for routinely searching any room other than that in which the arrest occurs—or for that matter, for searching through all the desk drawers or other closed or concealed areas in the room itself. Such searches in the absence of well recognized exceptions may be made only under the authority of a search warrant. Where, however the arresting officer inadvertently comes within plain view of a piece of evidence, not concealed, although outside of the area under the immediate control of the arrestee, the officer may seize it, so long as the plain view was obtained in the course of an appropriately limited search of the arrestee.

193. *Id.*

window (even a slightly open window).[194] The police can also legally stand or be in a place of public business and observe what transpires without crossing the Fourth Amendment threshold.[195]

A *fortiori*, where the police can legally observe activities or objects in an open field,[196] on a public street,[197] or in a car being

---

194. State v. Smith, 37 N.J. 481, 181 A.2d 761 (Sup. Ct. 1962), *cert. denied*, 374 U.S. 835 (1962); People v. King, 234 Cal. App. 2d 423, 44 Cal. Rptr. 500 (Ct. App. 2d Dist., 1965); Gill v. State of Texas, 394 S.W. 2d 810, 811 (Ct. of Crim. Appls. 1965). In People v. Bervtko, 77 Cal. Rptr. 217, 453 P.2d 721 (Sup. Ct. 1969) the court stated that the observation was legal because:

> The instant case involves observation by an officer from a place where he has a right to be and through an opening which defendant had provided through his arrangement of drapes covering his window. Peering through a window or a crack in a door or a keyhole is not in the abstract genteel behavior but the Fourth Amendment does not protect against all conduct unworthy of a good neighbor. Even surveillance of a house to see who enters or leaves is something less than good manners would permit. But it is the duty of a policeman to investigate and we cannot say that in striking a balance between the rights of the individual and the needs of law enforcement the Fourth Amendment itself draws the blinds the occupants could have drawn but did not. (77 Cal. Rptr. at 222).

See also Gil v. Beto, 440 F.2d 666 (5th Cir. 1971) (spotted drugs through open motel window); Ponce v. Craven, 409 F.2d 621 (9th Cir. 1969) (standing on motel walkways watched and overheard evidence through an open window); State v. Penna and Terrell, 5 Conn. Cir. 44,241, A.2d 385 (6th Cir. 1967). *See generally* United States v. Lanes, 398 F.2d 880 (2d Cir. 1968), *cert. denied*, 393 U.S. 1032 (1968); United States v. Lewis, 227 F. Supp. 433 (S.D.N.Y. 1964).

195. State v. La Duca, 89 N.J. Super. 159, 214 A.2d 423 (Super Ct. App. 1965); United States v. Source, 325 F.2d 84 (7th Cir. 1963); People v. Roberts, 182 Cal. App. 2d 431, 6 Cal. Rptr. 161 (Dist. Ct. App. 1960); People v. Rayson, 17 Cal. Rptr. 2d 243, 197 Cal. App. 2d 33 (Dist. Ct. App. 1961); Thorp v. Department of Alcoholic Beverages, 175 Cal. App. 2d 489, 346 P.2d 433 (1959). *See also* Cradle v. United States, 339 U.S. 56 (1950); United States v. Rabinowitz, 178 F.2d 962 (D.C. Cir. 1949), *cert. denied*, 339 U.S. 929 (1950).

196. Hester v. United States, 265 U.S. 57 (1924). *Hester* remains an important decision. It somewhat vitiates the Fourth Amendment's traditional touchstone - property rights - in favor of a reliance on the degree an individual's privacy has been invaded. In regard to observation of criminal activities by federal agents located in the open fields of the defendant's land the court concluded, "The special protection extended to the people in their persons, houses, papers and effects is not extended to the open fields." *Id.* at 59. One court has characterized *Hester* as meaning "it is not a search within the meaning of the Fourth Amendment to observe in a public place what is apparent for all the world to see." Caldwell v. United States, 338 F.2d 385, 388 (8th Cir. 1964), *cert. denied*, 380 U.S. 984 (1965).

A recent decision, Casey v. State of Nevada, 488 P.2d 546, 547 (Sup. Ct. of Nev. 1971) held it was no search for a state cattle inspector to conduct surveillance of defendant's uncle's open field: "Since *Hester*, the courts have quite consistently held that Fourth Amendment protections of privacy do not extend to open land, at least where the curtilage of a home is not breached or invaded in some way." This rule has been upheld even though the land was fenced Stark v. United States, 44 F.2d 946 (8th Cir. 1930); Tanney v. United States, 206 F.2d 601 (4th Cir. 1953); even though land posted with no trespassing signs McDowell v. United States, 383 F.2d 599 (8th Cir. 1967); and even though the evidence discovered was not in plain view Care v. United States, 231 F.2d 22 (10th Cir. 1956). *See also* State of Oregon v. Brown, 1 Or. App. Rpts. 322, 461 P.2d 836, 837 (Ct. App. 1969) (*en banc*) which upheld observation of defendant's marijuana garden as an open field investigation "even though the officers may be upon the private property of the individual." *See also* Riane v. United States, 229 F. 407 (9th Cir. 1924) *and* Koth v. United States, 16 F.2d 59 (9th Cir. 1926).

197. Trujillo v. United States, 294 F.2d 583 (10th Cir. 1961); State v. Collins, 150 Conn. Rpts. 488, 191 A.2d 253 (Sup. Ct. 1963); Coates v. United States, 413 F.2d 371 (D.C.

operated or parked in a public area,[198] it is not a search for the officers to seize what is plainly visible.

B. Plain View: Achieved by Surreptitious, Manipulative or Extra-Sensory Efforts.

In a varied group of cases, the courts have rigidly applied the physical presence doctrine to situations in which the police are technically in a legal location, but to secure a plain view, find it necessary to surreptitiously spy from behind ceilings and walls, to use trick devices, or to employ a variety of extra-sensory aids. In many of these decisions the courts ignore substantial indications that the observed individuals reasonably expected that they were safely engaged in a cloistered private activity. Indeed, the reasonableness of this anticipation is substantiated by the necessity for the police to resort to extraordinary surveillance efforts.

Furthermore, such courts overlook the purposeful character of the police surveillance. The Supreme Court in *Coolidge v. New Hampshire* emphasized that to escape the requirements of the Fourth Amendment the discovery of evidence in plain view must be "inadvertent."[199] "But where the discovery is anticipated, where the

---

Cir. 1969); United States v. Stable, 431 F.2d 1273 (6th Cir. 1970); United States v. Moody, 311 F. Supp. 756 (South Carolina 1970); Lederer v. Tehan, 441 F.2d 295 (6th Cir. 1971); Giacona v. United States, 257 F.2d 450, *cert. denied,* 358 U.S. 873 (1958); Marullo v. United States, 328 F.2d 361 (5th Cir. 1964); Sibron v. New York, 392 U.S. 40 (1968); Vale v. Louisiana, 399 U.S. 30 (1970). *Cf.* Terry v. Ohio, 392 U.S. 34 (1968) *and* Washington v. United States, 397 F.2d 705, 707 (D.C. Cir. 1968) (Judge Leventhal in his concurring opinion labels intensive visual surveillance and investigation in high crime areas "preventive patrolling" and expresses concern that too much street surveillance puts the police and the community in a confrontation posture).

198. Bushby v. United States, 296 F.2d 328 (9th Cir. 1961), *cert. denied,* 369 U.S. 876 (1962) (shot gun lying in rear of vehicle visible when door opened and dome light went on); United States v. Williams, 314 F.2d 795 (6th Cir. 1963)(bootleg whiskey visible when trunk popped open); People v. Manzi, 38 Misc. 2d 114, 237 N.Y.S. 2d 738 (Sup. Ct. 1963) (contraband seen in car); Theriault v. United States, 401 F.2d 79 (8th Cir. 1968) (burglary tools in bed of pick up truck); United States v. Williams, 446 F.2d 486 (5th Cir. 1971) (shotgun visible in car); State of Oregon v. Huddleston, 480 P.2d 454 (Ct. App. 1971) (stolen goods visibly placed in the bed of the truck); Orrion v. Erickson, 329 F. Supp. 360 (South Dakota 1971) (gloves used in robbery visible on front seat); Halls v. Craven, 325 F. Supp. 516 (C.D. Calif. 1971) (stocking mask used in robbery in plain view); Fitzpatrick v. Clark, 443 F.2d 916 (5th Cir. 1971) (hashish in plain sight); United States v. Chalk, 441 F.2d 1277 (4th Cir. 1971) (shotgun and dynamite spotted in car).

The above is merely a representative and recent sampling of cases holding that where an automobile is in a public place police officers in a legal position to do so can look inside the vehicle without that observation being considered a search. For an excellent discussion and documentation *see* Mascolo, *supra* note 180, at 400n.105 *et seq.*

199. Coolidge v. New Hampshire, 403 U.S. 443 (1971). *See* notes 160, 166, 190 *supra* and accompanying text.

police know in advance the location of the evidence and intend to seize it, the situation is altogether different."[200] In these situations the specific quest may become a search, and it is a distortion of the plain view doctrine to characterize this kind of surveillance as random observations visible in the normal course of the police officer's duty.[201]

The Toilet Opinions. The application of the physical presence—plain view doctrine to clandestine and deceptive surveillance of normally private areas has been illustrated with special clarity in a distinct group of mostly California cases generically labeled *toilet decisions.*[202]

In *People v. Norton*[203] and *People v. Young*[204] where police made a clandestine surveillance of doorless toilet stalls in a theater's (public park's) men's room the *Young* court held:

> They [homosexual activities] were conducted in the plain view of any member of the public who might happen to use the restroom. Had the police entered the public part of the restroom they could have observed such activities in the same way as any member of the public.
>
> . .[t]he fact that it was observed by the arresting officers from a vantage point concealed from public view from which the officers could conduct an effective vigil does not render the evidence inadmissable upon the ground that it was illegally obtained.[205]

In other decisions the police had a "plain view" of homosexual activity in "public" toilets while conducting surveillance from a win-

---

200. *Id.* at 470.

201. Mascolo, *supra* at note 180, at 416-417, describes purposeful surveillance as the primary ingredient in any search and concludes:

> . . . if [the police officer] engages in a mental quest for evidence of crime and if he relies upon his observations to assist in that quest then surely they should be classified as part of the quest itself. In short they should be designated as searches.
>
> Naturally there is another type of observation which has nothing to do with the search process and this might be called random or accidental observation. In the case of random observation there can be no search because the mental processes have not been set in motion. For example if an officer by happenstance comes upon evidence of crime, or likewise, if he observes a crime being committed in his presence, then his observations will not fall into the category of search.

202. *See* notes 203-213 *infra* and accompanying text. *See* notes 239-246 *infra* for a separate and contradictory line of toilet cases.

203. 209 Cal. App. 2d 173, 25 Cal. Rptr. 676 (Dist. Ct. App. 1962).

204. 214 Cal. App. 2d 131, 29 Cal. Rptr. 492 (Dist. Ct. App. 1963).

205. *Id.* at 494.

dow,[206] a two-way mirror,[207] a peephole,[208] through grillwork,[209] and while simply hiding.[210] In each of these cases the controlling factor was not the surveillance technique (except to the extent that the technique involved placing the officers physically in a legal non-trespassory location) but the potential visibility of the defendants to members of the public using the toilets.[211]

In the only Federal Court of Appeals treatment of a toilet surveillance fact situation, *Smayda v. United States* the Ninth Circuit held that police observation of closed toilet stalls (open three feet at the top and 18 inches at the bottom) in Yosemite National Park men's room by officers who peered through a concealed hole in the ceiling was not a search:[212]

> Here there was no physical search of appellant's person; only observation from a distance, albeit a short one. So far at least the Supreme Court has not extended the Fourth Amendment to such a situation. In every case there has been some physical unconsented to violation of a physical place, the property (either permanent or temporary) of the defendant or a non-consenting third party.[213]

---

206. People v. Holloway, 230 Cal. App. 2d 834, 839, 41 Cal. Rptr. 325, 328 (Dist. Ct. App. 1964):

Looking through a window is viewing that which is patent and visible to the general public. The fact that an officer may tend to observe more accurately than the public at large does not change the situation.

207. Townsend v. Ohio, 243 F. Supp. 777 (N.D. Ohio 1965).
208. People v. Hensel, 233 Cal. App. 2d 834, 43 Cal. Rptr. 865 (Dist. Ct. App. 1965).
209. People v. Maldonado, 240 Cal. App. 2d 812, 50 Cal. Rptr. 45 (Dist. Ct. App. 1966).
210. People v. Heath, 266 Cal. App. 2d 754, 72 Cal. Rptr. 457 (Dist. Ct. App. 1968); People v. Crafts, 13 Cal. App. 3d 457, 91 Cal. Rptr. 563 (Dist. Ct. App. 1970).
211. *But see* Mitchell v. State, 120 Ga. App. 447, 170 S.E.2d 765, (Ct. App. 1969) in which the court explicitly balances the public's interest in apprehending and deterring homosexual activities in public restrooms and the individual's interest in not being watched while he is engaged in the hopefully private process of relieving himself. The court frankly concludes "the public's interest in its privacy we think must to that extent be subordinated to the public's interest in law enforcement." 170 S.E.2d at 766.
212. 352 F.2d 251 (9th Cir. 1965), *cert. denied,* 382 U.S. 981 (1966).
213. *Id.* at 255. A persuasive dissent by Judge Browning argues that it makes no difference if a member of the public using the facility in a normal way could have observed the defendant's activity. The occurrence and validity of a search is measured in large part by the activities of the police. *Id.* at 259.
The *Smayda* decision provoked a flurry of law review comment mostly critical. *See* Note, *Fourth Amendment Application to Semi-Public Areas: Smayda v. United States,* 17 HASTINGS L. REV. 835 (1966); Note, *Public Toilet - Not an Unreasonable Search,* VAND. L. REV. 945 (1966); Note, *Police Surveillance of Public Toilets,* WASH. & LEE L. REV. 423 (1966).

This line of *toilet cases* relies heavily on the rationale of the physical presence doctrine. Each decision implicitly or explicitly concludes that the police had a right to be in the position they were in when they observed the incriminating acts. These holdings ultimately rest on the clearly fictional assertion that a toilet stall in a men's room unoccupied by normal users is not a constitutionally protected area (or in the words of the *Heath* decision, not an area in which the defendants could reasonably expect to have privacy)[214] because a member of the public from a vantage point other than that of the police officers could, with difficulty and significant forewarning, observe a small part of what the police saw.

Extra-Sensory Aids. In a now classic line of decisions beginning with *Olmstead v. United States* and culminating in *Silverman v. United States* and *Katz v. United States*,[215] the Supreme Court was impelled by the rapid advance of extra-sensory auditory equipment (used by law enforcement agencies to penetrate individual security

---

214. *See* note 210 *supra.*

215. The major Supreme Court decisions in this line began with Olmstead v. United States, 277 U.S. 438 (1928), a 5-4 decision which held that the Fourth Amendment does not encompass the interception of an individual's words because the words are not material things and because they were seized without trespass on the defendant's property. In Goldman v. United States, 316 U.S. 129 (1942), with Justice Murphy dissenting and some reluctant concurrences, the Court refused to reconsider *Olmstead* and held that the use of a wall microphone by federal agents to intercept conversations in an adjoining room was not a Fourth Amendment issue. In Silverman v. United States, 365 U.S. 505 (1961), the Court struck at the heart of the "propertied privacy" concept. A spike mike which penetrated the wall of the defendant's apartment and thereby intercepted his conversations was held to be a search and seizure. The Court made clear that conversations could be the object of a search and seizure. By characterizing the mike's penetration of the wall as a formal entry the Court also undercut the physical intrusion - trespass doctrine. *See also* Clinton v. Virginia, 377 U.S. 158 (1964). In between *Silverman* and *Katz* the court dealt with several other cases in which the tension between sophisticated auditory surveillance technology and the property underpinnings of the Fourth Amendment were highlighted. Lopez v. United States, 373 U.S. 427, 446 (1963) (Brennan, J., dissenting); Massiah v. United States, 377 U.S. 201 (1964); Hoffa v. United States, 385 U.S. 293, 313 (1966) (Warren, C.J., dissenting); Osborne v. United States, 385 U.S. 323, 394 (1966) (Douglas J., dissenting); Berger v. New York, 388 U.S. 41 (1967).

By 1967 the stage had been set for the Supreme Court's declaration in *Katz.* Indeed one commentator could predict in 1966,

> Thus the Court seems on the brink of a landmark ruling defining a comprehensive positive right of privacy from unreasonable surveillance. The rising concern over surveillance devices, alongside continued inaction by Congress on electronic eavesdropping increases the likelihood that such a ruling will come soon.

WESTIN, *supra* note 10, at 360.

Katz abandoned physical intrusion as the linchpin of search and seizure in favor of an inclusive, subjectively oriented, standard of privacy. The Fourth Amendment protects people not places when a person "justifiably relies" that a given activity will not be subject to government intrusion.

For the best account of the development and proliferation of the electronic eavesdropping devices that largely impelled these decisions, see WESTIN, *supra* note 10, at 73-78.

without physical presence) to conclude that if an individual's security from arbitrary police intrusion was to be maintained, the protections of the Fourth Amendment would have to be triggered by concerns other than property rights or the existence of a physical intrusion. With a few exceptions,[216] the courts have not applied the wisdom of auditory surveillance concepts to visual observations aided by extra-sensory devices.[217] Generally, the courts insist that once the police are in a location they are entitled to be in, they can observe objects in their plain view even if that view is effected by the use of the most imaginative and sophisticated techniques.[218]

For example, the law regarding observation and the use of artificial light remains virtually untouched since the Supreme Court's holding in *United States v. Lee*.[219] *Lee* approved the Coast Guard's use of a search light to inspect a ship at sea. "Such use of a search light is comparable to the use of a marine glass or a field glass. It is not prohibited by the Constitution."[220]

Where the use of a flashlight has made possible exogenous inspections of the interior of a house,[221] a garage,[222] a chicken

---

216. See notes 83-90 *supra* and accompanying text.

217. One possible explanation for the Court's reluctance to treat visual surveillance in the same manner as auditory surveillance is that until very recently the state of the art in extra-sensory visual surveillance devices (mostly flashlights and binoculars) could not match the array of microminiaturized microphones and other wiretapping equipment used for auditory surveillance. See WESTIN, *supra* note 10, at 70-78. However, with the continued development of the electronics industry and Vietnam has come the marketing of advanced visual surveillance systems, split screen and instant replay video tape, miniaturized cameras, etc. See GOULDEN, *supra* note 27, and BARKAN, *supra* note 41.

The Orbis III system, for instance, "contains a sophisticated camera which can penetrate tinted glass or dark glasses worn by the car's occupants. It is tied to a computerized vehicle registration list and produces automatic ticketing of speeders." Hentoff, *The Politics of Privacy(1)* The Village Voice, March 9, 1972, at 29. For an earlier account of the Orbis System, see N.Y. Times, July 9, 1969 at 70.

218. Where the police officer need only shift position, bend over, or stoop to make an inspection, courts have little difficulty in justifying the inspection on the basis of the plain view doctrine. For example, in James v. United States, 418 F.2d 1150 (D.C. Cir. 1969), the court held that an officer who had to stoop down to look into a garage was not conducting a search:

That the policeman may have to crane his neck, or bend over, or squat, does not render the doctrine inapplicable, so long as what he saw would have been visible to any curious passerby.

In accord see Ashby v. Florida, 245 So.2d 225, 227-8 (Sup. Ct. 1971) which reversed a lower court opinion, 228 So.2d 400 (Dist. Ct. App. 1969), and held that it is not a search to look through a crack in a garage since the officer looked inside the garage from a position he had a legal right to be in.

219. 274 U.S. 559 (1927).

220. *Id.* at 563.

221. State v. Plummer, 5 Conn. Cir. 35, 241 A.2d 198 (Cir. Ct. App. Div. 1967). (A flashlight inspection from a fire escape on which the police had a right to be, exposed the defendant in bed with a man to whom she was not married).

222. United States v. Wright, 449 F.2d 1355 (D.C. Cir. 1971). See notes 225-226 *supra* and accompanying text. *Compare* United States v. Vilhotti, 323 F. Supp. 425 (S.D.N.Y. 1971). See note 252 *infra* and accompanying text.

coop,[223] and on frequent occasions, an automobile,[224] the courts have characterized this observation as in plain sight of the police and hence not a search. A most recent decision, *United States v. Wright*,[225] upholds a flashlight inspection of a garage where the officers, who were legally standing outside the garage, directed their beam through an 8 to 9 inch crevice and discovered a stolen transmission. The defendant contended that the police officers' visual observation, particularly when aided by a flashlight, was a search. But the court said that regardless of whether the transmission could be considered in plain view to start with or whether the officer took a closer look at a challenging situation, no Fourth Amendment rights were involved. Although the court recognized that *Katz* defines a Fourth Amendment situation in terms of reasonable expectation of privacy, the decision implicitly adopts the test that this expectation of privacy from visual surveillance is a function of whether or not a person rightfully outside the garage could find some means to look inside.[226]

Observation made possible by magnification has been treated by the courts in much the same manner as the artificial light situations. Regardless of either the extent of the invasion of privacy made possible by magnification or an individual's expectation of privacy, no court has held magnification to be an independent determinant of a search.[227] The Supreme Court's dictum in *On Lee v. United States* is often cited by lower courts.

> The use of bifocals, field glasses or the telescope to magnify the object of a witness' vision is not a forbidden search and seizure even if they focus without his knowledge or consent upon what one supposes to be private indiscretions.[228]

---

223. Safarik v. United States, 62 F.2d 892 (8th Cir. 1933).

224. See Mascolo, *supra* note 180, at 402-403 & n.110. Recent cases upholding a flashlight inspection of an automobile include Dorsey v. United States, 372 F.2d 928, 931 (D.C. Cir. 1967),

> We do not think the need to employ a visual aid at night in the form of a flashlight converts this from lawful into unlawful conduct . . . . If policemen are to serve any purpose of detecting and preventing crime they must be able to take a closer look at challenging situations as they encounter them.

Marshall v. United States, 422 F.2d 185,188 (5th Cir. 1970), "The plain view rule does not go into hibernation at night"; Walker v. Beto, 437 F.2d 1018 (5th Cir. 1971); Parks v. State 46 Ala. 722, 248 So.2d 761 (Ct. Crim. App.1971). *Compare* Pruitt v. State, 389 S.W.2d 475 (Ct. Crim. App. 1965) and State v. Charbonneau, Cr4-10315 (Conn. Cir. Ct. 1965) (unreported).

225. United States v. Wright, 449 F.2d 1355 (D.C. Cir. 1971).

226. *Id.* at 1363.

227. *See* Hodges v. United States, 243 F2d 821 (5th Cir. 1957) *and* Johnson v. State, 2 Md. App. 300, 234 A.2d 464 (Ct. Spec. App. 1967).

228. 343 U.S. 747, 754 (1952). *On Lee* was the first informer, electronic eavesdropping case.

A recent Pennsylvania state court decision provides a very sharp picture of the kind of intrusion visual surveillance with magnification can entail.[229] In *Commonwealth of Pennsylvania v. Hernley*, an FBI agent suspecting that football gambling forms were being printed inside the defendant's shop, realized that the windows were too high for a man to see in, climbed a four foot ladder positioned 35 feet from the shop, and with the use of binoculars, observed incriminating activities. Reversing the lower court decision which excluded the agent's testimony, the court held that since *Katz* is not retroactive[230] the standard to be applied in the instant case is the physical presence test—a window observation does not involve a physical intrusion on the premises, and is therefore permissible. Furthermore, the Court suggested that even if *Katz* did apply,

> ... our case presents the situation in which it was incumbent on the subject to preserve his privacy from visual observation. To do that the appellees had only to curtain the windows. Absent such obvious action we cannot find that their expectation of privacy was justifiable or reasonable. The law will not shield the criminal from observation where the action shows such little regard for his privacy.[231]

The *Hernley* and *Wright* cases are apt models of the significant intrusion into an individual's reasonably anticipated privacy that inevitably occurs,when his right to privacy is defined only in terms of where the police are located and not in terms of the purpose, technique and effect of the police surveillance.[232] Judge Montgomery dissenting in *Hernley* asserts:

> I believe that these defendants were subjected to an unreasonable search when the FBI agent used a ladder to obtain

---

229. Commonwealth v. Hernley, 263 A.2d 904, 216 Pa. Super. 177 (Super. Ct. 1970), *cert. denied*, 401 U.S. 914 (1970).

230. Desist v. United States, 394 U.S. 244 (1969) (held that *Katz* was not to be applied retroactively).

231. 216 Pa. Super. at 181-182.

232. *See* notes 239-253 *supra* and accompanying text; *see also* United States v. Wright, 449 F.2d 1355, 1367 (D.C. Cir. 1971) (Wright, J., dissenting) and Fullbright v. United States, 392 F.2d 432, 435 (10th Cir. 1968), *cert. denied*, 393 U.S. 830 (1968). The court held that the use of binoculars by alcohol tax investigators to watch the defendant operate a still was not a search. However the court offered this qualification:

> By this we do not mean to say that surveillance from outside a curtilage may under no circumstances constitute an illegal search in view of the teachings of *Katz*.

a view into the premises otherwise not available to the public. I strongly believe that to hold otherwise would be to unreasonably restrict the right of our citizens to feel safe in leaving their windows uncurtained to the skies.[233]

Montgomery concludes that if the *Katz* rationale is applied in the visual sphere as it has been in the auditory sphere, magnification and "close motion pictures" of an individual will be proscribed in most instances.[234]

C. Reasonable Expectation of Freedom From Visual Surveillance

As stated earlier the reasonable expectation of privacy standard made triumphant in *Katz* has had less influence on lower court decisions dealing with visual surveillance than it has had in other areas of search and seizure law because of the tendency on the part of many courts to measure the reasonableness of the expectation by the physical presence tests of the plain view doctrine. Since *Katz*, only three Supreme Court cases have dealt significantly with the plain view doctrine and none have been particularly helpful.[235] *Harris*[236] and *Chimel*[237] speak to a fact situation in which the plain view rationale is used to supplement an admittedly legal search already in progress. *Coolidge*,[238] by emphasizing the common sense underpinnings of the plain view doctrine—e.g., that police who are lawfully performing their duty can, like anyone else, take notice of what they happen to see—does at least serve to distinguish the rationale of the plain view doctrine from the kind of purposeful visual observation that occurs when police overcome an otherwise defective observational location by using non-technological and technological intrusive surveillance techniques.

A handful of cases both pre- and post-*Katz* have defined a right to visual privacy by weighing all the elements that bear on the reasonableness of the police officer's visual intrusions.

A separate line of *toilet cases* has been responsible for much of the law in this area. In *Bielicki v. Superior Court*, the Supreme Court of California excluded testimony of a police officer who used a pipe which extended to the roof to spy on occupants of toilet stalls in an

---

233. 216 Pa. Super. at 182-183.
234. *Id.* at 183.
235. See discussion in United States v. Wright, 449 F.2d 1335, 1363 (D.C. Cir. 1971).
236. *See* note 166 *supra*.
237. *See* notes 163 and 166 *supra*.
238. *See* notes 166 and 190 *supra*.

amusement park's rest room.[239] The same court affirmed and extended *Bielicki* shortly thereafter in *Britt v. Superior Court.*[240] *Britt* involved a virtually identical fact situation (although here the police took motion pictures); however, the state attempted to distinguish *Britt* and *Bielicki.* In *Britt,* "the illegal activities were clearly observable to any person of the general public who might have entered the men's room at that moment."[241] The court did not deal with this constitutionally protected area argument but instead rested its opinion on the nature and effect of the police surveillance:

> The crucial fact in *Bielicki* was neither the manner of observation alone nor the place of commission alone, but rather the manner in which the police observed a place . . . .
>
> [C]landestine observations by police officers of premises devoted to common use by the public—such as for example, the shopping areas and public hallways and elevators of the department store here involved is not prohibited by our decision in *Bielicki.* But it is equally clear that authority to maintain clandestine surveillance of common use public places and persons therein is not the equivalent of a license to surreptitiously invade the right of personal privacy of persons in public places. Man's constitutionally protected right of personal privacy not only abides with him while he is a householder within his own castle but cloaks him when as a member of the public he is temporarily occupying a room . . . .[242]

Although *Bielicki* and *Britt* were misread and distinguished in a long line of subsequent California *toilet cases,*[243] two recent decisions have followed *Britt.*[244]

---

239. 371 P.2d 288, 21 Cal. Rptr. 552 (1962), *rehearing denied* (1962).

240. 58 Cal. App. 2d 469, 374 P.2d 817, 24 Cal. Rptr. 849 (1962).

241. 374 P.2d at 818.

242. *Id.* at 819. For a further discussion, see *Clandestine Police Surveillance of Public Toilets Held to be Unreasonable Search,* COLUM. L. REV. 955 (1963).

243. *See* text accompanying notes 202-210 *supra.*

244. In addition to State v. Bryant, 287 Minn. 205, 177 N.W. 2d 800 (1970), Brown v. State, 3 Md.App. 90, 23 8 A.2d 147 (Ct. Spec. Apps. 1968) held it was a search when a police officer on routine inspection of a tavern lavatory saw a known addict standing in a partially enclosed toilet and peeked over the top to discover narcotics parphernalia. The evidence was excluded as an illegal search and seizure on the grounds that the defendant had a reasonable expectation of privacy. Contrast this decision with James v. United States, 418 F.2d 1150 (D.C. Cir. 1969) and Ashby v. Florida 245 So.2d 225 (Sup. Ct. 1971). A policeman may "crane his neck, bend over or squat" without making the plain view doctrine inapplicable. The juxtaposition of these cases suggests that it is not only the method of police surveillance or the

In *State v. Bryant*,[245] the Supreme Court of Minnesota excluded evidence obtained when a police officer used vents in the ceiling of a department store lavatory to observe the defendant's engaging in "sodomy." Paraphrasing *Katz* the Court concluded,

> What a person knowingly exposes to the public even in his own home or office is not a subject of Fourth Amendment protection. But what he seeks to preserve as private even in an area accessible to the public may be constitutionally protected. While the *Katz* case involved evidence obtained by listening and the case before us involves evidence obtained by visual observation, we think the results are the same.[246]

A few recent cases have asserted that reasonable expectations of freedom from visual surveillance in the home will also be protected from observation by police officers occupying a position in which they have a right to be.[247] Dicta from a California state court of Appeals decision, *Vidaurri v. Superior Court*, suggests that:

---

security that the observed area provides against public visibility that determines when a search occurs. A separate factor is the sanctity of the observed activity or area. Under this theory a bathroom will get more judicial protection than a garage.

245. 287 Minn. 205, 177 N.W.2d 800 (1970).

246. *Id.* at 209. For an analysis of State v. Bryant, *see Criminal Law: Unreasonable Visual Observation Held to Violate Fourth Amendment,* 55 MINN. L. REV. 1255 (1971).

247. State v. Kent, 20 Utah2d, 1, 10, 432 P.2d, 64, 69 (1967) is an early case reaching this conclusion on the facts. A police officer with permission of the motel manager secreted himself in the attic from where he could observe defendant's bathroom and bedroom. The holding is best expressed by the dissent which labeled the decision a

> shocking conclusion that a peace officer who was where he had a lawful right to be without any physical trespass or invasion into the domain of the defendant and without the use of extrasensory aids simply observed what he could with his eyes and ears and made an unreasonable search.

The case most often cited for the proposition that a visual search is not measured by the physical intrusion of the viewer is Texas v. Gonzales, 388 F.2d 145, 148 (5th Cir. 1968). In dictum (since the facts of the case make clear that the police were standing illegally outside the defendant's window when they looked inside) the Fifth Circuit offered this exegesis,

> The court has increasingly discarded fictional property concepts in resolving the issues of privacy and public security. The existence of a search does not depend on a trespass under local property law. All that is necessary is an actual intrusion into a constitutionally protected area. . . . *Brock* teaches that this intrusion can be accomplished visually."

The District Court in Gil v. Beto, 323 F. Supp. 1264, 1267 (W.D. Texas 1970), *aff'd. on narrow grounds,* 440 F.2d 660 (5th Cir. 1970) speculated that if *Katz* were retroactive, then on the facts in the instant case it might have held that it was a search for a police officer to stand on a motel's walkway and look through a partially open window.

... a person who surrounds his backyard with a fence and limits entry with a gate, locked or unlocked, has shown a reasonable expectation of privacy for that area ... and does not give up that reasonable expectation of backyard privacy simply because a trespassing police officer might stand at the gate and look in to their yard . . . . [248]

Another recent California case, *Kirby v. Superior Court*, also in dicta, posits that whether or not a police officer can look into a motor vehicle is determined by the defendant's reasonable expectations of privacy manifested in the security of the vehicle from visual surveillance.[249]

Very few decisions have intimated that a search occurs where the police officer who is legally occupying a given area uses extrasensory devices to make possible the discovery of an activity that would otherwise remain private. The first and most important decision to reach this result is *Pruitt v. State*.[250] There an officer made a traffic stop, checked the defendant's license, and without probable cause beamed his flashlight into the back of the defendant's car revealing illegally transported liquor. The Court concluded,

Had he seen the wine visible to his naked eye lying on the front seat of the automobile, then the evidence would have been admissible for it would have been secured without the need of a search . . . . We think however that the search actually started when the officer shined or flashed the flashlight in the back of the car.[251]

Another interesting decision is Cohen v. Superior Court, 5 Cal.App. 3d 429, 435, 85 Cal. Rptr. 354, 358 (Ct. App. 1970) holding that where the police looked into the defendant's apartment from the fire escape the determinative question is not the extent of the physical intrusion necessary to reach the observation point but was a factual question of whether defendants could reasonably anticipate to be free from uninvited visual intrusion through the fire escape window. *See also* Edwards v. State, 38 Wis.2d 332, 156 N.W. 2d 397 (1968) and People v. Willard, 238 Cal.App.2d 292 47 Cal. Rptr. 734 (Ct. App. 1969); in both cases the courts denied a search despite the physical trespass on the land underneath defendants' window from which location the police looked inside the house. The courts considered how much of an intrusion this visual observation constituted and concluded that since the windows were open and plainly visible from the street, it was merely in the officer's plain view to watch from directly outside the window. *See also* People v. Martin, 45 Cal.App.2d 755, 290 P.2d 855 (1955), a case which also ignored the illegal location of the police observers. However, here the area observed was an office and the police implicitly had probable cause.

248. 13 Cal.App.3d 550, 553, 91 Cal.Rptr. 704, 706 (Ct. App. 1970).

249. 8 Cal.App.3d 591, 87 Cal.Rptr. 577 (Ct. App. 1970). An officer seeing a curtained van parked suspiciously in a business district after hours, parted the curtains and found the defendant with a nude and crying 14 year old boy.

250. 389 S.W.2d 475 (Tex. Crim. App. of Texas 1965). For a full discussion of *Pruitt* see Mascolo, *supra* note 180, at 423-424. *Pruitt* has been criticized in some subsequent decisions. See Walker v. Beto, 437 F.2d 1018, 1020.

251. 389 S.W. 2d at 476. For an identical holding see State v. Charbonneau CR4-10315 (Conn. Cir. Ct. 1965). The opinion is unreported but it is discussed in Mascolo, *supra* note 180, at 425.

United States v. Vilhotti, a District Court decision, intimates that on the law it is in agreement with *Pruitt.* The defendant sought to exclude testimony of contraband spotted during an FBI flashlight search of his garage.

> [M]odern methods of surveillance and the density of urban living necessitate abandonment of the element of physical invasion as a *sine qua non* of a Fourth Amendment violation. The two most important variables in deciding whether a visual search contravenes the Fourth Amendment are accessibility to view and the nature of the premises . . . . While the [FBI agent's] vantage point was a well traveled public right of way, it would be distorting the plain view doctrine to hold that it encompasses peering through cracks in a boarded window.[252]

On the facts the court held it was no search to use a flashlight to peer into an abandoned garage with "visible gaps in the boards" covering the window.[253]

The several decisions just discussed represent a serious attempt to protect personal privacy in the context of police visual surveillance. Several common concerns emerge from these decisions. First, an individual must demonstrate a desire and an expectation of freedom from visual surveillance (he builds a fence, draws his curtains, boards up a garage, transports an item under darkness, *etc.*). The reasonableness of that anticipation will then be measured by two threshold questions. What are the nature of the premises? Arguably, society has a greater interest in protecting a bathroom or a house than a garage or a motor vehicle. And how accessible, in fact, are these activities to visual surveillance? Can the activities or objects be routinely seen by the public (and thus the police) from common public areas without taking any purposeful or unusual action? Or are these activities susceptible to observation only after taking extraordinary actions, *e.g.*, intruding on the subject's land or buildings, using surreptitious or deceptive viewing techniques (two way mirrors, air vents, *etc.*) or employing technological and non-technological visual aids (zoom lens, search lights, infra red surveillance systems, helicopters or simply ladders, tunnels, *etc.*)? A sensitivity to these criteria will prevent the courts from being finessed by clandestine and

---

252. *See* note 224 *supra.* 323 F.Supp. at 431.
253. *Id.* at 431. Recall the statement in Fullbright v. U.S. 392 F.2d 432 (10thCir. 1968), *cert. denied* 393 U.S. 830 (1968), that in some circumstances using a flashlight might be the gravamen of the search. *See* Barnes V. State, 25 Wis.2d 116, 130 N.W.2d 264 (1964).

deceptive observational techniques and outflanked by technologically sophisticated visual surveillance systems.[254]

D. Observation and Electronic Surveillance Systems

Occasionally, a detailed analysis will make a brief conclusion appropriate. Let us, then in summary fashion, apply the varying doctrines of visual surveillance to the specific facts of a Mt. Vernon style camera system.

A workable construct would involve the following assumptions. In a legal and literal sense the camera is the eye of the police. The camera makes observations without a search warrant. Furthermore, camera surveillance of this type cannot readily meet the requirements of any of the exigent circumstance doctrines.[255] Therefore, if the cameras search at all, the search is *per se* unreasonable. Moreover, camera observations would normally be made without even reasonable suspicion. Although reasonable suspicion is not legally recognized as grounds for a search, in many of our cases the courts were influenced by the logic of the police officer's actions.[256]

---

254. *See* Lopez v. United States, 373 U.S. 427, 446 (1963) (Brennan, J. dissenting) and Osborne V. United States, 385 U.S. 323, 329 (1966) (Douglas, J. dissenting). Brennan bemoaned the fact that the Court's attempt to protect individual security and privacy through its application of the search and seizure law, had been "outflanked by the technological advances of the very recent past." 373 U.S. at 471.

255. In the analogous case of auditory surveillance Justice Stewart observed:

It is difficult to imagine how any of those doctrines could ever apply to the sort of search and seizure involved in this case. Even electronic surveillance substantially contemporaneous with an individual's arrest could hardly be deemed incident to that arrest. Nor could electronic surveillance without prior authorization be justified on the grounds of hot pursuit. And, of course, the very nature of electronic surveillance precludes its use pursuant to the suspect's consent.

Katz v. United States, 389 U.S. at 357-358.

256. For instance, in the plain view cases, notes 194-198 *supra*, particularly where the police spy into open windows or look into defendant's property the opinions suggest that it was the logical and common sense action for a police officer to take. Particularly in cases like Dorsey v. United States, 372 F.2d 928 (D.C. Cir. 1967); James v. United States, 418 F.2d 1150 (D.C. Cir.1969); and Ashby v. Florida, 245 So.2d 225 (Sup. Ct.1971), the courts sustain visual intrusions into areas not easily visible on the technical grounds of plain view. However, the officer's reasonable suspicion to inspect is implicitly persuasive. Thus to repeat the court's conclusion in *Dorsey*

We do not think the need to employ a visual aid at night in the form of a flashlight converts this from lawful into unlawful conduct. . . .If policemen are to serve any purpose of detecting and preventing crime they must be able to take a closer look at challenging situations as they encounter them.

372 F.2d at 931.

Supreme Court decisions in *Katz*[257] and *Terry v. Ohio*[258] teach that the Fourth Amendment offers the same security to an individual whether he be in a house, a bathroom or on the street. In every case, the individual is free from arbitrary state intrusion in those activities or areas in which he has a reasonable expectation of privacy.

Thus the central question becomes what privacy can an individual reasonably expect to have while on a public street. Surely, an individual cannot reasonably expect to be free from observation.[259] It seems unassailable that the courts will always affirm what the logic here demands—that a police officer be allowed, indeed be expected, to patrol and observe what transpires in areas fully open to the public.[260]

---

257. Katz v. United States, 389 U.S. 347 (1967). For purposes of emphasis it may be helpful, once again, to quote the operable words,

> For the Fourth Amendment protects people, not places. What a person knowingly exposes to the public, even in his own home or office, is not a subject of Fourth Amendment protection. . . But what he seeks to preserve as private, even in an area accessible to the public, may be constitutionally protected.
> *Id.* at 351, 352.

258. Terry v. Ohio, 392 U.S. 1 (1968) held that an officer who justifiably is investigating suspicious behavior may "pat down" the outside of a suspect's clothing to disarm him of weapons.

However the court made it clear that merely because an individual is in a public place he is not stripped of Fourth Amendment protection:

> This inestimable right of personal security belongs as much to the citizen on the streets of our cities as to the homeowner closeted in his study to dispose of his secret affairs.

Id. at 9. And later the Court concluded:

> Unquestionably petitioner was entitled to the protection of the Fourth Amendment as he walked down the street in Cleveland.

Id. at 9. *See also* Carroll v. United States, 267 U.S. 132 (1925); United States v. De Re, 332 U.S. 581 (1948); Henry v. United States, 361 U.S. 98 (1959); Rios v. United States, 364 U.S. 253 (1960); Beck v. Ohio 379 U.S. 89 (1964).

259. Even observation from a vantage point 22 feet overhead. In Commonwealth v. Hernley, 216 Pa. Super. 177 (Montgomery, J., dissenting) it was asserted that when the federal agent used a ladder to get a better vantage point from which to spy on the defendant it was a search. However it is significant that the agent in *Hernley* had a specific target and that target was relying on the fact that there existed no elevated vantage point from which a person could look through his windows. In the Mt. Vernon camera situation the use of a utility pole to mount the cameras is theoretically well publicized and is not part of a particular prying into one person's property. Only the most resolute imagination could conceive of a court ruling in the analogous situation of police use of a street platform for traffic direction that it was search for the police officer to inadvertently spot incriminating objects on the floor of a passing car.

260. *See* discussion of police presence and observation of public places, notes 194-198 *supra* and accompanying text.

On the other hand, it is entirely possible on the logic and the law that the courts at a future time will conclude that a person walking on a public street has a reasonable expectation not to be subjected to telescopic surveillance.[261] Were the police to use the system's telescopic capability to read a pedestrian's lips or documents, identify contraband or evidence, or detect incriminating characteristics of body and dress not otherwise observable, it is at least a tenable contention that a court would conclude that the individual had been searched.[262]

The same analysis reaches a parallel conclusion in regard to the camera's low light level capability. Under the circumstances just delineated, police use of a light intensification process to pierce the darkened interior of an individual's car[263] or a pedestrian's partially opened coat might be considered a search.[264]

Finally, if we assume that the cameras can be used to look into the windows of private residences,[265] a strong argument can be made that this kind of surveillance, in certain circumstances, is a search. Simply stated, if the householder takes steps to guard his windows in such a way that only a creature patrolling many feet above the street

---

261. Of course the individual scrutinized must have *manifested* an actual expectation of privacy. As one law review note concluded:

> Any activity or information exposed to the public by virtue of being too visible or too loud is not worthy of protection despite the individual's intentions.

Note, *From Private Places to Personal Privacy: A Post-Katz Study of the Fourth Amendment Protection,* 43 N.Y.U. L.REV. 968, 981 (1968). Therefore, the individual should have concealed, disguised, miniaturized or in some way ensured that the object or activity would escape normal detection.

262. The likelihood of a legal search occurring is increased if the camera operator manipulates the controls to combine and vary the angle of the cameras, the zoom lens and the instant replay capability to systematically track and focus on one person in the purposeful, target specific manner associated with a search. *See* Coolidge v. New Hampshire, 403 U.S. 443 (1971).

263. *See* Masculo, *supra* note 180.

264. In Barnes v. State, 25 Wis.2d 116, 130 N.W.2d 264 (1964), the court ruled that when the police arrested the defendant for a traffic violation it was part of the search to use a flashlight to peer inside the defendant's overcoat.

Although visual observation by magnification and visual observation by light intensification are quite similar they do differ in one critical aspect. While in the surveillance area not every object is exposed to telescopic surveillance every object is exposed to light intensification. To this extent entering the surveillance area is much like entering a well lit street or shopping center. Of course, this difference cannot be taken too far. For if the reasonableness of an expectation of privacy is measured by how often or how completely the police scrutinize a given activity, then, ultimately no expectation of privacy could meet the reasonableness test.

265. Observing a person through the windows of a public place like a store or restaurant is not substantially different from watching that person on the street.

Likewise watching a person in a motor vehicle is much like watching a pedestrian. *See* notes 195, 198 *supra,* and accompanying text. *See also* Kirby v. Superior Court, 8 Cal.App.3d 591, 87 Cal.Rptr. 577 (Ct.App. 1970), where a curtained motor vehicle provided privacy from visual scrutiny.

and capable of vast magnification and light intensification could pierce the security of his home then a court sensitive to the individual's intentions, the nature of the area observed and the manner of observation could quite persuasively characterize this surveillance as a search.[266]

Manifestly, one is left with the inevitable conclusion that the Fourth Amendment provides only the most narrow and tangential obstacles to police deployment and use of sophisticated remote controlled twenty-four hour camera surveillance equipment in public areas.

PART IV: QUESTIONS OF PUBLIC POLICY

An analysis of the implications for our society that widescale electronic visual surveillance involve must be prefaced by a restatement of where the law is not. It seems clear after our discussion that the commands of the First and Fourth Amendments do not proscribe, at least in any significant way, the kind of surveillance conducted in Mt. Vernon. Although the impact of other constitutional amendments cannot be substantively discussed here, a few comments, by way of outline and definition, seem in order.

The Fifth Amendment which, among other things, bars the state from compelling an individual to incriminate himself has "never been given the full scope which the values it helps to protect suggest . . . ."[267] Specifically, the privilege applies to state action that compels communications or testimony but it has been held inapplicable to the kind of real or physical evidence that a suspect would produce before the cameras.[268]

Another element of Fifth Amendment protections based in part on the self-incrimination clause and more directly on the Fifth Amendment's due process clause requires that any confessions introduced in a criminal prosecution be voluntary.[269] Coercion sufficient to taint the confession can be psychological as well as physical.[270] In

266. For a discussion of visual intrusions of a house, see notes 174-182, 247-248 and accompanying text.

267. Schmerber v. California, 384 U.S. 757, 762 (1966).

268. In *Schmerber*, a closely divided Court held that the self incrimination clause did not bar the involuntary withdrawal of blood and admission in evidence of the analysis. In the more nearly analogous case of United States v. Wade, 388 U.S. 218, 222 (1967) the Court held that, "compelling the accused to merely exhibit his person for observation by a prosecution witness involves no compulsion of the accused to give evidence having testimonial significance."

269. Brown v. Mississippi, 297 U.S. 278 (1936) was the first Supreme Court scrutiny of confessions.

270. See Asheralt v. Tennessee, 322 U.S. 143 (1944) and Watts v. Indiana, 338 U.S. 49 (1949).

the instant case, repeated showings of the videotaped account of the incident to the accused in order to extract a confession from him, would almost certainly render any subsequent confessions inadmissible.[271]

The Sixth Amendment's protections of counsel and confrontation provide no apparent obstacles to the deployment and operation of a camera surveillance system but the Amendment does present real issues that go to the nature and extent of the state's use of camera produced evidence. For instance, based on the Supreme Court's decisions in *United States v. Wade*[272] and *United States v. Gilbert*,[273] (holding that an accused is entitled to the presence of counsel at any critical stage in the prosecution, including a pre-trial lineup), it is very likely that a suspect's attorney would have to be present at any showing of the videotape to prosecution witnesses.[274] Another important question, bearing on Sixth Amendment protections, is can the video tape be shown in court, and if so, under what conditions.[275]

The amorphous concept of a constitutional right of privacy poses a final legal hurdle to the proliferation of the Mt. Vernon type surveillance systems. A constitutionally impelled broad based right of privacy was most forcefully articulated in *Griswold v. Connecticut.*[276] The seven to two Supreme Court opinion held that a statutory scheme which made it illegal for married couples to use contraceptives (or for doctors to prescribe contraceptives) was an unconstitutional invasion of the right to privacy. Justice Douglas based his plurality opinion on the existence in the Bill of Rights of zones or penumbras of privacy. In a much recognized concurrence, Justice

---

271. Of course under Escobedo v. Illinois, 378 U.S. 478 (1964) and Miranda v. Arizona, 384 U.S. 436 (1966) a suspect could have his lawyer present during the showing of the film and could demand to be left alone.

272. 388 U.S. 218 (1967).

273. 388 U.S. 263 (1967).

274. *See* Simmons v. United States, 390 U.S. 377 (1968), which suggested that photographic identifications can be a critical stage of the prosecution.

275. For one of the very few legal discussions of the use of videotape, see Note, *Judicial Administration—Technological Advances—Use of Videotape in the Courtroom and in the Stationhouse*, 20 DEP L. REV. 925 (1971). Generally, courts have held videotape admissible without expert testimony. See *id* at 943 for cites to numerous cases so holding. For two somewhat dated but colorful descriptions of videotape use in legal settings, *see* TIME MAGAZINE (Dec. 22, 1967) at 49 and TIME MAGAZINE (Dec. 29, 1967) at 38.

A rather exotic characterization of a Sixth Amendment problem is presented in the DePaul Law Review, *supra* at 947. In Santa Barbara, Calif., police used a video tape system to record interrogations of drunken drivers. The next day after viewing the tape almost all of the defendants pleaded guilty. This *de facto* trial produces what the author characterized as an alternate system of justice in possible conflict with the requirements of the Sixth Amendment.

276. 381 U.S. 479 (1965).

Goldberg sought to fortify this substantive due process approach to privacy by pointing to the Ninth Amendment as proof that when the framers drafted the first Eight Amendments they were not denying the existence of equally fundamental but unspecified liberties. In the years since *Griswold*, subsequent opinions have not strengthened the *Griswold* privacy doctrine in either breadth of applicability or clarity of formulation.[277] Particularly relevant for our purposes is the unwillingness of the courts to use the *Griswold* doctrine in its confrontations with the two major threats to privacy that developed in the late 60's—a continuing pattern of government intrusion by electronic surveillance and intrusion by the government's increasing collection, control and dissemination of personal data.

In the interests of completeness, it might be added that there appear to be no significant statutory or tort limitations on the right of the police to photograph people in public places.[278]

Finally, it should be noted that judicial regulation of television surveillance systems is not only inhibited by the lack of protective substantive law; it is further limited by the marked ineffectiveness of the adversarial process in confronting new technologies. The speed of

---

277. Hufstedler, *The Directions and Misdirections of a Constitutional Right of Privacy* 26 RECORD 546, 558-562 (October, 1971). A number of commentators have suggested that the Griswold doctrine was never clear or persuasive. *See generally Symposium on the Griswold Case and the Right of Privacy,* 64 MICH. L. REV. 197 (1965). Of course, see Black's dissent in Griswold v. Connecticut, 381 U.S. at 507.

The article by Shirley M. Hufstedler, *supra* suggests that any constitutionally substantiated right of privacy rests on a trilogy of decisions: *Griswold v. Connecticut;* Stanley v. Georgia, 394 U.S. 557 (1969), in which the court overturned the defendant's conviction for possession of obscene films and held that the defendant had a constitutional right to view pornography in his home; and Rowan v. Post Office Department, 397 U.S. 728 (1970) which upheld a statute allowing a receiver to designate material as offensive and obscene and thereby shut off any future mail from that sender. In effect the Supreme Court held that the recipient's right of privacy must prevail.

278. However, see former section 940 of the N.Y. Criminal Code which specified those circumstances under which the police were authorized to photograph an individual. This section and its replacement section 160.10 Criminal Procedure Law has been amended to regulate only fingerprinting and not photography. *See* amended L. 1971 c.762, §7 eff. Sept. 1, 1971. For cases interpreting §940, see Gow v. Bingham et. al., 107 N.Y.S. 1011, 57 Misc. 66 (Sup. Ct. 1907); Hawkins v Kuhne, 153 App.Div. 216, 137 N.Y.S. 1090 (Sup. Ct. App. Div. 1912). In Fidler v. Murphy, 113 N.Y.S.2d 388 (Sup. Ct. 1952), the court held that photographing a person in a case not provided for by law constituted a cause of action for assault against the police. Here a police lieutenant had the plaintiff shackled and photographed after a dispute arose over the operating weight of the defendant's truck. United States v. Kelly, 55 F.2d 67 (2d Cir. 1932). *See also* Kietmann v. Time, 284 F. Supp. 925 (C.D. Calif. 1968) where reporters in concert with the police gained entrance to the plaintiff's home and photographed him in the midst of his "healing act." In the rather extraordinary case of York v. Storey, 324 F.2d 450 (9th Cir. 1963), the Court of Appeals upheld a cause of action when a woman went to the police station to make a complaint and was subsequently photographed in the nude and the photographs were passed around by the police officers.

technological change,[279] its complexity[280] and its frequent partnership with government[281] combine to frustrate effective courtroom evaluation.

Having concluded, for reasons of substance and procedure, that the courts are unlikely to unilaterally regulate camera surveillance, let us now, in a normative setting, catalogue the competing interests involved in electronic visual surveillance.

The advantages of camera surveillance are concrete and prominent while the disadvantages that inevitably accrue to a society that electronically watches, magnifies and records the comings and goings of its citizens are intangible, amorphous and distant. For example, if we take Mt. Vernon's experience to be representative, then camera surveillance has a very significant deterrent effect on street crime.[282] Additionally, this kind of surveillance is arguably more effective in the detection and identification of criminals.[283] Once in court, the

---

279. The degree and speed of our present technological change is unprecedented. For example, in 1940 the Science Section of the National Resources Committee could state, "From the early origins of an invention until its social effects the time interval averages about 30 years." Green *The New Technological Era: A View from the* Law BULLETIN OF ATOMIC SCIENTISTS 11 (Nov. 1967). In the same article Green concludes, "But we know today that technological advance is so rapid that we do not have this 30 year interval. The shorter interval between the origins of a technology and the time its social effects are felt means that the practice of technology with intrinsic hazards will result in more injury to more people at an earlier time. Lawyers have recognized that during this time lag adequate justice may not be done on behalf of persons injured by the new technology . . . ." *Id.* at 14.

280. Green, *Technology Assessment and the Law; introduction and perspective,* 36 G. WASH. L. REV. 1033 (1968) ". . . modern technology produces insidious forms of hazards which do not produce instant dramatic injury but which operate slowly and cumulatively, so that the existence of hazards and concomitant injuries may not become manifest for many years or perhaps a generation." *Id.* at 1037.

281. Green, *supra* note 280, at 1043 posits that Big Science (the generic label for high technology products of the government, industrial partnership) is reviewed by the courts within the framework of government criteria. "When the government through the legislative and the executive controls a technology (both by developing and policing it) the courts are inclined to constrain liability within the range specified by the government. . . ."

What this means basically, is that in these technological areas effective protection of the public against the burdens and risks of the technology passes from the courts to the legislative and administrative arenas. If the public interest is to be protected at all, it must be in the formulation of legislation, of administrative standards. *See* Casner v. Hecla Mining Col. 19 Utah2d 364, 431 P.2d 792 (Sup. Ct. 1967) despite uncontraverted evidence that any exposure to radiation may cause harm, the court refused to find a causal connection between the radiation exposure and alleged radiation injury where the exposure was within limits established by government authority.

282. *See* notes 49-50 *supra* and accompanying text.

Mt. Vernon's experiment gives no indication that street crimes increase outside the surveillance area. In Mt. Vernon, a cameraless block on 4th Street was used as a control. Street crimes on that block did not increase during the surveillance year. However if one accepts the contention that many street crimes are committed by heroin addicts, it would follow that these individuals would merely shift the locale of their crimes to non camera areas. A full test of this theory must await future camera programs.

283. So few incidents occurred during the surveillance year, *see* notes 22-23 *supra* that this contention was not adequately tested. Still, logic insists that the camera's light intensifica-

prosecution's ability to present a filmed account of the accused's crime would logically lead to more convictions.[284]

Another projected benefit of camera surveillance involves increased police efficiency. The monitors provide senior police and civilian officials with up-to-the-second information. As mentioned earlier, the cop's on the beat effectiveness seems to benefit from an awareness that someone at the stationhouse is watching.[285]

Most significantly, many residents of Mt. Vernon approved of the camera system.[286] They felt that the camera surveillance area was a safer place in which to do business, to shop and simply to walk. Police in Mt. Vernon (and Olean, N.Y.) seemed gratified that a Big Brother reaction never developed in any force.

Competing with this truly impressive array of projected crime fighting advantages are a panoply of subjective negative effects. Our worst fears rest on two premises. First, assume, as all indications suggest, that electronic visual surveillance systems modeled on Mt. Vernon will be enthusiastically embraced by many communities in the next few years.[287] The result might well be patrol by electronic eyes of all parts of business districts in medium and large cities. In many communities, residential areas will have the benefit of this increased police protection.[288] The development and deployment of still more perspicacious surveillance units is naturally a very real possibility but one that will not be assumed herein.[289]

Our second premise deals with the nature of the government—citizen relationship in the America of the 1970's. Simply stated, the argument runs that the government has an interest in every indivi-

---

tion, magnification, instant replay, slow motion and delayed replay capabilities would contribute to the detection and apprehension of criminals.

284. Theoretically a taped account of the suspect activity also protects the defendant. In Mt. Vernon and Santa Barbara, *see* notes 23 and 275 *supra* the existence of a video taped record convinced the defendants to plead guilty.

285. *See* text after note 21 *supra*.

286. *See* notes 33-36 *supra*.

287. *See* notes 40-58 *supra*.

288. *See* note 59 *supra*. As noted earlier the Guller Report will conclude that surveillance systems of the Mt. Vernon type are adaptable to and appropriate in many residential areas. Certianly in the largest cities apartment styled residential districts are very amenable to camera surveillance. The National Academy Engineering Report, *supra* notes 22 and 39, made no distinction between business and residential areas in New York's 71st precinct.

Regardless of the business residential distinction it is of course true that in most cities the Black community lives in and around much of the business district. (This could present a nice equal protection problem.)

289. What a number of commentators have loosely referred to as "Vietnam goodies"—technological devices developed for Vietnam and now marketed domestically—include electronic sensors and infra-red viewers that may greatly increase the effectiveness of future surveillance systems, *see* Barkan, *supra* note 41. The Orbis III system with its alleged ability to visually pierce dark or tinted glass may represent an already operational state of the art improvement on the Mt. Vernon type camera system.

dual's behavior that exceeds a mere expectation of lawfulness. In a society of governmental largesse, a citizen's behavior is reviewed not only for criminal content but for a determination of government controlled status and benefits.[290] It seems apparent that the government has an interest in monitoring the activities of a citizen receiving welfare or social security benefits. The same is true for a student on scholarship, a businessman receiving government loans or holding government licenses or a professional regulated by a quasi-governmental association; in short, any American of school age or over.[291]

Alan Westin has explained the universal effect of surveillance in this way:

> Though the general principle of civil liberty is clear many governmental and private authorities seem puzzled by the protest against current or proposed uses of new surveillance techniques. Why should a person who has not committed criminal acts worry whether their conversations might be accidentally overheard by police officers . . . The answer of course, lies in the impact of surveillance on human behavior . . . .
>
> When a person knows his conduct is visible he must either bring his conduct within accepted social norms in the particular situation involved or decide to violate those norms and accept the risk of reprisal.[292]

---

290. For the most forceful discussion of the role of government largesse in our society, see Reich, *The New Property* 73 YALE L. J. 733 (April, 1964) critiquing the Supreme Court's decision in Fleming v. Nestor, 363 U.S. 603 (1960) in which a badly split court (5-4) held that social security benefits are not an accrued property right and thus can be revoked. Reich asserted that:

> The philosophy of *Fleming v. Nestor* . . . resembles the philosophy of feudal tenure. Wealth is not owned or vested in holders. Instead it is held conditionally, the conditions being ones which seek to insure the fulfillment of obligations imposed by the state. Just as the feudal system linked lord and vassal through a system of mutual dependence and loyalty, so government largesse binds man to the state. Reich, *supra* at 769.

See also HARBRECHT (with BERLE), TOWARD THE PARAPROPRIETAL SOCIETY 16-17 (1960) and FREIDMAN, LAW IN A CHANGING SOCIETY 372 (1959).

291. Wyman v. James, 406 U.S. 309 (1971) is an outstanding illustration of the collision between citizen claims of privacy and the state's need for information conditioned on the continuation of government benefits. Here a welfare recipient objected to mandatory home visitations claiming that such visits constituted the kind of search prohibited by the Fourth Amendment. In effect the Supreme Court concluded that home inspections were a reasonable requirment for continued receipt of welfare benefits.

292. WESTIN, *supra* note 10 at 57, 58.

Given the potential for widespread camera surveillance and the stake each of us has in the frequency and "quality" of government surveillance, a number of very legitimate fears arise.

A primary group of concerns can be conveniently grouped under the label of police abuse. As long ago as 1948, the Supreme Court was impelled to remark, in the context of the Fourth Amendment,

> The right of privacy was deemed too precious to entrust to the discretion of those whose job is the detection of crime and the arrest of criminals. Power is a heady thing; and history shows that the police acting on their own cannot be trusted . . . . [293]

To begin, police can use a Mt. Vernon type surveillance system to read a pedestrian's lips or to read documents in his possession. More generally police can direct the cameras to observe and magnify people in their apartments, cars or on the street in situations where one anticipates freedom from surveillance or at least freedom from the close scrutiny that the cameras are capable of.

Secondly, one might well fear police use of the cameras to enforce dormant or inconsistently utilized statutes. Jaywalking, spitting or failing to license your dog might, for the first time, become the objects of systematic police attention. The prospect of total enforcement of all laws is not a uniformly happy vision.

> Few groups, it appears, so fully absorb the loyalties of members that they will readily accept unrestricted observability of their role performance . . . . Resistance to full visibility of one's behavior appears . . . . to result from structural properties of group life. Some measure of leeway in conforming to role expectations is presupposed in all groups. To have to meet the strict requirements of a role at all times, without some degree of deviation, is to experience insufficient allowances for individual difference in capacity and training and for situational exigencies which make strict conformity extremely difficult.[294]

---

293. McDonald v. United States, 335 U.S. 451, 445-456 (1948). Dr. Guller discounted the possibility of police abuse: "The police have great potential for abuse right now. These cameras are no more dangerous than tools the police presently own. The public must be vigilant but the police must be trusted." Guller, *supra* note 6

294. WESTIN, *supra* note 10 at 58 quoting from MERTON, SOCIAL THEORY AND SOCIAL STRUCTURE 341-53 (1957) Westin continues, "Even though the authorities may accept evasion of the rules, the experience will be psychologically taxing on both the observed person and the authorities, since the latter must accept whether or not to act against the

Sophisticated visual surveillance systems could also be used for round-up or dragnet arrests. For instance, a review of two weeks of video tapes would vastly improve police capability to identify and then arrest on sight any person who had appeared in the surveillance area at a certain time and who met certain characteristics.

One might reasonably fear that police abuse of the system would lead to increased dossier building. In a way not presently practicable, the police could use widescale surveillance systems to track associational ties and mark the day to day habits of revolutionaries, activists, homosexuals, and other people of police interest.

Even if one were to discount the possibility of police abuse the deployment throughout our urban areas of electronic surveillance units introduces very real questions concerning the psychological and social well being of our society. We have already suggested that in an environment where all of us are justly worried about behavior inconsistent with government sponsored or controlled benefits, intensive surveillance may produce serious behavior modification. Within a surveillance area, we may alter or entirely suspend certain associations or activities. Eventually, these associations and activities may be deterred even outside the surveillance area.

In addition to very rational reasons for modifying personal behavior when observed by agents of the government, social scientists document that individuals vary their behavior in surveillance settings for very subjective, psychological reasons.[295] Every person has undoubtedly experienced the uneasy insecure feeling of being watched. Particularly when a person is spied on without being able to contemporaneously watch his observer, a process of serious behavior modification can result.

> In the asymmetrical case, where a person is being spied upon by direct or indirect means he may greatly modify his conduct if he suspects he is being observed even though he does not know the identity of the particular audience that might be observing him. This is one of the possibilities celebrated in Orwell's *1984* and its possibility is one of the forces operative in socially controlling persons who are alone.[296]

---

non-complying person and must measure the effects of not acting on the group perception of authority." WESTIN, *supra* note 10, at 58. For a full discussion of the "emotional release" that occurs when privacy allows minor non-compliance with social norms. *See* WESTIN at 35.

295. GOFFMAN, *supra* note 1, at 243.

296. *Id.* at 16n.4.

Westin has characterized asymmetrical observation as an especially dehumanizing process because it is without the "softening" and "game" aspects of face to face confrontations.[297]

Visual surveillance may lead to an abridgement of personal spontaneity. Individuals will not give free range to their expressions, laughter and movements when they anticipate detailed visual scrutiny by the police. Erving Goffman has analyzed the relationship between spontaneity and observation:

> In American society, it appears that the individual is expected to exert a kind of discipline or tension in regard to his body showing that he has his faculties in readiness for any face to face interaction that might come his way in the situation. Often this kind of controlled alertness in the situation will mean suppressing or concealing many of the capacities and roles the individual might be expected to display in other settings. Whatever his other concerns, then whatever his merely situated interests the individual is obliged to "come into play" upon entering the situation and to stay "in play" at least until he can officially take himself beyond range of the situation.[298]

A final subjective and psychologically oriented value threatened by intensive visual surveillance is an individual's sense of anonymity. While the courts have occasionally given legal content to this value,[299] it is expressed in its most forceful and natural form when an individual walks a street assured that his image and intentions are not a subject of intimate police scrutiny. "Knowledge or fear that one is under systematic observation in public places destroys the sense of relaxation and freedom that men seek in open spaces and public arenas."[300]

---

297. WESTIN, note 10 supra at 59. Fried, Privacy 77 YALE L. J. 475, 490 (1968) spotlights another type of harm produced by asymmetrical observation. "An unseen audience is more threatening to privacy and the values it nourishes because of the possibility that one may forget about it and let down his guard as one would not with a visible audience."

298. GOFFMAN, supra note 1, at 24-25.

299. See Talley v. California, 362 U.S. 60 (1960). See also Brennan's dissent in Lopez v. United States, 373 U.S. 427, 446 (1963) and discussion note 215 supra and accompanying text.

300. WESTIN, supra note 10, at 31. Westin defines anonymity as occurring when an individual in a public place enjoys freedom from identification and surveillance.

> He may be riding on a subway, attending a ball game, or walking the streets; he is among people and knows he is being observed: but unless he is a well-known celebrity he does not expect to be personally identified and held to the full rules of behavior and role that would operate if he were known to those observing him. In this state the individual is able to merge into the situational landscape.

214 / ROBERT R. BELAIR and CHARLES D. BOCK

The preceeding overview of the very personal, psychological harms that might predictably flow from intensive electronic surveillance of public streets leads us to the last and most general theme of this paper. To the extent that America adopts the ethic of a watched society, we inevitably lose the sense of participatory democracy and trust that privacy nourishes. If one accepts the "Westinian" definition of privacy ("privacy is the claim of individuals, groups or institutions to determine for themselves when, how and to what extent information about them is communicated to others")[301] then manifestly, we selectively share or deny personal information about ourselves (privacy) to others depending on how intimate we desire to become with those people. We share personal information about ourselves with another person because we believe that person will not then act in a manner contrary to our interests. We establish trust in that person. Professor Fried, in *Privacy*, a philosophical exegesis of the Westin concept of privacy, asserts that once a person has complete surveillance of someone that surveillance extinguishes any possibility of trust.[302] In a similar way, it is reasonable to suggest that once a state chooses to watch its citizens intensively any sense of trust and participation existing between a government and its citizens is gravely undermined.

Ultimately, what is in conflict on the public streets are fundamental values of liberty and security. Camera systems free us from fear of harm to our persons and property. They provide a new kind of liberty, albeit incomplete, to walk the city streets at any hour. On the other hand, some measure of liberty is sacrificed. For it is certain that if we do walk those streets any unconventional act of dress or demeanor will be marked and recorded. The question to be answered then is just how high a price are we willing to pay for technology's newest contribution to law and order?[303]

Id. at 31 . *See also* Beaney, *The Right to Privacy and American Law,* 3 LAW AND CONTEMP. PROB. 253, 258 (1966). Beaney cites the increasing tendency to invade the anonymity of both the "renowned" and the "obscure common man."

301. WESTIN *supra* note 10, at 7.

302. Fried, *supra* note 297, at 484.

303. Space does not permit an analytical treatment of the statutory or administrative responses that might be made to the push for television surveillance systems. If we decide that the advantages of the cameras are too significant to ignore it seems obvious that Congress, the state legislatures or the LEAA could impose a number of restrictions. For instance the cameras could be strictly limited to use in high crime and business areas. Secondly the advanced telescopic capabilities of the Mt. Vernon system could be eliminated within future installations. Mt. Vernon officials have not contended that the cameras magnification capability was critical. However the prospect that a pedestrian's features can be displayed in detail across the width of a monitor is an upsetting and intrusive vision. Thirdly street scenes might be videotaped only when an incident of police interest appears to be developing. Video tape represents perhaps the most serious threat for police abuse.

8 | COMMERCIAL INFORMATION BROKERS

JOHN P. FLANNERY*

I. INTRODUCTION

> [Your] privacy has been invaded to the point where you've just been stripped of everything, right in public and you have no self respect left and ... very little of anything else after you've been ground up in the machine.[1]

Privacy is not a term of universal definition, but rather relates to an individual's experience and his culture. To the average American, the term implies solitude or quiet or "social distance," no doubt as a reaction to our densely populated, commercial society. The concept of control is fundamental to an American definition of privacy. Professor Westin has incorporated this concept when he describes privacy as the "claim of individuals, groups, or institutions to determine for themselves when, how, and to what extent information about them is communicated to others."[2] While there are varied instrusions into "privacy," we will focus exclusively on commercial information brokers and will not deal with credit bureaus *per se*.[3]

Within the commercial sphere, we find various government and private agencies wresting control from the individual by selling and exchanging information about him, without his consent and often

---

*Staff member, *Columbia Human Rights Law Review*.

1. Transcript from WABC-TV Broadcast, *Assault on Privacy*, Jan. 8, 1972, at 19 [hereinafter referred to as ABC Transcript].

2. WESTIN, PRIVACY AND FREEDOM 16 (1967) [hereinafter referred to as WESTIN].

3. *See* Note, *Credit Investigations and the Right to Privacy: Quest for a Remedy*, GEO. L. J. 509 (1969). *See also The Zone of Privacy: Although Individual Dignity Must Be Preserved, Business In Our Easy Credit Economy Needs Information For Survival*, 44 J. AM. INS. 29 (1968); *Hearings on H.R. 16340, Before the Subcommittee on Consumer Affairs of the House Committee on Banking and Currency*, 91st Cong., 2d Sess. (1970) (the bill would enable consumers to protect themselves against arbitrary, erroneous, and malicious credit information); *Hearings on S.823, Before the Subcommittee on Financial Institutions of the House Committee on Banking and Currency*, 91st Cong., 1st Sess. (1969).

with irrevocable damage. The state governments readily provide accident records, motor vehicle registrations and employment information.[4] The federal government sells lists of names and other information and occasionally does not know the purchasers.[5] Private agencies supplement this government data with information they have compiled, bought or otherwise obtained, and then sell these compilations.[6] Private agencies may also get information from services they perform. For example, two companies that prepare tax returns have used income tax information, without the consent of their customers, for solicitation purposes.[7] Other private agencies have been charged with selling information to employers about the political views of potential employees.[8]

Several of these intrusions would have been impossible if the information was manually handled and manually disseminated. The task of compiling and categorizing data manually would be too burdensome to be worthwhile. However, the information is in fact manipulated by computers which may create authoritative but inaccurate reports and which facilitate the indiscriminate transfer of data. Furthermore, the use of computers is increasing[9] and the available figures understate the actual growth.[10] It has been forecast that the "nation one day will all be cabled [giving] access to knowledge and computing power for everyone who can afford a TV set."[11] The security of present computerized data may be preserved by the use of specialized programming techniques when the file is first created[12] or at the time of access to the data.[13] However these methods do not protect against interceptions of data by electromagnetic radiation monitoring, physical security wiretapping, equipment failure, operat-

---

4. *See* notes 53-57 *infra* and accompanying text.

5. *See* notes 24-52 *infra* and accompanying text.

6. *See* notes 58-73 *infra* and accompanying text.

7. *See* notes 74-85 *infra* and accompanying text.

8. *See* notes 88-90 *infra* and accompanying text.

9. *See* Note, *Computerization of Government Files: What Impact on the Individual?* 15 U.C.L.A.L. REV. 1371, 1388 (1968).

10. These figures are a very rough index of computer growth. Since 1967 in addition to a tremendous growth in the *numbers* of computers the capacity and speed of the computer has drastically increased with the "third generation" of computers. For example, an IBM S360/95 of the third generation has a memory core, retrieval capability, etc., which is much greater than that of the IBM S140, a second generation computer.

11. Mr. Hammer, Univac's director of Computer Science, called the enabling technique, "circulating memory" theory which consists of a flow of information through the cables past a community of users. *"Wired City" by 1975, Developer Predicts,* COMPUTER WORLD, May 12, 1971, at 1.

12. GIRS, General Informational Retrieval System, is an example of a software device that might be used to this end. *See* Carrol, *Multi-Dimensional Security Program for a Generalized Information Retrieval System,* 39 AMERICAN FEDERATION OF INFORMATION PROCESSING SOCIETIES 571-577 (1971) [hereinafter referred to as 39 AFIPS (1971)].

13. *See* Hoffman, *Formulary Model for Flexible Privacy and Access Controls,* 39 AFIPS 587 (1971).

ing system software bugs, personnel, or administrative procedures.[14]

There is a need, therefore, to provide the individual with an opportunity to secure his privacy by giving him the means to control information about himself. He must be allowed to confront his files, and to correct or expunge data in these files. In the following discussion, we shall describe the commercial data collection and dissemination practices of the government and private sectors. Without knowledge of these methods, the individual cannot protect his privacy. Following a brief survey of the difficulties with tort and other remedies, we shall consider the most viable alternative, *viz.*, legislation. In particular, three legislative responses will be considered: The Freedom of Information Act (FOIA),[15] the Postal Revenue and Federal Salary Act,[16] and the Fair Credit Reporting Act (FCRA).[17] These acts have been chosen for discussion because they are the primary legislation dealing with the problems of control of data.

II. INFORMATION AVAILABLE FROM THE STATE AND FEDERAL GOVERNMENT

At the federal, state and city levels, information is collected by various agencies, *e.g.*, licensing, taxation, automobile registration, workmen's compensation bureaus. Almost all of the states and the federal government have freedom of information statutes regarding the form and manner of information to be collected and disseminated.[18] These laws assume that the rational citizen has a "right to know" the data collected in order to more fully participate in government. In addition, the government wishes to avoid a credibility gap which might result from a "closed door" policy. The wording of these statutes may be broad, as is the Florida Freedom of Information Act,[19] or more elaborate in describing rules for the disclosure (or withholding) of information, such as the Federal Freedom of Information Act.[20]

---

14. *Id.*
15. 5 U.S.C. § 552 (1971).
16. 39 U.S.C. § 4009 (1964).
17. 15 U.S.C. §§ 1681 *et seq.* (1970).
18. At least forty-two states have codified Freedom of Information provisions. Freedom of Information Center, State Access Statutes, Report No. 202, June 1968 (available from the School of Journalism, University of Missouri in Columbia).
19. FLA. STAT. ANN. § 119.01 (1960):

All state, county and municipal records shall at all times be open for personal inspection of any citizen of Florida, and those in charge of such records shall not refuse this privilege to any citizen.

20. 5 U.S.C. § 552 (1971).

In applying these statutes, a balancing test is frequently employed, weighing the "right to know" against the individual's right to privacy. Often, the privacy of the subject is subordinated to the right to know. In *Accident Index Bureau v. Hughes*,[21] the New Jersey State Commissioner of Labor and Industry barred public inspection of workmen's compensation records, contending that state policy was the re-employment of the injured or disabled and not the promotion of agencies such as Accident Index, which sold these records to prospective employers and labelled such workers as "malingerers" or "accident prone." The majority of the court felt that the commissioner had frustrated a "legitimate interest," *i.e.*, the revelation of information. The contrary opinion was expressed by Justice Francis in his dissent:

> The right to inspect a public record is a broad one but it is not unlimited; It is not absolute under all circumstances. Denial of inspection and copying for a purpose detrimental to the public interest or in conflict with the public policy . . . is proper.

The Federal Freedom of Information Act poses a similar balancing problem by virtue of its presumption of disclosure.[23]

A. Federal Government Disclosure

The federal government disseminates information which may be divided into two broad categories: 1) *individual* personal information or discrete information and 2) *statistical* or *generic* information. The first category might contain, for example, the names and addresses of licensees, and other particular information such as the type of automobile or boat that is registered. On the other hand, *statistical* data is normally thought of as non-personal, non-specific information. However, inadequate procedures in one government agency coupled with a computer's capacity to collate data, permit one to obtain discrete information. To the extent that this is true, the two categories merge.

1. Individual Information. There are several subdivisions of discrete disclosure: confidential information, information that should be confidential but is disclosed for promotional purposes, and information for political solicitation.

---

21. Accident Index Bureau v. Hughes, 46 N.J. 160, 215 A.2d 529 (Sup. Ct. 1965).
22. *Id.* at 532-533.
23. *See infra* notes 117-140 and accompanying text.

Income tax information is thought to be confidential but there is no assurance of privacy:

> The confidentiality of tax returns is maintained by a statute that has all the containing qualities of a sieve. Tax returns are fully available to state tax officials, to any Congressional committee 'authorized to investigate returns,' and to anyone authorized by Executive Order.[24]

Furthermore, the Internal Revenue Service (IRS) collects data on "known militants and activists" to uncover tax evasion;[25] a practice that the IRS has readily admitted.[26]

Other practices that should be confidential but are disclosed for promotional purposes include sales by the IRS of lists of gun owners pursuant to the 1968 Gun Control Act[27]; the sale of the names and addresses of returning veterans to local insurance companies;[28] and the sale by the Federal Communications Commission (FCC) of lists of licenses granted and of license applicants to unknown purchasers.[29] A former Secretary of Transportation, whose lists of

---

24. Countryman, *The Diminishing Right of Privacy: The Personal Dossier and the Computer*, 49 TEX. L. REV. 837, 857 (1971). [hereinafter referred to as Countryman].

25. Wall, *Special Agent for the FBI*, NEW YORK REVIEW OF BOOKS 12, 19 (Jan. 27, 1972).

26. N.Y. Times, Jan. 13, 1972, at 1.

27. A gun collector discovered the practice. Required to register with the Internal Revenue Service pursuant to the requirements of the 1968 Gun Control Act, he received solicitations from a sports supply shop that used the identical address label used by IRS. This seemed to make it easy to locate and steal weapons kept unprotected. The IRS had been selling lists containing the names and addresses of 143,000 gun collectors and dealers. (This policy has been partly discontinued. The IRS continues to sell lists, but only about gun dealers, not gun collectors.) See Hearings on H.R. 2730 and Similar Bills Before the Sub-comm. on Postal Operations of the House Comm. on Post Office and Civil Service, 91st Cong., 2d Sess., ser. 91, pt. 28, at 69 (1970) [hereinafter referred to as *Hearings on H.R. 2730 and Similar Bills*].

28. Dez Ingold, Acting Director for the Selective Service System in a letter dated March 19, 1970, to Congressman Horton concerning mailing lists noted that,

> [a]bout fifteen years ago, a Congressional investigation was made because certain local boards had been furnishing the names and addresses of recently returned veterans to local insurance companies... [and] In the past six months, an incident of such sale of names was brought to the attention of one of our state Directors. After a complete investigation and FBI report, the employee who has sold the names was discharged.

Hearings on H.R. 2730 and Similar Bills, supra note 27, at 81. Now the Selective Service System does not disclose any addresses of registrants unless authorized. 32 C.F.R. §1606.32 (1971). Authorized addresses are only used to forward official mail to the registrants. 32 C.F.R. § 1606.21 (1971).

29. The FCC files are sold by two firms that do not inform the FCC who the buyer is. The copy is sold by a private firm, the Cooper-Trent Division of the Keuffel and Esser Company, and the tape is sold for $55.00 per reel by the Department of Commerce's

680,000 licensed pilots and registrations were sold through the Federal Aviation Administration (FAA) and the U.S. Coast Guard (U.S.C.G.),[30] admitted:

> [We have] no control over the use of information which is released to the public under the provisions of the Freedom of Information Act. In fact, under the Act, we are not permitted to release information selectively, based on judgment as to the propriety of the use which will be made of the information requested.[31]

It has been suggested that this behavior results from the Department's desire to promote aviation.[32]

While the Civil Service Commission has stated that it will not tolerate having people use personnel lists for political solicitation,[33] the Veterans Administration has been ordered to give Vietnam Veterans Against the War a list of returning veterans for solicitation purposes.[34]

The Civil Service Commission has files on ten million federal job applicants and additional files on 1.5 million individuals suspected of subversive activities.[35] In addition to the investigative files, the

---

Clearinghouse for Federal Scientific and Technical Information. *Hearings on H.R. 2730 and Similar Bills, supra* note 27, at 81.

It is interesting to note that the FCC also maintains 11,000 names and addresses of organizations and individuals whose qualifications for FCC broadcast license "are believed to require close examination." Reasons for being on the list are license suspension, the issuance of a bad check to the FCC, or stopping payment on a license fee check after failing a commission examination, or, and this seems to be the danger, the individual's relation to other agencies which put him (her) on one of their lists. *Human Rights Linked to DP Responsibility*, COMPUTERWORLD, May 22, 1971, at 2. For further discussion of commingling, *see infra* notes 121-125, and accompanying text.

30. *Hearings on H.R. 2730 and Similar Bills, supra* note 27, at 75.

Information is sold on boats for the following jurisdictions: New Hampshire, Washington, Alaska, the District of Columbia and Guam. Any individual or organization requesting copies of these records is provided the record upon payment of a search and copying fee.*Id.*

31. *Hearings on H.R. 2730 and Similar Bills, supra* note 27, at 76.

32. *See* Hogan, Rehnquist, Mondello, *Rights in Conflict–Reconciling Privacy with the Public's Right to Know,* 63 LAW LIB. J. 551, 556 (1970).

33. *Id.* at 562.

34. The VA has furnished data tapes to several organizations that assist returning veterans. The five organizations are the American Red Cross, the American Legion, the Veterans of Foreign Wars, the Disabled American Veterans, and the American Veterans of World War II. *Hearings on H.R. 2730 and Similar Bills, supra* note 27, at 79. In an unpublished order, Judge Gesell allowed the use of the tape to the Vietnam Veterans Against the War. Vietnam Veterans Against the War v. Veterans Administration, Docket No. 2277-70 (D.D.C., Oct. 14, 1971). Counsel for Vietnam Veterans was of the opinion that Judge Gesell wouldn't have compelled disclosure if the tape wasn't already being produced. Interview with Mr. Becker, counsel for the Vietnam Veterans, in New York City, Feb. 22, 1972.

35. Countryman, *supra* note 24, at 861.

Commission maintains files which are objects of strict disclosure rules.[36] Despite these strict rules one can still obtain information from private sources beyond that permitted by the agency regulations.[37]

If an employee or an agent of the employee wants to look at his personnel folder, the agency must remove all medical information, test materials, investigative, loyalty and security investigative reports, as well as the confidential questionnaires and employment inquiries.[38] To protect the integrity of the file an agency representative must be present while the employee or his representative examines the folder.[39] It is anticipated that in the near future, the records of the Civil Service Commission will be computerized. Mr. Mondello, counsel for the Commission, contends that investigative files should not be computerized but should be retained in their present forms. If computerized at all, Mr. Mondello believes that there should be at the least an annual update of all computer files,[40] including a printout of each individual's file to be mailed to the employee in order to allow him to correct any errors. In the case of a dispute, the file would be flagged and attention would be directed to the problem. The anti-computerization attitude reflects the fear that the information will be automated without proper screening or controls.[41]

2. Statistical Information. Statistical information is provided primarily by the Census Bureau of the Department of Commerce which, pursuant to constitutional authority, enumerates the population for the purpose of apportioning representatives.[42] The decennial census has become more than an "apportionment" census and includes statistics on sex, race, national origin, number of TV's, and number of rooms. A failure to answer questions on the census can result in a

---

36. The Commission maintains four types of files: official personnel folders, appeals files, retirement files, and leave records.

The official personnel folder is the most comprehensive of these files and only information concerning the position title, grade, salary, and duty station is made public. No information is released if it is sought for solicitation. 5 C.F.R. § 294.702 (1971). Upon agency or commission appeal certain "specifically identified" information in the file, for example, the individual's name, is withheld from disclosure. 5 C.F.R. § § 294.801 (b) (5), 294.802 (c) (5) (1971). Finally leave records are not available to anyone without the written consent of the individual. 5 C.F.R. § 294.1101 (1971).

37. Despite government precautions, a privately owned firm in Washington, D.C., specializes in providing computer tapes with a detailed personal description of over 3 million federal employees. *Hearings on H.R. 2730 and Similar Bills, supra* note 27, at 6.

38. 5 C.F.R. § 294.703 (a) (1971).

39. *Id.*

40. Interview with Anthony Mondello Esq., Counsel for Civil Service Commission, in New York City, Dec. 10, 1971.

41. ABC Transcript at 16.

42. U.S. CONST. art. I, § 2, cl. 2.

criminal penalty.[43] Besides the decennial census, the Bureau conducts surveys for other agencies. Although there is no criminal penalty for failure to complete these questionnaires, this request for information may be intimidating and intrusive.[44]

This burgeoning fact gathering, which reflects the growth of the Bureau's legislative mandate,[45] has created problems. It has been said that the problems of the individual are ignored by the planners who require these statistics:

> if these people [planners] could read some of the letters which the people they represent have sent Congress, they would begin to realize the urgency of the problem. They would have some understanding of the impact on individuals, of the threats, the official intimidation and harassment to provide personal information about themselves. They would realize that the brunt of these programs is falling on such groups as the poor, the sick, the disabled, the illiterate, and the elderly.[46]

In addition, the statistics that result from these questionnaires "have tended to make facts into norms."[47]

It is generally believed that the information provided by the Census Bureau is *generic* not *specific* because use of census information is ostensibly restricted to statistical purposes[48] and any other disclosure results in criminal penalties.[49] However, the Bureau's breakdown of information into homogeneous small area statistics and its use of categories may provide particular data about an individual.

For example, the Census Bureau makes available tracts which list geographic areas containing 4,000 to 7,000 persons with similar education and income.[50] The Bureau has determined that one way to protect the individual is to set a broad range on the categories distributed in Bureau reports. It has established the rule that the upper limit of a category is 1 3/4 to 2 1/2 times the lower limit, for example, the category 5 - 9. However, the Bureau rule does not provide for

---

43. 13 U.S.C. §§ 221-224 (1964).

44. *See* MILLER, THE ASSAULT ON PRIVACY: COMPUTERS, DATA BANKS, AND DOSSIERS 154 (1971) [hereinafter referred to as MILLER].

45. The bureau now reports on industry, business, agriculture, governments, on crime and on defective, dependent and delinquent classes. 13 U.S.C. §§ 101-61 (1964).

46. 116 CONG. REC. 17,719 (1969) (remarks by Senator Ervin).

47. BOORSTIN, THE DECLINE OF RADICALISM: REFLECTIONS ON AMERICA TODAY 18 (1970).

48. 13 U.S.C. §9(a) (1964).

49. 13 U.S.C. § 214 (1964).

50. *Hearings on Privacy in the Mail Before the Subcomm. on Postal Operations of the House Comm. on Post Office and Civil Serivce,* 91st Cong., 2d Sess., ser. 90, pt. 42, at 5 (1968) [hereinafter referred to as *Hearings on Privacy in the Mail].*

minimum frequencies within a category, *i.e.*, the number of items in a category might be only one.

The truly intrusive nature of this technique of information dissemination is apparent in the following example. Several years ago the Census Bureau provided a "statistical" list of one hundred and eighty Illinois doctors. The list was broken down into more than two dozen income categories, and each category was further subdivided by medical specialty and area of residence, thereby making it possible to identify individual doctors.[51]

Statistical information can become specific when the Census Bureau does not provide subcategories but when supplementary information is available from other sources. It has been said that cross-tabulating the statistical categories by computers

> may make it feasible for a person or organization with certain of the same information on some of the people to identify many of them in the tabulation. . . . With a computer the comparison and identification become far more feasible.[52]

The solution to this problem rests on altering the present disclosure rule of the Bureau which might be done by making a frequency provision per category.

B. State Government Disclosure

The state provides information and may pursue a commercial interest in disseminating the data. Specifically, the state dispenses and sells motor vehicle registrations[53] and in some cases allows the purchaser to microfilm the original forms.[54] Among non-commercial state practices are New Jersey's distribution of the names and addresses of licensed drivers to a nationwide organization in return for the present addresses of parking ticket delinquents,[55] and its dissemination of workmen's compensation reports.[56] In addition, as a result of "right to know" statutes, information concerning births and deaths can be compiled nationally in a form useful for sales promotion.[57]

---

51. MILLER *Supra* note 44, at 151.

52. 39 AFIPS 578, 581 (1971).

53. *See* Lamont v. Comm. of Motor Vehicles, 269 F. Supp. 880, 883-884 and n.6 (S.D.N.Y. 1967).

54. One year R. L. Polk & Co., when they were denied the registration, made arrangements with the Commissioner to copy the M.V.-50 form which contains most of the information that is contained on motor vehicle registrations. This resulted in an allegation that the Commissioner had "developed a personal acquaintanceship." *Hearings on H.R. 2730 & Similar Bills, Supra* Note 27, at 56-57.

55. *Hearings on Privacy in the Mail, supra* note 50, at 31.

56. *See supra* notes 21-22, and accompanying text.

57. *Hearings on H.R. 2730 and Similar Bills, supra* note 27, at 56-57.

C. Private Agencies as a Source

The activities of private agencies which provide information may be divided into three categories: collection, handling and dissemination. Collection of information by these agencies is facilitated by the right to know statutes. In addition, other methods are used such as the compilation or purchase of telephone and city directories, or the deception of the public in order to obtain the information. Handling of data generally means the collation or exchange of the information. Dissemination usually means distribution at a "reasonable" price to any interested buyer. These processes have been subject to abuse in three principal areas: mailing lists, income tax information, and employment.

1. Mailing Lists. Mailing lists of consumers are compiled from masses of personal data and sold at the cost of gross intrusion upon individual privacy. The methods of securing this information are, as indicated above, based on right to know statutes, the compilation or purchase of directories, and misleading statements.

One example of deceptive collection practices occurred when Metromedia, through its subsidiary O. E. McIntyre, sent out a form letter which read:

> All you have to do is to send in this questionnaire in the enclosed postage paid envelope—nothing else is needed. The questionnaire is short and easy to fill out. There is *nothing to buy* and we should assure you that no salesman will call on you.[58]

The individual was given the opportunity of winning "1,111 magnificent gifts" by completing the three page questionnaire which contained several hundred questions about the individual and members of his family. Specific questions were concerned with travel, books read, type and number of cars owned, employment and salary, and even the kind of fuel used in the addressee's home.[59] The responses sought by the questionnaire were apparently for the purpose of compiling mailing lists to facilitate merchandise sales despite representations to the contrary in the covering letter.[60]

Often an agency may depend on both right to know statutes and directories. R. L. Polk & Company, which claims that outside the government, "no one handles and organizes so many separate pieces

---

58. *In re* Metromedia, Inc., No. C-1864 (Feb. 17, 1971) [hereinafter referred to as FTC Metromedia Complaint].

59. *Id.* at 4-6.

60. *Id.* at 7.

of information,"[61] obtains a great deal of information by compiling "city directories" and buying lists of every motor vehicle registered in the U.S.[62] Polk maintains 200 million names in its "marketing services division" and can provide 10,000 lists of organizations and individuals that may be purchased in manuscript form or gummed labels.[63]

Most of the files that are maintained by these agencies are available to everyone pursuant to right to know statutes. However, a mere list of names and addresses is of no value unless it can be refined into categories. For example, the lists may be collated with other data; the most elementary compilers use the Census Bureau to refine their information.[64] A director of the Census Bureau has said that direct mail advertisers and others "frequently make use of small-area statistics to classify their own mailing lists according to certain characteristics."[65] Reflecting an appreciation for more specific information, Polk has a "current market value index," that rates a family from 0 to 9 on the basis of the number and type of car the family owns,[66] and a "household census list," which has particular, not statistical, information on 24 million families. This information is stored on magnetic tape.[67] In addition, R. H. Donnelly maintains the "Donnelly

---

61. Polk is divided into several divisions: city directory division, bank directory division, and Marketing Services Division. The information described *infra* notes 62, 63, 66, 67 and the accompanying text are derived from the efforts of these three divisions. The descriptions and statistics discussed are the result of an interview with Don Marine, Manager of Data Processing and Production Methods, R. L. Polk & Co., Detroit, Michigan, March 13, 1972.

62. Compiling the city directories provides 69 million files including the name, address, marital status, occupation, place of employment, telephone number, and whether the place of residence is owned or rented for every resident over 18 years of age. The motor vehicle file contains almost 60 million names, 75 percent of the nation's car and truck owners. In addition to this Polk also publishes a bank directory twice a year which includes information about banks, bank officers and financial statistics.

63. *Hearings on H.R. 2730, supra* Note 27, at 56.

64. *Hearings on Privacy in the Mail, supra* note 50, at 32.

65. *Hearings on Privacy in the Mail, supra* note 50, at 32.

66. The index has been described as:

a program of checking the value, as listed in the standard used car manual, of each car registered to a family, adding up the figures if there is more than one car, and then assigning each of the 41 million car-owning families in the United States a number, from 0 to 9, that represents the total value of its automobiles.

Hearings on H.R. 2730, supra Note 27, at 58. (estimated annual expenditure for current consumption)."

67. This certainly compromises a "precision marketing tool" because the extent of information included is surprising. The information obtained when Polk is assembling its city directories comprises the information for the household census list and consists of "occupation of head of household and all persons over 18, marital status, wife's name, whether wife works, number of children, age range of children, total persons in the household, total employed persons in the household, occupancy status (owner or renter), primary families, sub-families, and secondary families, type of dwelling (single or multiple), length of residence

Quality Index" of some 50 million names based on car registrations and telephone directories.

After collection is completed, important questions arise concerning the use of information and the cost of such use to the individual. It has been reported that *Reader's Digest* used a computer-generated mailing that told non-subscribers the names and addresses of their neighbors who subscribed.[68] Other solicitations have detailed more personal information, such as income, job or business, and bank balance[69] as part of their manipulation of potential purchasers. One might feel that such control over buyers has gone too far when, for example, the Dunhill Company sells mailing lists of eight-to-fifteen year old girls, for 2¢ per name, because the young women "are at a highly impressionable age and . . . starting to form lifetime buying habits."[70]

---

at current address, age of structure, telephone number if there is a phone, spending index (estimated annual expenditure for current consumption)." *Hearings on H.R. 2730 & Similar Bills Supra* note 27, at 58.

68. MILLER, *supra* note 44, at 96.

69. Paul Zurkowski, Executive Director of the Information Industry Association of America and many others received such a letter. Professor Miller reprinted the letter to Mr. Zurkowski, changing the name and address included in the letter:

Dear Mr. Zurkowski:

I'm amazed at the number of my friends who have dramatically increased their incomes in just the past few months! John and Joana Q. Public of 325 Orchard Way in Suburbia tell me their August income in a new business venture they created from what had been a part-time job was $2050. That's a big jump from John's previous $1380/mo. at NASA.

Bob Babbitt of 225 Main Street in Anytown quit managing a fleet of trucks for Icicle Ice Company in December 1968 to start his own business. By August of '69 he had reached a monthly income of $3750.

Three years ago you and Mrs. Zurcowski bought your present home. The Publics and the Babbitts were homeowners too. It was when their ownership responsibilities caused money problems, that they sought to make more.

Most (people) started out with no more money than the few hundred dollars you have in the bank right now. Few of them had two cars like the Zurkowskis do. Usually they had a car less desirable than your '67, or no car at all, when they decided to "rise above it."

However after making a careful household-by-household study of Washington residents with incomes in the critical $12,500 to $19,500 range, I have selected you and Mrs. Zurkowski as possibly being among the few who will take positative action if given the opportunity.

I look forward to telling you how I've doubled my income since retiring from the Air Force (full colonel) in July.

Id. at 96-97.

70. Vance Packard noted that there were tens of millions of youngsters who spent over $500 a year. THE NAKED SOCIETY 153 (1964). This has certainly increased.

Approximately 15 billion pieces of mail were sent to addresses obtained from prepared and commercially available mailing lists.[71] Congressman Cornelius E. Gallagher estimates that $240 million of the $321 million deficit sustained due to third class mail is a result of commercial mailings.[72] Given the intrusive nature of the direct mailings and the cost of commercial mail to the American citizen, one may conclude, as did Congressman Gallagher, that

> A man should be able to release his name for purposes of receiving some merchandise or service without fearing that his mail will begin to swell with circulars and 'spectacular' offers within two or three months.

2. Income tax information. While present federal law forbids disclosure of income information by government agents (unless in strict confidentiality),[74] there is no restriction on those who prepare income tax forms, *e.g.*, private accountants or lawyers.[75] The use of tax information for purposes other than filing returns has been described in one editorial as a "breach of privacy of which the ordinary taxpayer probably isn't even aware."[76] Richard Werntz of Computer Data Processing described the firms which disclose tax information as serving

> Two masters, and their duplicity is a breach of confidence with the American public. . . . [W]e have long felt that financial institutions, department stores, insurance companies and others who have stepped into the income tax field have apparent conflicts of interest with their public, and should at least be restricted from using the confidential information to sell goods and services, and possibly restricted from entering the business of tax preparation.[77]

Weisenberger Financial Services broadly described in its newsletter[78] two approaches, personal and impersonal, for using income tax

71. *Hearings on H.R. 2730, supra* note 27, at 21.

72. *Hearings on Privacy in the Mail, supra* note 50, at 30.

73. *Id.* at 30.

74. 26 U.S.C. § 6103 *as amended* (Supp. V. 1970).

75. Of the 75 million returns filed in 1970 it is estimated that almost one half were prepared by someone other than a taxpayer. 117 CONG. REC. S3968 (daily ed. Mar. 29, 1971) (remarks of Senator Mathias).

76. The Evening Sun, Apr. 12, 1971, at A10.

77. Letter from Mr. Werntz to Senator Mathias, March 29, 1971, on file in Senator Mathias' office.

78. Weisenberger Financial Services Newsletter, Aug. 12, 1970 [hereinafter referred to as Newsletter].

preparation as a screening device to find clients for mutual funds, insurance, or money management. Among users of the personal approach, two companies, H & R Block and Benevest, stand out. In 1970, H & R Block had 4,349 offices producing $80 million[79] and it was estimated that they handled 10% of all individual tax returns.[80] The Federal Trade Commission alleged that data obtained for tax returns was given by H & R Block to a wholly-owned subsidiary which compiled mailing lists. The lists were to be used to contact individuals for the sale of mutual funds and life insurance.[81] Although H & R Block discontinued this program, the choice did not result from concern for individual privacy. Rather, it resulted from a judgment that "the package which combined mutual funds and life insurance was 'too sophisticated' for the company's market at this time."[82] In 1970 Benevest, Inc.,[83] prepared tax returns for 40,000 individuals and subsequently contacted the same 40,000 for the sale of life insurance and mutual funds.[84]

If a store or bank wants to develop sources of information the way Benevest and H & R Block have, it can ask Digitax, Inc., to provide it (the bank or store) with appropriate forms and the necessary computer services. Gary D. Ritter, president of Digitax, described their customers' needs:

> They see it much more as a vehicle for getting into other business, getting traffic, than for being profitable *per se* from the actual preparation of returns.[85]

The impersonal approach, *i.e.*, not face-to-face, is provided by Fiscal Systems, Inc., which prepares a Tax Pak for customers to complete. The tax returns are computer-prepared from forms filled out by the customer.

---

79. 1970 Annual Report for H & R Block at 19.

80. Newsletter, *supra* note 78, at 3.

81. *In re* H & R Block, (June 30, 1971) (proposed complaint) [hereinafter referred to as FTC H & R Block complaint]. The name of the subsidiary was J.B. Grossman, Inc. Included on one list was the name, address and occupation of the customer. Only customers that earned more than a certain stated income were included on this list. Other lists contained only the names and addresses of the customer. Then Grossman supplied these lists to H & R Block Financial Services, a joint venture between H & R Block and Pennsylvania Insurance Company.

82. Wall Street Journal, Mar. 17, 1971, at 1.

83. Benevest, Inc. in San Francisco is a subsidiary of Beneficial Finance Co. Newsletter at 3.

84. Newsletter, *supra* note 78, at 5. Actually 100,000 individuals were contacted at first but because Benevest felt that 60,000 were bad credit risks for the "instant refund" program, only 40,000 returns were prepared.

85. Newsletter, *supra* note 78, at 4.

3. Employment Information. The *Wall Street Journal* noted that, "Out of fourteen employees who were recently fired from one discount store for thievery, eight strolled across the parking lot and got jobs in a supermarket in the same shopping center."[86] In response to this situation, "mutual protective associations" were formed. These organizations trade names of former workers in order to screen job applicants. Korvettes' parent corporation, Spartan Industries, has adopted an extensive plan for exchanging information through a subsidiary, Stores Prevent Inc., a "security service organization"[87] which maintains a computer bank of names, birth dates, social security numbers and other data on all former Spartan employees dismissed for stealing. This service is offered to other firms nationwide who are requested to reciprocate by submitting similar information in order to keep alleged shoplifters from employment.

In addition to alleged shoplifters, political "undesirables" may be kept unemployed on the basis of information lists. Political lists are maintained by several groups: the Institute for American Democracy, Group Research, Inc., the Anti-Defamation League, American Security Council, and the Church League of America.[88] Some of these organizations try to sell their information. A firm in Dayton, Ohio, called Agitator Detection, Inc., advertises a "sure-fire method for keeping radical America out of work" and asserts that they "have complete, computerized files on every known American dissident. . . . and all 160 million of their friends, relatives and fellow travelers."[89]

An organization known as the Church League of America, headed by Edgar Bundy, collects information on left-wing people and boasts of its over seven million cross-indexed files of political suspects, its "working relationship" with "leading law enforcement agencies," and its cooperation with undercover agents. In hearings before the Constitutional Rights Subcommittee of the Judiciary, a letter described the service that the Church League of America provides:

> American businessmen are faced with a grave problem. . . .
> Our working forces include more than a few radicals, socialists, revolutionaries, communists and trouble-makers of all sorts. The colleges and schools are educating and training thousands more who will soon be seeking employment.
> The hiring and training cost to industry for individual workers runs into many thousands of dollars. Before they

---

86. Wall Street Journal, Feb. 5, 1970, at 19.
87. Interview with Mr. Riccio, Mgr., in N.Y., Nov. 12, 1971.
88. Interview with Charles Baker, Director of Institute for American Democracy, Dec. 10, 1971.
89. See Donner, *The Theory and Practice of American Political Intelligence,* NEW YORK REVIEW OF BOOKS, at 27n.6, April 22, 1971.

are employed, their educational and professional back-grounds are screened most carefully. On the other hand, little if anything is done to determine their philosophy of life. In many cases this is of paramount importance.

The Church League of America is non-denominational, non-political, and tax exempt. For 32 years we have been intensively researching the activities about which management would be well-advised to be aware. Our files are the most reliable, comprehensive and complete, and second only to those of the FBI which, of course, are not available to you. . . .

We can supply you with all the data regarding your people that you may deem advisable. . . . In return we seek cooperation to the end that we may modernize and keep abreast of what appears to be an ever-growing need.

My office will be glad to send a representative at your request to go into this delicate matter at greater length.[90]

III. AVAILABLE REMEDIES

There are several non-legislative means which have been suggested or used to assure an individual's right to privacy. The following brief discussion provides a catalogue of these available or potential remedies.

A. TORT AND OTHER REMEDIES.

Warren and Brandeis first described the invasion of privacy as a tort in an article published in 1890.[91] They determined that the press was exceeding proper boundaries of decency and that private individuals should be protected from unjustifiable infliction of mental pain and distress caused by publication of personal information. This right of privacy was distinguished from defamation in terms of remedy, and truth was not deemed a defense. While Georgia was the first state to recognize a common law right to privacy in a commercial appropriation context,[92] some states such as New York would not recognize a right at common law that would protect an individual from

having his picture published . . . or his eccentricities commented upon either in handbills, circulars, catalogues, periodicals or newspapers. . . .[93]

---

90. *See* C. PYLE, UNCLE SAM IS WATCHING YOU, 57-58 (1971).

91. Warren & Brandeis, *The Right to Privacy*, 4 HARV. L. REV. 193 (1890).

92. Pavesich v. New England Life, 122 Ga. 190, 5 S.E. 68 (1905).

93. In the case cited a picture of a bountiful young woman was used to advertise flour without her consent. Roberson v. Rochester Folding Box Co., 171 N.Y. 538, 544; 64 N.E. 442 (1902).

However, New York later passed a bill that forbade commercial appropriation without consent[94] and thirty-five states now have protection from commercial appropriation either as a common law right or by statute.[95]

In Prosser's opinion, Warren and Brandeis were referring to more than just commercial appropriation. Prosser therefore divided the tort into four categories: (1) intrusion, (2) appropriation, (3) false light, and (4) public disclosure of private facts.[96] Extension of the privacy tort to instances of intrusion into a person's life has received some support in the courts recently[97] and appropriation has been applied when a person's picture is used for commercial purposes.[98] On the other hand, public disclosure of private facts has not been consistently applied.[99]

There are several problems with the tort remedy. It has been suggested that the pursuit of a remedy for invasion of privacy in a public court is somewhat incongruous;[100] that it is difficult to assess damages in a privacy action;[101] that there is a gap between defamation and privacy so that "someone who has been injured by the misuse of information often must run the risk of having his claim fall between the conceptual tools of privacy and defamation."[102] The tort of privacy is further confused when one considers it in relation to First Amendment privileges.[103]

---

94. N.Y. CIVIL RIGHTS LAW § § 50-51 (McKinney 1948).

95. PROSSER, LAW OF TORTS 831-832 (3d ed. 1964).

96. *See generally* Prosser, *Privacy,* 48 CALIF. L. REV. 383 (1960).

97. Two cases that are especially relevant are Pearson v. Dodd, 410 F.2d 701 (D.C. Cir. 1969), *cert. den'd.,* 395 U.S. 947 (1969) and Nader v. General Motors Corp. 25 N.Y. 2d 560, 307 N.Y.S. 2d 647, 255 N.E.2d 765 (1970). In the Dodd case, Drew Pearson, a columnist, had published information stolen from Senator Dodd's file. In the *Nader* case, GMC had repeatedly intruded into Nader's life. Dicta in *Dodd* approved the extenson of the privacy tort to instances of intrusion. *Dodd, supra* at 704. Subsequently, the court in a narrow holding in *Nader* relied on *Dodd* and held that GMC had intruded into Nader's privacy.

98. *See e.g.,* Eick v. Perk Dog Food Co., 347 Ill. App. 293, 106 N.E.2d 742 (1952) (picture of a blind child used to advertise dog food).

99. There is a rigid standard that the disclosure must offend the community; however, the standard is applied inconsistently. A reformed prostitute pictured in a movie, the Red Kimono, that offensively illustrated her prior life was informed by the court that she could recover damages if she proved her allegations. Melvin v. Reid, 112 Calif. App. 285, 297 P. 91 (1931). A second case in New York refused recovery to a "has-been" child prodigy when the *New Yorker* did a profile of him as a clerk despite the fact that he had suffered "ruthless exposure." Sidis v. F-R Publishing Corporation 113 F.2d 806, 807 (2d Cir. 1940).

100. MILLER, *supra* note 44, at 202-205.

101. *Id.* at 202.

102. *Id. See also* Note, *Invasion of Defamation by Privacy, 23* STAN. L. REV. 547 (1971).

103. For example, consider Prof. Kalven's argument,

. . .it has been agreed that there is a generous privilege to serve the public interest in news . . . What is at issue, it seems to me, is whether the claim of privilege is not so overpowering as virtually to swallow the tort. What can be

Other non-legislative remedies are not without their difficulties. Contract and warranty are not useful in this area because of the lack of bargaining between the collector of data and his subject. Indirect collection methods militate against using a theory of implied warranty to guarantee the authenticity of the information. Perhaps a fiduciary obligation could be imposed on the data handler; the information would be the *res* of a trust under which the collector could use the data only for the benefit of the subject-beneficiary. However, it is an established legal principle that the subject matter of a trust must be a legally enforceable property interest.[104]

In addition to these remedies, self-regulation is a possible source of protection. However, there has been no response by data process managers to the challenge made by Sir John Wall, Chairman of the Board of International Computers:

> Will you state openly that because you are responsible for the threat to privacy you will act responsibly to combat and minimize that threat?[105]

Paul Zurkowski of Information Industry Association (I.I.A.), a three year old trade association of companies in the information business, has recognized the problem and has suggested that a code of ethics is the only way self-regulation can be fostered. However, he feels that I.I.A. is a relatively young organization and has other problems to solve before it can effectively regulate itself.[106] In any case, it is doubtful that an organization could effectively regulate itself without a background of close cooperation with the federal government.[107]

---

left of the vaunted new right after the claims of privilege have been confronted?

See Kalven, *Privacy in Tort Law—Were Warren and Brandeis Wrong?* 31 LAW AND CONTEMP. PROB. 326, 335-336 (1966).

104. *See, e.g.,* 1 G.G. BOGERT & G.T. BOGERT, THE LAW OF TRUSTS AND TRUSTEES § 111, at 562-563 (2d. ed. 1965); 1 A. SCOTT, THE LAW OF TRUSTS §§ 74-77 (3d. ed. 1967). Professor Westin has suggested that information about oneself could be considered personal property over which only the individual or his agent should have control. As property, the information could be collected only with due process of law. WESTIN, note 2 *supra*, at 339-344. On the contrary Professor Miller writes that personal and real property notions are irrelevant to the personal values involved in privacy. MILLER, *supra* note 44, at 226-231.

105. Address before Spring Joint Computer Conference, Atlantic City. *See* COMPUTER WORLD, May 26, 1971, at 1.

106. Interview with P. Zurkowski, Executive Director of IIA, Dec. 10, 1971.

107. One obvious example is the National Association of Securities Dealers (NASD), a private trade association of over the counter dealers registered in August 1939 and the primary regulating instrument of the securities business established under the Maloney Act of 1938, 15 U.S.C. §§ 78o, 78o-3, 78g, 78gg, an amendment to the Securities Exchange Act of 1934, 15 U.S.C. §§ 77b-77e, 77j, 77k, 77m, 77o, 77s. § 3 of the certificate of incorporation

B. *Relief Provided by Legislation*

New premises must be established to provide guarantees for individual privacy in data collection and dissemination. The Federal Trade Commission has relied on existing legislation that prohibits false, misleading and deceptive statements[108] to control misuse of information.[109] In addition, improper use of income tax information by income tax preparers, *e.g.*, for solicitation, is the subject of proposed amendment to the tax law.[110] Senator Mathias has proposed a bill that would make disclosure of a client's tax data for purposes other than filing his return, a misdemeanor, punishable by $1000 fine or a year in prison.[111] A bill proposed by Senator Mark O. Hatfield requires the consent of an individual for the sale or distribution of personal information; but the exceptions to the Hatfield rule reduce it to a bill of little effect.[112]

Commentators have suggested the creation of a federal agency[113] to protect individual privacy in the data collection area. Such an agency would establish the criteria for data classification, disclosure and the means for individual challenges to information collection. In addition, the agency would require minimum standards of conduct and electro-mechanical safeguards for each level of data classification; create a system of remedies which may include correction and destruction of files; and generally supervise data collection, storage and transfer.

Three present legislative enactments may provide relief for the subject of information collection: the Freedom of Information Act,[114] the Postal Revenue and Federal Salary Act of 1967,[115] and the Fair Credit Reporting Act.[116] These laws are the primary source of protection now afforded individuals to stop undesired intrusions into their private lives and authenticate records being kept about them.

---

indicates that the association is primarily concerned with the enforcement of ethical standards and practices in the investment banking and securities business and unlike the SEC, NASD can impose several different sanctions including money penalties. NASDM, Rules ¶2301 (1971).

One should note that the rules that regulate credit bureaus through the Fair Credit Reporting Act arose in part from the practices of the Associated Credit Bureaus (ACB).

108. 15 U.S.C. § 52 (1970). *See* FTC Metromedia Complaint, *supra* note 58, and FTC H & R Block Complaint, *supra* note 81.

110. Wall Street Journal, Nov. 24, 1971, at 1, col. 5.

111. S. 1387, 92d Cong., 1st Sess. (1971).

112. The bill, for example, has exceptions allowing distributions permitted by federal statute or if the lists are distributed for law enforcement purposes. S.969, 92d Cong. 1st Sess. (1971).

113. MILLER, *supra*, note 44, at 248; WESTIN, *supra* note 2, at 396.

114. 5 U.S.C. § 552 (1971).

115. 39 U.S.C. § 4009 (1964).

116. 15 U.S.C. § § 1681 *et seq.* (1970).

1. Freedom of Information Act (FOIA). The Freedom of Information Act provides for public disclosure of agency records and thereby places an individual's privacy in a precarious position. There has been criticism of the FOIA because of its poor draftsmanship.[117] Although the Justice Department has aided the public in understanding the Act,[118] the Department's memorandum does not have the force of law.

Disclosure under the Act has aided public ascertainment of important information.[119] However, there are instances in which the agencies fail to fulfill FOIA's mandate for disclosure.[120] For example, agencies may avoid disclosure of data by methods such as "commingling." When information exempt from disclosure is mixed with information that is not exempt, the non-exempt information may also become unavailable,[121] despite case law to the contrary.[122] For example, information may be classified as "Compiled for Law Enforcement Purposes" and thereby come within the "Law Enforcement exception,"[123] or "In the interests of National Defense" and come within another exception.[124] Information kept in law enforcement files may be exempt even if it is never used in enforcement proceedings.[125]

Congress has provided for individual protection in the event of "clearly unwarranted invasions of privacy" of any person[126] and the

---

117. Prof. Davis noted, "even though no reasonable person could have intended such a result, the Act in clear terms requires disclosure of non-commercial and non-financial information furnished to the government with a good faith understanding that it will be kept confidential." K.C. Davis, *The Information Act: A Preliminary Analysis*, 34 U. CHI. L. REV. 761 (1967).

118. The Justice Dept. drafted a memorandum describing and construing the FOIA. See Atty. General's memorandum on the Public Information section of the Administrative Procedure Act. See reprint, 20 Ad. L. REV. 263 (1968).

119. In Sousie v. David, 28 Ad.L.2d 609 (D.C. Cir. 1971), Chief Judge Bazelon said that the Garwin Report, an "independent assessment" of the SST, was subject to public disclosure unless it was "inextricably intertwined" with the decision making process. The court went on to find the report free of any encumbrance that might prevent disclosure. For a description of how the Nixon administration allegedly kept the Garwin Report secret, see McCLOSKEY, TRUTH & UNTRUTH 75-84 (2d ed. 1972).

120. *See* Nader, *Freedom from Information: The Act and the Agencies*, 5 HARVARD CIVIL RIGHTS – CIVIL LIBERTIES LAW REVIEW (1970); Note, *The Freedom of Information Act and the Federal Trade Commission: A Study in Mis-feasance*, 4 HARVARD CIVIL RIGHTS–CIVIL LIBERTIES LAW REVIEW 345 (1969).

121. Nader, *supra* note 120, at 9-10.

122. The court held it is a violation of the FOIA to withhold documents from public inspection on the grounds that part are exempt and part are not exempt. Suitable deletions may be made before providing the documents. Wellford v. Hardin, 27 Ad.L.2d 844 (D.D.C. 1970).

123. 5 U.S.C. § 552 (b) (7) (1971).

124. 5 U.S.C. § 552 (b) (1) (1971).

125. Cowles Communication, Inc. v. Dept. of Justice, 28 Ad. L. 2d 768 (N.D. Calif. 1971).

126. 5 U.S.C. § 552 (b) (6) (1971).

deletion of identifying details, opinions, administrative staff manuals, and instructions to staff. During the hearings, sentiment was expressed favoring a broader privacy protection in view of the possible abuse of "great quantities of files containing intimate details about millions of citizens."[127] One department wanted to drop the word "clearly" and another suggested the elimination of the words "clearly unwarranted" in order to broaden the privacy protection.[128] The regulations of several agencies do provide broader privacy protection than that required by the statute[129] and, as a rule, the individual can get his own records.[130]

However, mere access to files is insufficient protection against invasions of an individual's privacy. A procedure must be established to permit an individual to confront his record, to expunge erroneous material and to control dissemination of personal information. Congressman Edward I. Koch introduced a bill in 1969 which did provide these elements. The purpose of the bill is to apprise individuals of records concerning them which are maintained by government agencies.[131] It provides that the individual will be notified that the "agency maintains or is about to maintain a record concerning said individual."[132] It also requires that one agency will not disclose data to another without consent of the individual;[133] that the agency main-

---

127.. H. REP. NO. 1497, 89th Cong., 2d Sess. 11 (1966).

128. Note, *Freedom of Information: The Statute and Regulations,* 56 GEO. L.J. 193-194 (1967).

129. Federal Maritime Commission exempts "all personnel and medical records and all private, personal, financial or business information contained in other files which if disclosed to the public, would invade the privacy of any person. . . ." 46 C.F.R.   503.35(f) (1972). The National Transportation Safety Board discourages disclosure of any record identifiable with a person:

> Any of the following may be withheld . . . personnel and background information personal to any officer or employee . . . medical histories and information concerning individuals, including applicants for licenses, . . any other detailed record identifiable with a particular person.

14 C.F.R. § 401.23 (1971).

130. The Atomic Energy Commission allows an individual access to his own file: "Information in such files which is not exempt from disclosure pursuant to other provisions of this section will not be withheld from the individual concerned. . . ." 10 C.F.R. § 9.5(a)(6) 1971). Similarly the Air Force: "When the sole and exclusive basis for withholding information is protection of an individual's personal privacy, the information should not be withheld from him. . . ." 32 C.F.R. § 806.5(g)(3) (1971). However, while the Civil Service Commission makes the employee's medical file available to him or his representative, the Commission withholds "medical information concerning a mental or other condition of such a nature that a prudent physician would hesitate to inform a person suffering from it. . . ." 5 C.F.R. § 294.401(b) (1971).

131. H.R. 4375, 92d Cong., 1st Sess. (1971).

132. *Id.*   § 552 (a)(1).

133. *Id.*   § 552 (a)(2).

tain a record of and grounds for the inspection of files;[134] and that an agency allow an individual to provide supplemental information.[135] The ordinary enforcement procedure of the FOIA,[136] *i.e.*, judicial relief, is applicable. However, the bill provides no protection against commingling, is vague regarding the procedures for inspection[137] and may require a public proceeding for challenging the collection of private information.

Senator Birch Bayh introduced a bill which would alleviate some of the shortcomings of the Koch Bill.[138] Bayh suggested that the individual be allowed to "remove erroneous material of any kind"[139] and challenges would be heard by a "federal privacy board."[140]

Although these legislative provisions for confrontation will not eliminate all injury, they guarantee safeguards for the individual. In light of the too widespread practice of disclosing information, however, better standards must still be devised to determine whether information should be released at all.

2. Avoidance of Commercial Solicitation. The "right to be let alone" has been recognized as the "most comprehensive of rights and the right most valued by civilized men."[141] One aspect of this right is the individual's control over interference with his life. Distinctions have been drawn between an individual's right to privacy in public and in his own home, and between commercial free speech and non-commercial free speech. These distinctions determine the degree of control which a person may exert.

Justice Burton recognized that an individual cannot always demand the same amount of privacy that he secures in his home when he is in public. In *Public Utilities Commission v. Pollack,*[142] a case in which passengers claimed an infringement of their constitutional right to privacy by the use of radio on public vehicles, he stated:

> [H]owever complete his right of privacy may be at home, it is substantially limited by the rights of others when the possessor travels on a public thoroughfare or rides on a public conveyance.[143]

Justice Douglas, however, dissented:

---

134. *Id.* § 552 (a)(3).
135. *Id.* § 552 (a)(5).
136. *Compare Id.* § 552 (b) *with* 5 U.S.C. § 552 (a)(3) (1971).
137. Interview with Larry Baskir, Esq., Chief Counsel to the Constitutional Rights Subcommittee of the Senate Committee on the Judiciary, Washington, D.C., Dec. 10, 1971.
138. S. 975, 92d Cong., 1st Sess. (1971).
139. *Id.* § 552 (a)(6).
140. *Id.* § 2 (a).
141. Olmstead v. United States, 277 U.S. 438, 478 (1928).
142. Public Utilities Commissioner v. Pollack, 343 U.S. 341 (1952).
143. *Id.* at 464.

[A]n individual even in his activities outside the home . . . has immunities from controls bearing on privacy. . . .[144]

The street car audience is a captive audience. It is there as a matter of necessity, not of choice. One who is in a public vehicle may not of course complain of the noise of the crowd and the babble of tongues. One who enters any public place sacrifices some of his privacy. My protest is against the invasion of privacy over and beyond the risks of travel.[145]

Similarly, in the criminal area, Courts have discussed "place" as a relevant consideration with respect to Fourth Amendment rights,[146] i.e., that one cannot expect to assert privacy in an open field[147] or to prevent transmission by a conversant of an allegedly "private" conversation.[148] Justice Stewart, writing for the majority in *Katz*, however, noted that the emphasis should not be on "places," "for the Fourth Amendment protects people, not places."[149]

In addition to the higher degree of control which an individual can exert in his home, his control of solicitations directed to him is basically related to the law that has developed concerning distinctions between commercial and non-commercial speech. Ordinances restricting handbilling, door-to-door solicitations and obscene mailings are constitutionally permissible when they control commercial activities. These bars on commercial solicitation may allow an individual to free himself from unwanted intrusions.

---

144. *Id.* at 467. Mrs. Jacqueline Onassis in a countersuit in which she is trying to enjoin a photographer from invading her privacy took a unique stand on privacy:

> . . . Mrs. Onassis said that shopping was a private activity, although it took her to a public store; that visiting a friend was private, although she had to go through public streets, and that a walk alone in Central Park was private, although the park was public. . . .

N.Y. Times, March 10, 1972, at 31, col. 3-4.
145. Public Utilities Commissioner v. Pollack, 343 U.S. at 468. Although Justice Douglas' view did not prevail in *Pollack,* in Griswold v. Connecticut, 381 U.S. 479 (1965), he found a state statute condemning the sale and distribution of contraceptives unconstitutional because of its interference with privacy:

> . . . specific guarantees in the Bill of Rights have penumbras, formed by emanations. From those guarantees that help give them life and substance . . . various guarantees create zones of privacy. (at 481-485).

This opinion has been subject to many interpretations ranging from merely marital privacy, to the privacy of the home, to a broad right of privacy.

146. Katz v. United States, 389 U.S. 347, 361 (1967) (Harlan concurring).
147. Hester v. United States, 265 U.S. 57 (1924).
148. Lopez v. United States, 373 U.S. 427 (1963).
149. Katz v. United States, 389 U.S. at 351.

The early cases which legitimized specified anti-solicitation ordinances rest on the distinction between commercial and non-commercial activities. As the Court in *Jamison* v. *United States*[150] wrote:

> [The states] may not prohibit the distribution of handbills in pursuit of a clearly religious activity merely because the handbills invite the purchase of books ... or the raising of funds.... The states can prohibit the use of the streets for the distribution of purely commercial leaflets, even though such leaflets may have "a civic appeal or a moral platitude" appended ....[151]

Similarly, the Supreme Court has held a city ordinance forbidding door-to-door soliciting invalid as a denial of freedom of speech and the press when applied to the activities of Jehovah's Witnesses.[152] But the Court noted that the ordinance in question "was not solely directed at commercial advertising."[153] In a later case, *Breard* v. *Alexandria*[154] the Court decided that a "legitimate [commercial] occupation may be restricted or prohibited in the public interest"[155] after it balanced the "householder's desire for privacy" with the publisher's "right to distribute publications in the way that ... brings the best results."[156] Observing that "the usual methods of solicitation—radio, periodicals, mail, local agencies—are open"[157] the Court concluded:

> It would be, it seems to us, a misuse of the great guarantees of free speech and free press to use those guarantees to force a community to admit the solicitors of publications to the home premises of its residents.[158]

In view of the extended use of mailing lists, attention must be focused on the ways that an individual may withdraw his name from a list to stop someone from sending commercial mail to his home. In the area of mailings of obscene materials, some contend that the commercial/non-commercial is unwarranted. The Court in *Ginzburg* v. *United States*[159] wrote:

---

150. 318 U.S. 413 (1943).
151. *Id.* at 417.
152. Martin v. Struthers, 319 U.S. 141 (1943).
153. *Id.* at 142 n.l.
154. 341 U.S. 622 (1951).
155. *Id.* at 644.
156. *Id.*
157. *Id.* at 632.
158. *Id.* at 645.
159. 383 U.S. 463, 474 n.16 (1966).

Commercial activity, in itself, is no justification for narrowing the protection of expression secured by the First Amendment.

It is misleading, however, to say that the "commercial feature" of the obscene materials was not relevant to the Court's decision because the Court did observe the publications against a "background of commercial exploitation."[160]

In *Rowan v. U.S. Post Office Department*,[161] there was a significant shift in the law. Prior to *Rowan*, only the government had authority to determine whether material was obscene[162] and therefore barred from the mail, whereas *Rowan* allows the addressee to determine whether the material is "provocative."[163] Once such a decision is made, any householder may insulate himself from advertisements that offer for sale "matters which the addressee in his sole discretion believes to be erotically arousing or sexually provocative"[164] under the Postal Revenue and Federal Salary Act of 1967.[165] In validating this statute, the Court balanced privacy and communication: "the right of every person 'to be let alone' must be placed in the scales with the rights of others to communicate."[166]

An examination of the *Breard* and *Rowan* cases reveals a basis upon which individual control over all mail solicitation could be established. *Breard* first drew the distinction that commercial solicitation was not necessarily a protected activity under the First Amendment. The Court in *Rowan* examined one aspect of such unprotected activity and authorized individuals to determine whether or not unwanted materials were deliverable. Although the statute challenged in *Rowan* dealt explicitly with materials categorized as "erotically arousing or sexually provocative," the Court found that the legislative history of the statute supports the prohibition of all future mailings, independent of any objective test:

> The section was intended to allow the addressee complete and unfettered discretion in electing whether or not he desired to receive further material from a particular sender.[167]

---

160. *Id.* at 466.

161. 397 U.S. 728 (1970).

162. The "Roth" test is the obscenity test enunciated in Roth v. United States, 354 U.S. 476 (1957). This test requires that three elements be present to determine whether the materials are obscene: (1) The dominant theme of the material taken as a whole appeals to prurient interest; (2) The material is offensive because it affronts contemporary community standards; (3) The material is without redeeming social value. 354 U.S. at 484, 489 (1957).

163. Chief Justice Burger determined that the valid statutory test is subjective because "what may not be provocative to one person may well be to another." Rowan v. Post Office, 397 U.S. at 737.

164. 39 U.S.C. § 4009(a) (1964).

165. *Id.*

166. Rowan v. Post Office, 397 U.S. at 738.

167. *Id.* at 736, 737.

The Court specifically extended the prohibition on delivery beyond "sexually provocative" materials:

> In operative effect the power of the householder under the statute is unlimited; he may prohibit the mailing of a dry goods catalog because he objects to the contents—or indeed the text of the language touting the merchandise. Congress provided this sweeping power not only to protect privacy but to avoid possible constitutional questions that might arise from vesting the power to make any discretionary evaluation of the material in a governmental office. In effect Congress has erected a wall ... that no advertiser may penetrate without [the citizen's] acquiescence.[168]

The Court thereby categorically rejected the argument that a vendor can send unwanted material wherever he chooses.[169] While earlier cases were generally concerned with door-to-door solicitation, the *Rowan* Court said that "the right to communicate must stop at the mailbox of an unreceptive addressee."[170] The Court noted that a lesser restriction would in effect sanction a form of trespass.

The Postal Revenue and Federal Salary Act is limited by its terms to "erotically arousing or sexually provocative" material, but the Court emphatically declared that the Act should be accorded a liberal interpretation. Although the Court did not have to reach this issue to decide the case, the dicta might well serve as a guide to the lower courts—thereby enlarging the sphere of an individual's privacy.

3. *Fair Credit Reporting Act (FRCA).*

A bank asks a credit bureau for information concerning a loan applicant to determine whether or not to grant the loan. The bureau reveals that the individual has been bankrupt, had an "undesirable account" and had been arrested and charged with being a "common and notorious thief." Furthermore, the bureau advises that extreme caution should be taken in dealing with the individual because of numerous inquiries concerning his "unethical business practices." As a result, the loan is not granted. Unknown to the bank, however, the "facts" reported by the bureau are erroneous.[171]

---

168. *Id.* at 728, 737.
169. *Id.*
170. *Id.* at 736, 737.
171. *See* Petitioners of Retailers' Commercial Agency, Inc., 342 Mass. 515, 518; 174 N.E.2d 376, 378 (1961).

Before the Fair Credit Reporting Act[172] was enacted the applicant might not know why his application was refused, and the bureau's name was kept confidential pursuant to agreement. Although its impact has not been universal, the Act attempts to satisfy the

> need to insure that consumer reporting agencies exercise their grave responsibilities with fairness, impartiality, and a respect for the consumer's right to privacy.[173]

The Act imposes disclosure requirements upon credit bureaus and all users of information. To some extent the credit bureaus adhered to the guidelines of the FCRA prior to its enactment, by virtue of their membership in the Associated Credit Bureaus (ACB),[174] and Senator Proxmire relied extensively on the ACB rules in his draft of the FCRA.[175] While the guidelines of the ACB and the FCRA are similar, the former does not have the criminal and civil penalties found in the latter.[176]

Under the Act, the consumer reporting agency must maintain "reasonable procedures"[177] to insure that the customer uses the information only for a permissible purpose. A permissible purpose arises only if the information is the object of a proper court order,[178] if a consumer gives his written consent,[179] or if insurance, employment, credit, government license, or a "legitimate business need"[180] is involved. Adverse information that is more than seven years old must be expunged,[181] and at the consumer's request a "consumer reporting agency" must disclose the "nature and substance" and, in some cases, the sources of information.[182] A consumer reporting agency must provide a consumer the opportunity to challenge the accuracy of his file and correct any errors[183] or file a statement if a subsequent reinvestigation does not resolve the dispute.[184]

Perhaps of most significance, the Act requires a consumer reporting agency to notify a consumer when a report based on public

---

172. Fair Credit Reporting Act, P.L. 91-508, 84 Stat. 1127-1136, 15 U.S.C. §§ 1681-1681t (1970), enacted Oct. 26, 1970, effective date April 25, 1971 [hereinafter referred to as F.C.R.A.].

173. F.C.R.A. § 602(a)(4), 15 U.S.C. § 1681(a)(4)(1970).

174. Denney, *Federal Fair Credit Reporting Act*, 88 BANKING L.J. 578 (1971).

175. *Id.* at 581.

176. *See* F.C.R.A. §§ 616, 617, 619 and 620, 15 U.S.C. §§ 1681n, 1681o, 1681q, 1681r (1970).

177. F.C.R.A. § 607(a), 15 U.S.C. § 1681e(a) (1970).

178. F.C.R.A. § 604(1), 15 U.S.C. § 1681(1) (1970).

179. F.C.R.A. § 606(2), 15 U.S.C. § 1681b(2) (1970).

180. F.C.R.A. §§ 604(3)(A)-(E), 15 U.S.C. §§ 1681b(3)(A)-(E) (1970).

181. F.C.R.A. § 605, 15 U.S.C. § 1681c (1970).

182. F.C.R.A. § 609, 15 U.S.C.§ 1681g (1970).

183. F.C.R.A. § 611(c), 15 U.S.C. § 1681i(d) (1970).

184. F.C.R.A. § 611(b), 15 U.S.C. § 1681i(b) (1970).

record information is "likely to have an adverse effect" on the consumer's employment. In the alternative, the agency need only maintain procedures to assure the currency of public record information.[185] Finally, the user of a consumer report obtained from a consumer reporting agency must notify the consumer that his credit, insurance or employment has been adversely affected either wholly or partly because of such report.[186]

Information provided by the state. A motor vehicle bureau's provision of the driving record of an applicant to an insurance company illustrates one application of the FCRA. The driving record qualifies as a "consumer report" because it is a written communication bearing on the "personal characteristics" of the consumer,[187] and the motor vehicle bureau qualifies under the Act as a "consumer reporting agency":

> Any person which for monetary fees ... regularly engages in the practice of assembling or evaluating consumer credit information ... for the purpose of furnishing consumer reports to third parties, and which uses any means or facilities of interstate commerce.[188]

Any insurance company which uses such report is obligated to notify the consumer if the report has a "partly or wholly" adverse effect on the consumer's insurance application.[189]

It has been questioned whether telephone directories or "city directories" such as those compiled by Polk & Co. violate the FCRA. An informal Federal Trade Commission opinion considered this problem:

> ... to the extent that they [city directories] only provide name, address, telephone number and information regarding marital status and number of children, such directories would not be consumer reports.[190]

On the other hand the staff opinion continues:

> ... to the extent that a "city directory" indicates whether a consumer owns or rents his place of residence, such a direc-

---

185. F.C.R.A. § 613(2), 15 U.S.C. § 1681k(2) (1970).
186. F.C.R.A. § 615(a), 15 U.S.C. § 1681m(a) (1970).
187. F.C.R.A. § 603(d), 15 U.S.C. § 1681a(d) (1970).
188. F.C.R.A. § 603(f), 15 U.S.C. § 1681a(f) (1970).
189. F.C.R.A. § 615(b), 15 U.S.C. § 1681m(b) (1970). 4 CCH CONSUMER CREDIT GUIDE ¶ 99,487 (1971). It is because motor vehicle reports do not clearly indicate "personal characteristics" that they are not the subject of a consumer report.
190. 4 CCH CONSUMER CREDIT GUIDE ¶99,525 (1971).

tory may well constitute a consumer report, because property ownership is a fact often considered as relevant to a person's credit worthiness.[191]

Information Provided by the Federal Government. The FCRA does not appear to hinder the flow of information from the federal government possibly because its information is not considered relevant to a person's credit-worthiness.[192]

There may be disclosure which runs in the other direction, *viz.*, from a "consumer reporting agency" to a governmental agency; but the disclosure must be for a permissible purpose.[193] For example, where the government decides to deny a VA or FHA loan based on information from a consumer reporting agency,[194] notice, as required by the FCRA,[195] must be made to the consumer by the appropriate agency.[196] If information is used for another purpose, *e.g.*, to facilitate the government's search for a fugitive, only identifying information may be disseminated.[197]

Information Provided in the Private Sector. The compilation of mailing lists by collating government and census data which reflect an individual's "personal characteristics,"[198] seems to be an activity regulated by the FCRA. However, the use of such lists is not among the enumerated "permissible purposes,"[199] and one might therefor conclude that the activity is prohibited.

---

191. *Id.*

192. Counsel for the FTC commented that, for example, boat lists obtainable from the Coast Guard in the Department of Transportation would not be a "consumer report" because such reports are not relevant to a person's credit worthiness unless possibly the style of boat could be used to this end. Interview with L. Goldfarb, FTC Staff Attorney, Washington, D.C., March 3, 1972.

193. F.C.R.A. § 604, 15 U.S.C. § 1681b (1970); FTC, Compliance with Fair Credit Reporting Act, Division of Special Projects of the Bureau of Consumer Protection at 16-17 (1971) [hereinafter referred to as FTC Guidelines].

194. One recent example of this is Housing and Urban Development's contract with the Retail Credit Company for information from Retail on those citizens who seek government insured loans. Washington Post, Dec. 8, 1971, at D19.

195. F.C.R.A. § 615(a), 15 U.S.C. § 1681(g) (1970).

196. 4 CCH CONSUMER CREDIT GUIDE ¶ 99,496 (1971).

197. F.C.R.A. § 608, 15 U.S.C. § 1681(f) (1970), FTC Guidelines at 17. ACB in its guidelines advises credit bureaus of this disctinction:

All of this explanation points up the importance of having such government agency representative complete a form on which he states the specific purpose of the report he is requesting from your credit bureau. Based on that form, you can decide whether he qualifies for a full report or identifying information only.

J. SPAFFORD, THE FAIR CREDIT REPORTING ACT 10 (1970).

198. F.C.R.A. § 603(d), 15 U.S.C. § 1681(a)(d) (1970).

199. F.C.R.A. § 609, 15 U.S.C. § 1681(g) (1970).

Nevertheless, the Federal Trade Commission has an ambivalent position regarding mailing lists. In an informal staff opinion, Michael Carson, an FTC Attorney with the Division of Special Projects, stated:

'. . . assuming that the list in question is used by credit granters for the mailing of, or otherwise soliciting offers to purchase items for personal, family or household use, it would appear that such a list is a consumer report or series of consumer reports when that list is disseminated to a third person. . . .[200]

It is of no consequence that such a list might include only favorable information because the definition "consumer report" encompasses favorable as well as adverse information. The opinion concludes that there is no "permissible purpose" either on the basis of a "credit transaction"[201] or a "legitimate business need" for issuing such lists unless an individual has first requested credit from the "would-be" user of the lists.

This opinion appeared to be undermined by a second opinion which concluded that when a user does submit a list of names to a "consumer reporting agency" and the "consumer reporting agency" deletes names that are not "credit worthy," the list can be used when the result is not to deny credit to those deleted from the list.[202] It would seem that the practice described in the first and second opinion are identical in effect, and the basis for distinction has not been articulated. As noted by Senator Proxmire:

There is virtually no difference between requesting a reporting agency to review its files and compile a list of all those who are credit worthy and asking a reporting agency to do the same thing from a list of names submitted to the agency by the client.[203]

Robert Breth, President of A. J. Wood Research Corporation described the purpose of these screening files as separating out a "goodie" list,[204] a practice antithetical to the "confidential" nature of the consumer report.[205]

---

200. 4 CCH CONSUMER CREDIT GUIDE ¶ 99,484 (1971).

201. F.C.R.A. § 604(3)(A), 15 U.S.C. § 1681(b)(3)(A) (1970).

202. 4 CCH CONSUMER CREDIT GUIDE ¶ 99,484 (1971).

203. Letter to M. Kirkpatrick, Chairman, FTC, Oct. 8, 1971. (photostat from Sen. Proximire's file).

204. Letter to Sen. Sparkman, Chairman, Commission on Banking, Housing and Urban Affairs, Sept. 17, 1971. (photostat from Sen. Proxmire's file).

205. Mr. Breth's reference was to the statement, "The consumer has the right to have information in his file kept confidential." *See* FTC Guidelines, *supra* note 229, at 26.

Although the issue is yet to be resolved by a formal commission ruling, the FTC staff has reversed its informal position. Mr. Carson, expressed the conclusions of the staff that:

> ... the clear statutory intent [of the FCRA] was to require some act on the part of the consumer indicating his permission for a consumer reporting agency to utilize his credit information in its files. ...

and the staff's recommendations therefore are:

> ... that consumer reporting agencies may not utilize nor grant access to their files without expressed or implied permission of the consumer involved.[206]

When income tax preparers use, for unrelated purposes, the information obtained from the consumer's tax forms, the FCRA often has been unable to intervene. Because it is clear the "consumer report" does not include:

> any report containing information solely as to transactions or experiences between the consumer and the person making the report,[207]

information obtained from the preparation of an income tax form is not a "consumer report." Furthermore, because the one who prepares the return is the one who uses the information to determine credit worthiness, the tax preparer who personally uses the information is not a "consumer reporting agency."[208]

Although the FCRA is concerned about information used to affect an individual's employment,[209] an employer who makes an independent investigation is not a "consumer reporting agency"[210] and is not regulated by the Act. Similarly, if an employer maintains computer files of those who shoplift and refuses to re-hire them in another branch store, he would not be within the scope of the FCRA.[211] However, if several independent companies agree to estab-

---

206. Letter to Mr. R. Breth, Senior V.P., A.J. Wood Research Corp., Oct. 6, 1971. (photostat from Sen. Proxmire's file).

207. F.C.R.A. § 603(d), 15 U.S.C. § 1681 a (d) (1970).

208. F.C.R.A. § 603(f), 15 U.S.C. § 1681(f) (1970).

209. See notes 186- 88 supra and accompanying text.

210. 4 CCH CONSUMER CREDIT GUIDE ¶ 99,447 (1971).

211. The reasoning would be similar to that allowing a company to maintain an internal blacklist preventing individuals from receiving credit in any of the firm's branches because of an invalid credit card or other appropriate reason. See 4 CCH CONSUMER CREDIT GUIDE ¶99,448 at 89,402 (1971).

lish a central file containing information on alleged shoplifters, the group would be a "consumer reporting agency."

Amendments. To fulfill the purpose of the Act, the consumer should be notified of an adverse result before the user receives the report. In addition after an adverse report has prevented an individual from obtaining a job, the employer should be required to hold open the position until the individual has an opportunity to investigate the report.[212] At present, an individual never sees his file. The agency merely discloses the "nature and substance of all information" to the consumer.[213]

To discover whether an agency has any information about himself an individual must literally go door-to-door to each agency and ask to see its files. An informal staff opinion notes that there is no provision in the Act that "would enable a consumer to ascertain the number of credit reporting agencies which collect and maintain his credit data."[214] Upon issuance of a report by a consumer reporting agency, the subject should immediately receive a copy. This would allow the individual to challenge the accuracy of the report and make corrections before any dissemination had occurred. In addition, the Act should provide that on request, an individual receive a true copy of his file in order to update the information and challenge any erroneous material.[215]

IV. CONCLUSIONS

At present, neither the Freedom of Information Act nor the Fair Credit Reporting Act can be used to stop what is considered a "harmless" or "required" dissemination of information by the government. In order to frustrate the flow of inaccurate information and more fully protect the individual's privacy, the FOIA should be amended with the Bayh Bill. As an additional safeguard, highly personal information, such as that maintained by the Civil Service Commission, should not be computerized.

---

212. Presently there is no obligation for the employer to hold open a job position which has been denied on the basis of a consumer report. *See* 4 CCH CONSUMER CREDIT GUIDE ¶ 99,429 (1971).

213. The pertinent section is F.C.R.A. § 609, 15 U.S.C. § 1681(g)(a)(2) (1970). *See* 4 CCH CONSUMER CREDIT GUIDE ¶ 99,428 at 89,386 (1971). An example of a satisfactory disclosure is:

A department store in this city told us that you were several months behind on your payment.

For additional examples *see* FTC Guidelines, *supra* note 193 (Appendix I).

214. 4 CCH CONSUMER CREDIT GUIDE ¶ 99,448 (1971).

215. Senator Hatfield has recognized the need to more adequately protect the individual and has proposed a bill, S.968 92 Cong. 1st. Sess. (1971), to amend the F.C.R.A. This bill would incorporate many of the proposals outlined above.

Because commercial solicitation may involve more than annoyance, an individual should be protected not only from obscene literature, but from any unwanted commercial mailings. A liberal application of the Postal Revenue and Federal Salary Act, as construed in the *Rowan* case, could effectively accomplish this objective.

While the FCRA protects the individual from mailing lists, state agency reports and certain employment practices, it has many shortcomings. It does not require the agent collecting the information to use it for a particular purpose, and it does not require that the subject's consent be obtained prior to disclosure. Under the present Act the individual does not have the right to confront his complete file, and any challenge to the file can arise only after a report has been disseminated. As suggested above, the individual must' be given notice of collection and the right to examine his file before dissemination.

The direction of the law in this area is difficult to predict. Absent an effort by the principals to discipline themselves, government regulation may be the only solution. These proposals above have been submitted because the respect for an individual's integrity and his right to control information about himself is presently considered inferior to the profit motive. The decision must now be made whether we will consider the long term social cost of present practices.

A